Jo Miles Schuman is an elementary school art teacher in Ann Arbor, Michigan, and a printmaker. She received her B.A. degree in creative arts from Antioch College and her M.A. in art from the University of Michigan.

ART FROM MANY HANDS

Multicultural Art Projects | by Jo Miles Schuman

Davis Publications, Inc.
Worcester, Massachusetts

Davis Publications, Inc.
Worcester, Massachusetts, U.S.A.

Printed in the United States of America
Library of Congress Catalog Card Number: 80-14665
ISBN: 0-87192-150-2

10 9 8 7 6 5 4 3 2 1

To

Irene Tejada,
Inspiring Teacher and Friend,

and to

The Students, Faculty, and Staff
of
Burns Park School
Ann Arbor, Michigan

CONTENTS

PREFACE

From ancient to modern times, people have used almost every conceivable material in their environments to bring beauty into their lives and the lives of others. I hope that through this book more people will become aware of these arts and crafts, which are our inheritance as world citizens.

It is not expected that students will be able to create pieces of art as fine as the examples shown them, which are usually the result of years of training and tradition. But when they work with materials with their own hands, students appreciate the skills of those artisans even more. At the same time, they enjoy the creative process themselves and gain some confidence in their own abilities. Exposing students to art from all over the world brings them the wonder of art in all its many forms, expands their knowledge of what art is, and shows them the variety of ways design problems can be solved. Inspired by these experiences, students often produce

Public school children enjoying their multicultural art exhibition at North Commons Gallery, Ann Arbor, Michigan. Photo by Jack Stubbs for the *Ann Arbor News,* March 22, 1973.

art of very fine quality that can stand on its own merits. This is true, however, only when students are helped to use the example as a springboard for their own personal expression, rather than as something to copy.

I also hope that in a world where differences in culture and ethnicity sometimes bring conflict, learning about cultural differences in arts and crafts can help students appreciate and respect one another. In America's communities and classrooms, where children of several ethnic backgrounds often live and work together, these arts can be a language of understanding.

If a child is unaware of the artistic aspects of his heritage, learning about them can be an impor-

Angela and Thea, third-grade students, work together on a Mexican art project.

tant growing experience. If he is already aware of this heritage, he might find pleasure and self-respect in sharing this knowledge. Children who are underprivileged in the sense that their community does not include minority groups need to experience the richness of creative expression in cultures other than their own.

Children should be proud of their own cultural heritage, not in the sense that it is the *most* beautiful, but in the knowledge that it *is* beautiful. They should also have the opportunity to see the art of other cultures. We should help them realize that the creativity of all peoples is to be valued.

Sadly, in the late twentieth century most people have lost—and still more are losing—the ability and the confidence to create objects of beauty with their own hands. In few areas of the world is art still a part of daily living, a skill everyone engages in and hands down through the generations. It is a wonderful and valuable part of the human spirit that sees and enjoys beautiful things. People in the past, even in circumstances of privation, devoted hours to decorating tools and clothing and homes that would serve practical purposes just as well if they were left unadorned. But today this enrichment of our lives is left to specialists—trained artists—or to the few who design the products that are mass-produced. Most of us no longer have confidence in our own hands. Children do, however, until they become aware that adults do not sit and draw or engage in other arts or crafts, and then they lose their motivation and their confidence.

This is not to say that specialists in art are a new phenomenon. Many early societies set apart people who were exceptionally talented in the arts to be specialists. The bas-reliefs in the Parthenon were not the work of the common man, and Japanese sumi-e artists spend many years perfecting their techniques. These arts are usually referred to as the fine arts, produced primarily for beauty rather than utility. Still, it is possible for students to engage in these arts, even though their own work is less skilled.

I have included in this volume projects based on both kinds of art—the fine arts, created by artists working as specialists in their societies, and the popular arts, handed down by tradition within groups and families. Tradition is really just another form of special training, and the quality of popular art work is often on the same level as that of fine art.

Schooled and unschooled, young and old, ancient and contemporary—the examples of art work chosen for this book come from many skilled hands.

ACKNOWLEDGEMENTS

In writing this book I have sought assistance from a great many people, all of whom have given generously of their time and knowledge. Some of the projects could not have been written at all without this substantial help.

Karin Douthit contributed many ideas and translated correspondence pertaining to the project on the flower-related arts of Germany. Yolanda Marino spent much time and was helpful in many ways with the projects on Puerto Rican arts and island maracas. The information concerning straw inlays was provided by Valentin Petrovich Kotov, Senior Artist of the factory which produces these inlays in Zhlobin, Byelorussia. Jody Hymes and Susan Walton of the Project on Asian Studies in Education at the University of Michigan, Ann Arbor, were very helpful with the Japanese projects and that on Way-ang Kulit. Hitoshi Uchida contributed information to the project on making Japanese fish prints. I am much indebted to Vee-Ling and Richard Edwards for their helpful comments on the section on Chinese arts and to Vee for the calligraphy that illustrates that project. Without Ingrid Cole's advice on constructing and dressing a tapestry loom, and that of Lois Kane on the art of tapestry weaving, that project could not have come to fruition.

Others who have read chapters and made helpful comments or given ideas or advice on projects are: Elsa Adamson, Mrs. Surjit S. Bakhshi, Rabbi Martin Ballonoff, Lisa Berg, Joan Blos, Susan Buchan, Mrs. Vincent Chrypinski, Madelaine Conboy, Mrs. Andrew Ehrenkreutz, Cecelia Ference, Richard Ford, Zelda Gamson, Marian Gillett, Ruth Gomez, Elaine Headly, Mimi Khaing, Rickie Lauffer, Marianna Lis, Scott McGuilliard, Paul Melton, Cyril Miles, Margaret Miles, Christella Moody, Arvilla Muirhead, Mr. and Mrs. Rudi Ong, William H. Peck, Eugene Power, Judy Rothman, Sao Saimong, Seiichi Sasaki, Elisabeth Schuman, Aliza Shevrin, Meredith Shore, Joyce Tinkham, May Uttahl, William Wiercbowskie, Gretchen Whitman, and Bill Zolkowski.

Others shared special skills: Julia Moore taught me how to create the dashiki diagramed in the project on tie-dyeing, and Mr. and Mrs. Stephen Kuchta shared their knowledge of gourd-raising and drying with me. Thanks to Vee-Ling Edwards, Joyce Tinkham, Marianna Lis, and Saburo Ikeuchi, who, by demonstrating their arts in the classroom, gave a wonderful experience to many students.

I am indebted to Jill Bace, Registrar of the Kelsey Museum of the University of Michigan; Richard Pohrt, of the Chandler-Pohrt Collection; Cyril Miles, Museum of African Art, Highland Park Community College; Donald A. Sellers, of Plymouth House Galleries; Eugene Power; and Mr. and Mrs. James P. Wong; all of whom went to some difficulty in order to let me photograph from their collections.

I am grateful to Amy Saldinger for translating the correspondence from Byelorussia, Janice Moore for her translation of an article relating to the Swedish cookie presses and for the pepparkaka recipe in that project, and to Terry Johnson for translating correspondence from Germany.

Fred Crudder processed much of my film and without complaining got the best possible prints out of even the earliest negatives. I enjoyed working with Julie Steedman, who took a number of the photographs in this book. They are Figures 1–3, 2–4, 2–5, 2–6, 2–29, 2–30, 2–31, 3–14, 4–43, 4–46, 4–53, 5–11, 5–51, 5–52, 5–54, 5–55, 5–56, 8–5, 8–6, 8–34, 8–35, 8–38, 8–39, 8–56, 8–57, 8–58, 8–59, 8–60, and 8–61. All other photos, unless otherwise credited, are by the author.

Ruth Beatty, Art Coordinator for the Ann Arbor Public Schools has been supportive throughout this endeavor.

Thanks to *Arts and Activities* for permission to publish some of my photos and material that first appeared in their magazine in January 1975 under the title "Mexican Bark Cutouts" (Figures 6–8, 6–9, 6–10), and to the Ramses Wissa Wassef Centre, Harrania, Egypt, for permission to publish photos of the tapestries woven at their Centre.

Parents of students at Burns Park School and friends traveling in other countries have enriched this book by obtaining photographs or pieces of art, often involving some hours of work or even discomfort. I must especially thank Nancy Rice for her contribution to the project on Swedish cookie presses; Elizabeth Arnold; Mary Clark; Edith Gesche; Tamiko and Yoshihiko Imamura; and Shirley Paul, who travelled by airplane from Mexico to the United States, cushioning a ten-pound, nineteen-inch clay sun on her lap all the way to get it here safely.

Thanks to John Stafford, who designed the shadow screen for the Indonesian Arts project, and to John Lillie and Alan Klein, who constructed the marionette theatre.

I am indebted to several faculty members of the University of Michigan who were my teachers: David H. Reider, who introduced me to the art of photography; Douglas Hesseltine, who gave advice on the line drawings; but most of all to Irene Tejada, whose appreciation of arts from many cultures has inspired enthusiasm and creativity in her students for many years. She read and commented on several chapters and contributed substantially to the projects on marionettes, shadow puppets, and the seed necklaces of Puerto Rico, as well as bringing many of the arts represented in this book to my attention.

A warm thank-you to everyone associated with Burns Park School in Ann Arbor, Michigan—parents, students, staff, and teachers—who have welcomed these ideas and helped make the art room an exciting and rewarding place in which to work.

I am grateful to my husband, Howard, to my daughter Beth, and to my sons, Marc and David, all of whom have contributed ideas, support, and help in countless ways over the past five years toward the completion of this book. (My husband, who is candid, urges me to note, however, that although he indeed edited parts of the manuscript and helped in many ways, he also provided a few road blocks to climb, chasms to leap, and other obstacles to overcome. Our partnership is never dull.)

I am grateful also to my parents, Max and Margaret Miles, who instilled in me a respect for, and appreciation of other cultures. Perhaps the earliest beginnings of this book can be traced to the influence of my grandfather, Henry Turner Bailey, whom I never knew, but whose silent studio I explored at an early age, coming across art pieces from many corners of the world that spoke of creativity in clay, paper, wood, and stone, in places far away from our small New England town.

Finally, I am indebted to all the artists, ancient and contemporary, a few known but most unknown, whose work illustrates and is the inspiration for the projects in this book.

Jo Miles Schuman
Ann Arbor, Michigan

1

A METHOD
FOR TEACHING
MULTICULTURAL
ART PROJECTS

BEGINNING THE PROJECT

Where does one begin? There are many beginnings. The study may start spontaneously, through a news clipping that describes art from another culture; through something a child or parent or teacher sees or does or brings to class; or perhaps through research on a particular culture that is part of a social studies unit. Whatever sparked the study, if children are to engage in an art project, showing them an actual piece of art brings the highest motivation and involvement.

Children feel a certain magic about the real thing. You hear their breath draw in, see their eyes widen, sense their respect and wonder when they can see and maybe touch an Inuit sculpture of smooth black stone, an intricate and vibrantly colored painting on amate paper from Mexico, or a hand-stamped and embroidered adinkra cloth from Ghana. Nothing can really substitute for this exciting experience.

Giving children this experience is not as difficult

1

FIGURE 1–1. Items found in secondhand shops: a weaving on a backstrap loom from Guatemala, a plate and a papier mâché bird from Mexico, a gold-leafed lacquerware owl from Burma, a Navajo silver and turquoise bracelet, and a toy papier mâché beast of burden from Japan.

as it might seem. Is there a secondhand shop in your community? You can find surprising things there—a seventy-five cent clay animal from Mexico with lovely hand-painted designs (it does not matter if there are small chips); a backstrap loom from Guatemala, which shows young students how cloth is created; an old Polish wycinanki design for two dollars, a treasure to be shared. These are chance finds, but as tourism grows, such small, inexpensive things become easier to find even if one cannot travel oneself.

Most cities have an increasing number of art import shops. Although larger items can be prohibitively expensive, smaller handcrafted pieces are often within a teacher's budget. Many shops are willing to lend items to a school for one day if they are assured that the pieces will not be harmed. They may require a refundable deposit against loss or damage.

We often live in a community without ever tapping its human resources. Has someone in your community traveled abroad? Are there foreign visitors to your town—students or business representatives who may have art objects to show or skills to teach? Are there Americans with ethnic backgrounds in your area who have knowledge of a traditional craft? Invite to the classroom a Japanese student who can demonstrate ink painting, a Chinese visitor who can show the growth of a language through calligraphy, a Native American who can demonstrate beadwork, or a Polish-American who has learned to cut wycinanki designs. Many people are willing and happy to give this valuable experience to your students, but you will have to search for them—they do not advertise these special skills. In most cities there are international organizations that might help you. You can also inquire at universities, which often have students and faculty from many countries.

Perhaps the art you wish to see can be found only in a museum or art gallery. Then you have to take the class to the art. Make arrangements in advance with the people in charge and ask a guide to explain the art work to the children. Take paper and pencils so that the students can sketch and bring home their impressions.

Failing an actual object, pictures are the next best thing. The public libraries are rich resource places. Most art books are beyond the budget of public schools, but public libraries often have a number of books with beautiful color illustrations for those with the curiosity to find them and the muscle to carry them home. If teachers request it, libraries will sometimes purchase or borrow books that are not in their own collections. The bibliography at the end of this book lists resource books relevant to most of the projects described.

Once you have chosen an art project, think about materials. Is the same material available, or can you create a substitute? If you are studying Pueblo clay pottery and the school is lucky enough to have a kiln, you can work directly in clay. Or you could even create your own outdoor kiln in the Pueblo manner, as this book describes. However, if you have seen an exhibit of African masks and sculpture carved from wood, you will realize that wood is not a practical medium to use at the elementary level. Papier mâché would be a good substitute. Children's enthusiasm is greatest when their materials are as close to the original as possible, but their imagination is boundless and can fill great gaps. Children are realistic and know that making sculpture of pure

FIGURE 1-2. Vee-Ling Edwards shares her knowledge of calligraphy with Dan, a fifth-grade student.

MATERIALS

gold is impossible in the classroom, but they are delighted to see their cardboard sculptures (inspired by ancient pre-Columbian art) transformed by an application of gold paint.

The budgets of most public schools require that materials be as inexpensive as possible. Most indigenous art uses materials that are found naturally in the environment. The school usually has paper, glue, paints, and other basic art supplies. But look further into your community for other, sometimes free, often more exciting materials. Look at the land where you live, at what grows there naturally and by cultivation; look at the industries, the stores, inside the homes.

In some areas, children can dig clay, an act that brings them to the source of their material. Slate for use in rock engravings can be found naturally. Sand can be colored and used for sand painting. Native grasses and weeds can be used for weaving and basketry. In many cultures, jewelry is made from natural objects that are often available: seeds, bones, shells, and feathers.

Visit the industries in your area. Sheets of aluminum, which are excellent for making African repoussé panels or Mexican tin figures, are waste material from offset printing. Iron foundries throw away large hunks of man-made sandstone, which is a perfect medium for young children to use for their own sculpture when they are studying Inuit carving. Look into the stores and services in your community. Round three-gallon containers from the ice cream store can be used as segments in a totem pole. Old rubber inner tubes can be cut into shapes and used for making prints.

Use waste products from the home. Cartons, boxes, and tubes can be bases for papier mâché sculpture. Aluminum TV dinner trays can be cut up and made into tin sculpture. Leftover balls of yarn become fine weavings.

TRYING IT OUT

After finding the inspiration (in the form of art pieces or illustrations) and the materials, go through the project yourself before presenting it to the class. There may be pitfalls in directions or construction that you cannot foresee unless you go through the steps first. The method may be too tedious or require a skill level too high for the age level you have in mind. (Sometimes, however, especially with older students, encountering difficulties and overcoming them together is a valuable part of the problem-solving aspect of the art process.)

In a few cases there may be dangers in the art materials that are not immediately apparent. In going through the steps first, the teacher encounters these and makes the process safer before presenting it to the class. For instance, taping the overly sharp edges on cut aluminum or learning the safest possible way to set up hot wax for batiking can help prevent accidents from occurring.

Do you want replicas of ethnic art, or do you want to use an art form as a basis for inspiring the child's own creativity? This is an important question, and the answer will vary according to the purpose of the project. My feeling is that only *rarely* should an art form be literally copied. If the group is studying a particular culture and wants to get as close to it as possible so the children can participate vicariously in an aspect of that culture, then the answer may be yes, make replicas. For instance, if the group is studying Indonesia, they may choose to make shadow puppets, as described in this book. Children enjoy doing research; choosing a story; learning its meaning in that culture; and using the particular shapes, symbols, and colors for each character. Children have some freedom to choose which characters to re-create. They can put on a performance, complete with instrumental accompaniment, for their schoolmates. The feeling created by attempting to make and use authentic puppets and simulating the rhythm of the gamelon is a valuable experience.

Even in this situation it is not a good idea to be rigid. Most children will find challenge enough in re-creating an intricate shadow puppet. However, an especially creative child may use the inspiration to create his own character, using his own symbols. This is how new forms are created within all societies, and sometimes they are then perpetuated by tradition. Such an innovation should be acceptable within the classroom, too.

TO COPY OR CREATE?

FIGURE 1–3. Kate copies a photograph of an Indonesian shadow puppet as part of a class project to put on a wayang kulit performance of an episode from the *Ramayana*. It proved to be a valuable experience in learning about another culture.

FIGURE 1-4. This two-headed bird-of-the-mountain design by a fifth-grade student was inspired by the Otomí Indian cutouts. It is the student's own personal expression, not a copy.

My own predilection, whenever possible, is to use the art form in question as a method of exploring new ways of seeing and of expressing *oneself*. Except for the previously mentioned "re-enactment," which can be very rewarding, most children get little satisfaction from a copy—it falls short of reality and has too little of themselves in it. Children should learn the method and especially the *spirit* in which the art form was made and then use this knowledge to create their own art work. For example, in making the amate paper cutouts described in Chapter 6, authentic bark paper cutouts are shown. The Otomí Indian method of making the paper is explained, and the method we will use to simulate it. Then we talk about traditional Mexican designs. We look at examples in *Design Motifs of Ancient Mexico* by Jorge Enciso. We talk about how some of these designs spring from natural forms (birds, lizards, flowers, and people), even though they are not realistically drawn, and how others are based on geometric shapes (zigzags, triangles, squares, and so on). The children are encouraged to make imaginative designs based on a natural form or an abstract shape of their choice. The resulting designs, because of the materials and the original inspiration, have the spirit of the Otomí Indian work, but are as varied as the children themselves and are very much their own personal expressions.

2
ARTS OF
WEST AFRICA

Although African masks and sculpture are what first come to mind when one thinks of African art, this vast continent with its many different nations and ethnic groups is rich in other arts as well. Bronze, gold, ivory, textiles, and leather are used; pottery-making, weaving, and many other skills have been carried on for centuries. The artist has traditionally held a place of respect and importance in the village. Art is an integral part of life, sometimes an expression of religious ideas through abstract symbols. Containers, tools, dwellings, and clothing are often designed to have special meaning to the society, and they are strong in color and design.

Many villagers, especially in Nigeria, Ghana, and Senegal, still create textiles in the traditional manner. These are often richly colored and patterned with vibrant energy. Each village has its own partic-

TEXTILES

7

ular style. The designs are created in several different ways: by painting, weaving, printing, tie-dyeing, resist-dyeing, and combinations of these processes. Projects for all age levels can be based on these arts.

Photographs of these textiles can be found in many books listed in the bibliography. There is an increasing interest in these fabrics; perhaps you can locate an import shop that will allow you to borrow and display cloth or clothing made in Africa.

Adinkra Cloth of Ghana

Adinkra cloth, made in Ghana, is decorated with stamped designs. The stamps are carved from a calabash, and handles for them are made of strong sticks (see Figure 2–2). The stamp is dipped in a black dye made from the bark of the badie tree and pressed on the cloth. Adinkra, the name of the dye, means "good-bye," and the cloth was originally worn when guests were departing or at funeral ceremonies. Traditionally, the glossy black designs were stamped on matte black or russet cloth because those colors were used for mourning. More recently, they are

FIGURE 2–1. Adinkra cloth from Ghana. Symbols are stamped within squared-off sections of cloth strips, and the strips are sewn together with colored thread. Collection of Charles and Julie Steedman. (See also color plate 1.)

FIGURE 2–2. Five adinkra stamps carved from calabashes. From the collection of Mrs. Betty Okuboyejo. Photograph by Susan Buchan.

FIGURE 2–3. Adinkra symbols. Clockwise from top left: Adinkra 'hene, symbol of royalty, the most important adinkra design; Aya, the fern, symbol of defiance; Hye wo nhye, symbol of forgiveness; Fihankra, symbol of safety or security in the home; Akoma, the heart, symbol of patience and endurance; Dwanimen, ram's horns, symbol of strength.

also stamped on white or brightly colored fabrics and used for decorative purposes.

First, the artist usually divides the cloth into squares by drawing lines with a comb dipped in the dye. Then symbols are stamped within these squares. Sometimes the cloth is divided into small squares and the symbol is stamped only once in each square, but more often each symbol is stamped several times within a larger square.

There are many traditional designs used in stamping, and Ashanti names designate their meanings. Therefore, the cloth is not only a beautiful item of clothing but carries a message as well. See Figure 2–3 for some of the traditional symbols and their names and meanings.

In one type of adinkra cloth, one very large piece of fabric is stamped. However, the usual, older method uses long strips of cloth decorated in repeated designs, which are then sewn together with brightly colored thread. The joining stitch uses a sequence of colors that is repeated at regular intervals. (See color plate 1.)

Making Adinkra Designs on Paper and Cloth

FIGURE 2–4. Max, age eight, concentrates on cutting a stamp from a slice of potato.

For young children, a potato stamp can substitute for one made from a calabash. In fact, using this method, older children and adults can also produce beautiful results. First slice a potato into ¾-inch slabs. Then the children can cut the slab into simple shapes with table knives or plastic picnic knives. Brush tempera paint onto the flat cut surface and press it onto colored construction paper. Emphasize how a pattern is built up by repeating very simple shapes.

If there is concern in your community about using food, such as potatoes, for an art project, you can cut the stamps from pieces of styrofoam trays, the kind used for packing meat in the supermarkets. The styrofoam can be cut in shapes with scissors, and interior lines, circles, and dots can be made by pressing into the styrofoam with a pencil.

Beginning at the second-grade level, children can work together on a group project to create a large piece of adinkra cloth in the traditional manner. It can be displayed in the school as a decorative hanging. But first, so that the children understand the process and will have something to keep of their own, it is a good idea to work on individual squares of cloth. Old cotton sheeting does nicely and can be dyed after printing, or the children can work directly on colored cloth. The stamps can be cut from potatoes or styrofoam (see Figure 2–4). Acrylic paint, which will not wash out after it has dried, should be used for printing. The square of cloth should be

FIGURE 2–5. Melissa, age eight, has brushed her potato stamp with acrylic paint and is stamping it in one square of her piece of cloth. The edge of a piece of cardboard was used to print the squaring-off lines.

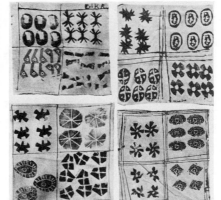

FIGURE 2–7. Four finished pieces of decorated cloth by second-grade students. Clockwise from top left: by Erik, Mira, Thea, and Katie.

FIGURE 2–6. The classroom teacher, helping at the dye table, rolls up Angela's sleeve just in the nick of time. Max and Daniel dye their cloth while Elizabeth waits for the color she wants.

FIGURE 2–8. Second-grade students print a strip of cloth for a large wall hanging. Rebecca is printing with a piece of styrofoam, and Molly is making a design by printing with the edge of a piece of cardboard.

placed on a thick pad of newspaper, which will help the stamp give a stronger impression. The typical adinkra cloth design is created within squared-off areas. These lines may be made by painting the edge of a piece of cardboard and pressing this against

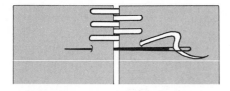

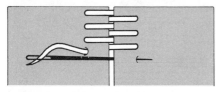

FIGURE 2-9. Diagram of the stitch used to join two strips of cloth.

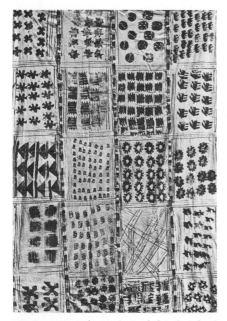

FIGURE 2-11. A section of the finished wall hanging inspired by adinkra cloth from Ghana. Each of thirty second-grade students stamped one square. The cloth was dyed bright blue and was then sewn together with red, orange, green, yellow, and black embroidery thread.

the cloth. Then fill in each area with one of the symbols: paint the black acrylic on the stamp with a brush, and press hard on the cloth. Repaint the stamp for each new impression (see Figure 2–5). Wash the brushes out immediately after use, before the acrylic dries. When the cloth is thoroughly dry, it may be dipped in a dye solution. Commercial dyes available in the grocery store work well, and plastic gallon milk containers, cut down, make fine dye pots (see Figure 2–6).

FIGURE 2-10. Second-grade students Jonathan, Rebecca, Susan, and Ori, under the supervision of a parent, take their turns sewing the cloth strips together.

To make a large hanging, tear a sheet into strips twelve inches wide and as long as the sheet. Mark off squares the length of the strip (every twelve inches) with a piece of cardboard. Each child fills in one square with his most successful stamp (see Figure 2–8). When thoroughly dry, the strips may be dyed a bright color. These strips can then be sewn together on a sewing machine or by hand. Although it takes time by hand, the traditional joining stitch (Figure 2–9) in a bright, repeated sequence of colors adds a great deal to the beauty of the cloth. One second-grade class completed theirs over a period of two weeks; parents helped by directing four children at a time during part of each day. They are very proud of the finished cloth, to which they all contributed so much (see Figures 2–10 and 2–11).

The parents who supervised the sewing enjoyed being involved in a school project. The children used doubled embroidery floss, just as it comes in the bundle. The threads were kept short, for safety's sake, so the children would not raise their needles too high and endanger the children next to them. Students preferred to sew towards themselves. As the work progressed, the ends of the strips were checked to be sure they were even. Between sewing sessions, the cloth, taped to a pole, was rolled up.

Older children from the fifth grade and up may want to duplicate more accurately some of the more complicated symbols used on adinkra cloth, learn their names and meanings, and create symbols that have special meanings for themselves. These symbols can be cut in potatoes, but since this stamp will not keep more than a day or two it may be better to cut the shape into linoleum for use over an extended period of time. Draw the design with a magic marker on a small piece of linoleum. Leave enough linoleum around the design so that the student can hold it easily while cutting. Observing the safety rule of *always cutting away from the hand that holds the linoleum,* cut away from the design with linoleum cutting tools, leaving the design raised. With heavy shears, remove the excess linoleum that had been used for holding the piece, and glue the design to a block of wood for easy handling (see Figure 2–12). A trial print with tempera paint on paper can show any changes that should be made in the stamps before the final printing. Finally, stamp the cloth using slightly diluted black acrylic paint, or roll black oil-base printing ink on the stamp with a brayer (Figure 2–13). Both methods produce a permanent washable design. Acrylic paint has the advantage of being water soluble before it dries, so that tools and hands can be easily cleaned. Oil-base ink requires turpentine for cleaning. As previously noted, first make the lines to separate the design into squares by inking the edge of a piece of cardboard and stamping with it. It is important to put a thick pad of paper under the cloth when printing. When it's dry, the cloth may be dyed any color. Children may make individual squares, or a group of students may make a large hanging.

FIGURE 2–12. A handle of scrap wood has been glued to a linoleum stamp for easier handling. This adinkra symbol is Aya, symbol of defiance.

FIGURE 2–13. Brian, nine, rolls oil-base printing ink on his adinkra stamp. This design is called Nsa, a motif from a cloth of that name.

Adire Eleko Cloth of Nigeria

FIGURE 2–14. Adire eleko cloth from Nigeria, of the olokun design, from the collection of Scott McGilliard and Susan Buchan.

Making Decorated Cloth in the Manner of Adire Eleko

The Yoruba people of southwest Nigeria make adire eleko cloth, a fabric with intricate white designs that stand out against the blue indigo dye. Adire eleko is created by placing a paste made of cassava starch and alum on white cotton. Sometimes the paste is painted on by hand with a feather or palm frond, and sometimes it is forced through a hand-cut zinc stencil. When the paste dries, the cloth is dyed with indigo. Although synthetic indigo dye is increasingly used, some villagers still make their own dye.

To make the dye, villagers chop and pound the indigo plant, dry it, and then combine it with potash in a complicated process that takes several days. The cloth is brown after being dipped in the dye and oxidizes to blue when hung in the sun. When the dye is dry, the cassava paste is removed; the paste has resisted the blue dye, creating the white design on a blue background. (Usually, since the paste is placed on only one side of the cloth, a little dye seeps in from the back, giving a bluish tint to the design.)

The Yorubas first draw lines that square off the material and then put designs within these boundaries. The designs are a combination of geometric lines (spirals, triangles, diagonals, dots) and shapes abstracted from natural forms (birds, flowers, snakes, fish). Fabrics made up of traditional combinations of these designs are given names. The adire eleko cloth pictured in Figure 2–14 is called olokun. It always includes the figures of birds around a stool seen here in a lower middle square. Color plate 2 shows a pattern whose name, translated, means "cloth with two patterns." Squares of abstract tortoise designs alternate with squares of birds, letters, and other symbols.

Before beginning the project, the children should study a piece of adire eleko, if it can be obtained, or photographs of the fabric.

Students from about fourth grade on can make their own resist-dyed cloth by using a paste made of six tablespoons of flour, one teaspoon of alum, and two cups of cold water.[1] This should be cooked

[1] Taken from *Contemporary African Arts and Crafts* by Thelma R. Newman. © 1974 by Thelma R. Newman. Used by permission of Crown Publishers, Inc.

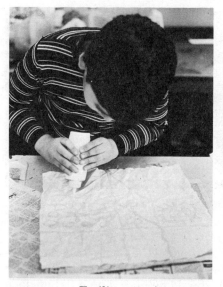

FIGURE 2–15. Emilio, age nine, uses a squeeze bottle filled with a specially prepared paste as a drawing tool. He first draws lines to square off his cloth and then creates designs in the squares.

FIGURE 2–16. James, seven, has dyed his cloth dark blue and is now scraping off the paste to reveal the white designs.

in the top of a double boiler. Stir it while it cooks until it becomes semitransparent and thickens somewhat. The designs may be painted on the fabric, but the somewhat glutinous paste is easier to manage if it is cooled slightly and put in a plastic squeeze bottle (mustard, hair dye, or soap bottles would do) and squeezed out. You can use the container as a drawing tool. After filling the bottle, test it first on newspaper to see if the consistency is right for drawing—not too thick to come out easily and not too wet. The paste should form a raised line. Beat in a little extra water if it is too thick; cool longer if it is too liquid.

Use any white cotton, such as old cotton sheeting, for making the designs. The children should have planned their design first, drawing it on paper equal in size to the cloth they will use. Remind them that the paste will be quite thick (⅛ inch or more) and that they should not make their figures too detailed. Place the cloth on a pad of newspaper. As they squeeze the paste onto the cloth, they can refer to their drawing. The application of paste should be

FIGURE 2–17. Designs inspired by adire eleko, created by sixth-grade students David and Sue.

FIGURE 2-18. A paste resist design by Wendy, eleven. Snake, flower, and leaf designs combine with geometric forms.

FIGURE 2-19. Samantha, five years old, brushes blue paint on a design drawn with a candle on light blue paper. You can tell that she has carefully observed the spiral and crosshatched designs of an adire eleko design.

Adire Eleso, or Tie-Dyeing

completed at one sitting; as the paste dries, it puckers the cloth so that there is no longer a flat drawing surface. The cloth should be placed on a flat surface to dry.

After the paste has dried *thoroughly,* for at least three days, place the material in a pot of commercial navy blue dye that has previously been made and cooled. A lighter color may not show enough contrast, and navy blue most approximates the indigo dye. After five minutes, rinse the cloth briefly under running water, place it between newspapers to blot up extra water, and then scrape off the now softened paste with a table knife or tongue depressor. Hang it up to dry. Since the paste resists only on the side on which it is placed some dye will seep in from the back. This gives a pleasing bluish tint to the design.

Very young children can make adire eleko designs on white or light blue paper instead of cloth. After being shown examples or photographs of the cloth, the children draw their own designs on the paper with a small candle or piece of paraffin (instead of cassava paste). When the drawing is complete, the paper is "dyed" by brushing on dark blue watercolor or diluted tempra paint. The wax resists the paint, and the design appears in good contrast against the dark blue.

In tie-dyeing a design is created by folding, bunching, or twisting material and then tying or sewing it very tightly so that the areas inside will resist penetration of the dye when the material is immersed in a dye bath. The art of tie-dyeing has been practiced for centuries in many parts of the world. Ancient examples of cloth decorated in this way have been found in South America, India, Japan, and China. Many countries in West Africa have a tradition of making beautiful fabrics through this art: Sierra Leone, Ivory Coast, Ghana, Togo, Senegal, Upper Volta, and Nigeria, among others.

In Nigeria, if the tied material is dipped in indigo, it is called adire (indigo) eleso (little stones) because often the pattern is created by tying in many rows of seeds or stones. In one traditional design, hundreds of tiny seeds are tied in concentric circles starting from the center of a very large piece of cloth.

Often, more than one technique is used in creating a design. Figure 2–20 shows a tie-dyed fabric from Togo. Rows of seeds were tied in, creating the small circles, and then the cloth was folded accor-

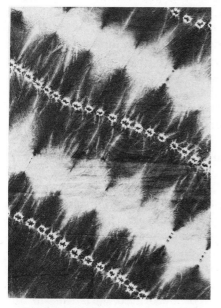 

FIGURE 2–20. Indigo blue tie-dyed fabric from Togo. Courtesy of Museum of African Art, Highland Park Community College.

FIGURE 2–21. Detail from a tie-dyed fabric made in Ghana. The diamond shape was created by tying small pleats in the cloth, the marbleized background by tying the cloth in a tightly bunched ball. Collection of the author.

dian style and either tied or sewn to create the larger diagonal pattern. After being tied, it was dyed in indigo. See color plate 3.

The fabric in Figure 2–21 is from Ghana. The large diamond, which is three feet long, was made by folding and tying the material in narrow pleats. The surrounding marbelized pattern was made by bunching the material into a tight ball and wrapping it with string. The cloth was immersed in green and gold dyes.

The tie-dyed fabrics are worn in a wide variety of traditional styles: wraparound skirts, robes, shirts, and head wraps. The fabrics are now also made into Western style dresses and shirts.

Making Tie-Dyed Fabric Designs

Many items can be decorated with the tie-dye method. Students can design wall hangings or decorate T-shirts, pillow covers, or curtains. Some of the students in the class may want to make a dashiki. The dashiki is a traditional African shirt worn by men, but it is becoming popular now in America for both men and women. There is an excellent film for younger elementary school children called *The Blue Dashiki,* which may be available through your library.[2] It tells the story of a young boy in the city who sees a dashiki in a store and earns the money to buy it. But children enjoy *making* a piece of clothing themselves that they can wear with pride.

Instructions for making a dashiki are given in Figure 2–25. The dashiki design is very simple and can be cut out and sewn in a few minutes. Plain white cotton cloth works best. Old sheeting is fine, but if it is *too* old, the fabric may be weak and tear easily. Avoid synthetic fibers, which often do not take the dye very well. On the junior high level, the students can sew the dashiki themselves; in elementary school, teachers or parents can do the machine sewing. Stitching by hand is rarely strong enough to allow for wearing. When the dashiki has been made, it may be decorated with the tie and dye method.

Students should experiment with tie-dying on

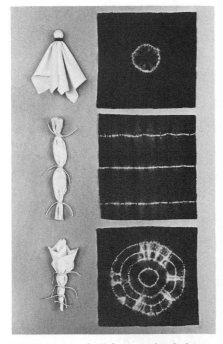

FIGURE 2–22. Articles on the left are tied in the manner that produced the results shown on the right. From the top down: a marble, secured with a rubber band; accordian fold bound with string; a long point tied in four places with string.

2 *The Blue Dashiki, Jeffrey and His City Neighbors.* Encyclopedia Britannica Educational Corporation, 425 N. Michigan Avenue, Chicago, Ill. 60611.

scraps of cloth before they make their final wall hanging or decorate a dashiki. Essentially, the material is tied *very tightly* in certain areas with string or rubber bands, so that when the cloth is dipped in dye the tightly gathered places resist the dye and form a pattern. Pulling the string hard against a slab of wax will increase its ability to resist the dye. Tying around marbles or beans makes small circles. Folding accordian style and tying makes different linear patterns. Try dipping a twisted and tied point of cloth in a light colored dye and then just the tip of the same area in a darker dye—this gives a sunburst with a deeper colored center (see Figure 2–22). Experiment and see what happens.

Commercial dyes, which are available in most grocery stores, should be mixed ahead of time. Make strong colors by using less water than indicated on the package. Add salt to make them more colorfast. Plastic gallon milk containers are good for storing dye, and more of the same containers cut in half make good dye pots. Dip tied fabrics in the dye until the fabric is a shade darker than you want it to be. Rinse out excess dye. Let the pieces dry thoroughly before untying.

If the tie-dyed fabric is to be a wall hanging, it should be ironed and then glued or sewn to a dowel along the top edge. Leave just enough dowel extending at either side to tie on a length of yarn for hanging (see Figure 2–24).

A dashiki should be ironed with a cloth dipped in diluted vinegar *before* it is washed the first time. This increases colorfastness. Wash separately from other clothing.

At first, tie-dyeing has many accidental qualities. If children are disappointed in the way it turns out, they can retie the cloth and dip it in deeper colors for a different effect. If it is still not satisfying, they can use the color as a background and print over it using potato or linoleum cuts and textile paint. (See the directions for making adinkra cloth.) A border around the neck, sleeves, or bottom edge may be all it needs. African fabrics frequently combine several different methods of textile design in one piece.

Dashikis may also be decorated with batiked de-

FIGURE 2–23. This design by Myles, age twelve, in orange, red, and blue, was achieved by folding the cloth and dipping in the tips and edges. It was then unfolded, folded again differently, tied with rubber bands, and dipped again.

FIGURE 2–24. Kristen's multicolored marbleized wall hanging was created by tying bunches of fabric in a few places and then crumpling up the entire cloth into a ball and tying it again.

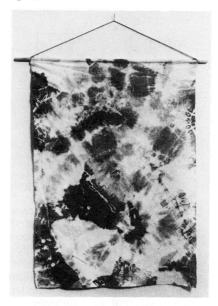

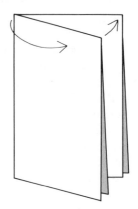

FIGURE 2–25. Directions for making a dashiki:

1. Double cloth lengthwise and hold against person for whom dashiki is to be made. For long sleeves, let it go from wrist to wrist; for shorter sleeves, cut at forearm. Cut at any desired length, leaving an extra inch for hemming.

2. Fold cloth over again, very precisely, matching all corners.

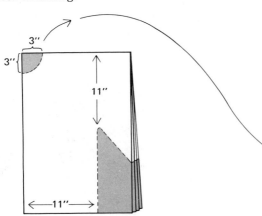

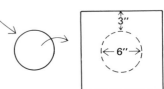

3. Cut on dotted lines to make neck opening three inches out and down from the corner. Mark this line first with a compass. Cut out piece to make sleeve: the folded dashiki should be eleven inches wide for an average student, ten inches for a slight student, and twelve inches for a heavier student. Carry this cut up to eleven inches from the shoulder and then curve down to make sleeve, as in diagram.

4. Take the circular piece that was cut from neck hole in step 3 and place in the middle of another piece of cloth. Cut out a hole of the same size. Discard both round pieces. The margin should be at least three inches beyond the hole all around. This will be interfacing for the neck.

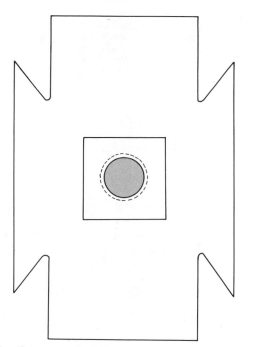

5. Open up dashiki and fit hole in square piece directly over hole in dashiki. Sew together to make facing.

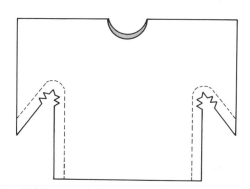

6. Fold material down with *facing inside*. Sew on dotted line under arms and down the sides. Cut *V*-shaped notches out of edge under arm.

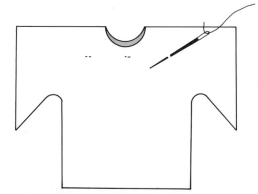

7. Turn right side out. Turn facing inside and tack-stitch at corners and front so that it will lie flat inside.

8. Hem sleeves and bottom to desired length. Decorate the dashiki by tie-dye method or by the batik process described in Chapter 5.

FIGURE 2–26. Jill's dashiki is blue and green. The front center was picked up in a long point and tied in three places with string. It was gathered and tied around the neck, sleeve ends, and bottom to produce the parallel lines.

signs. Wax batiking is a similar process to the Nigerian adire eleko, or cassava paste resist designs, described earlier. The country most associated with batiks is Java, and directions for making them are given in the section on Indonesian arts in Chapter Five.

ANCIENT AND CONTEMPORARY METAL WORK OF NIGERIA

Items made of bronze were produced in Africa as early as 2500 B.C., and work was done in iron as early as 400 B.C. Copper, gold, and silver were used as well. With these metals and varying techniques, tools, weapons, containers, weights for weighing out gold, and jewelry of all kinds were made.

Beginning in the fifteenth century and continuing through the nineteenth, the Nigerian kingdom of Benin created many beautiful, realistic sculptures in bronze. Artists made portraits of royal figures that rank among the finest sculptures of the world. The palace walls and doors in Benin were covered with bronze plaques, in relief, with decorated backgrounds. These plaques provided historical records of events in the empire: scenes of hunting, battles, family life, and symbolic animal forms. Figure 2–27 is a portion of one of these panels from Benin. The leopard spots are suggested by an overall decorative pattern of large circles, and tiny dots suggest fur. The background of dots and a floral pattern is typical of the Benin bronze panels.

Both the portraits and the panels were made with the lost-wax process. In this process, a sculpture is made of wax over a base of clay. The wax sculpture is modeled in very fine detail. The wax is then covered with a mixture of clay and charcoal. When this mold of clay and wax is heated, the wax melts and flows out of tubes set in the clay. Molten metal is then poured into the space left by the "lost wax." When the metal cools, the clay is broken away. This leaves the metal sculpture, which is then refined and polished. The lost-wax process of making bronze sculpture and jewelry is still used in Nigeria and in many other parts of Africa.

In Oshogbo, Nigeria, a Yoruba artist named Asiru Olatunde has become famous for his work in aluminum counter-repoussé panels. He achieves a relief design in metal that resembles the Benin work of centuries ago, but he does it by a very different me-

FIGURE 2–27. Bronze plaque with leopard. Benin, Southern Nigeria, seventeenth century. Courtesy of Linden-Museum, Stuttgart.

thod. Instead of modeling the sculpture in wax and casting it in bronze, he works with aluminum. When he hammers on tools placed on the face of the panel, the metal expands so that unhammered areas are raised into relief. This is called *counter*-repoussé. (In the more common form of repoussé, the raised areas are pushed out from the back.) Olatunde first sketches his designs on paper. He then uses simple tools to create a richly textured aluminum panel. In the panel shown in Figure 2–28, it looks as if he may have hammered on a nail set to form the background and used something like a screwdriver for the lines. Before hammering the background, Olatunde makes designs on the parts to be raised, such as patterns on clothing (typical Yoruba textile designs can be recognized) and fur and feather patterns on birds and animals. His designs, like the Benin bronzes, often show village scenes or animals. The background is enriched with designs derived from nature: leaves, stars, and insects. Many of his ideas come from Yoruba folklore. Like the carved wooden doors that have been made by Yoruba people for decades, his designs illustrate aspects of Yoruba daily life, history, and traditions.

Olatunde does commissioned work for churches (using such themes as Noah's ark or Adam and Eve), banks, universities, exhibitions, and museums. His panels are appreciated and purchased by both his own townspeople in Oshogbo and art collectors in other parts of Africa, Europe, and the United States.

FIGURE 2–28. Aluminum counter-repoussé panel by Asiru Olatunde, Oshogbo, Nigeria. Collection of the author.

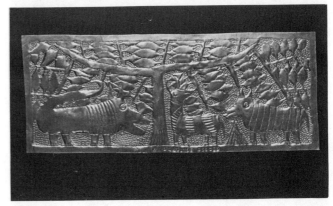

Sheet aluminum, 0.020 gauge, can be purchased at a reasonable price in hardware stores. (Do not use the tooling aluminum in art supply stores, as it is much too thin for this project.) However, if your community has an offset printing company, you may be able to get a few sheets of aluminum free. Although aluminum is often recycled now, the company may donate one or two large used sheets, which would be ample for your project. Aluminum offset plates come in several thicknesses. For this project use the thickest plate, at least 0.008 inches. With steel wool and scouring powder, remove ink from the surface of the aluminum before beginning the project.

Making Aluminum Counter-Repoussé Panels

FIGURE 2–29. Brian has taped the edges of his panel to preserve a border and transferred his design to the aluminum with carbon paper. Now he is making impressions on the design by hammering a nail with a stick of hardwood.

FIGURE 2–30. After impressing eye and flipper lines on his turtle design, Theodore uses a nail to fill in the background. This raises the unhammered areas.

Cut the aluminum sheets into rectangles about 3½ x 5 inches. This work calls for patience, and this is large enough for fifth- or sixth-grade students. Make a ½-inch border around the aluminum by folding one-inch masking tape over the edges. This will preserve a border of unhammered aluminum and also prevent students being cut by the sharp corners.

Next, work out a design on paper the size of the aluminum plate minus the border. The students should not try to get many small figures on this size plaque. One central animal, person, or design is probably best. Older students, of junior high age, may want to work on a larger panel. A large panel could show a group of people or a jungle, grassland, or river theme that includes a background of leaf, grass, or wave patterns. When the drawing is completed, it should be taped to the aluminum over a piece of carbon paper and transferred by pencil.

Remove the paper after transferring the design and place the aluminum over a thick pad of newspaper. Being careful not to penetrate the metal, create designs *on* the figures. Feathers, fur, spots, or clothing and features are typical designs. Pressing hard with an old ballpoint pen (that no longer contains ink) can make lines; tapping with a hammer on various metal objects (nails, nail sets, bolts, and screwdrivers) can create eyes, fish scales, and feather designs. This is done with a somewhat lighter touch than the subsequent hammering out of the background. If there are not enough hammers to go around, use eight- to ten-inch sticks of hardwood for hammers.

Once the designs on the figures have been completed, fill in the background with deeper, quite closely packed impressions. This will raise all the unhammered areas. A sharp nail will penetrate the aluminum (especially if you are using offset printing plates). It is better to use a dulled nail (hammer the point flat), the *head* of a finishing nail, or a nail set or bolt. The nail sets and bolts give pleasing round impressions without the danger of making holes that pierce the panel. If the impressions are too close together, the effect is poor; if they are too far apart, the metal will not raise properly.

When you have filled in the background, remove the tape and mount the panel by nailing it with small ⅝-inch no. 18 wire nails to a piece of wood. Lumber companies will often allow schools to use their scraps; if you are using scraps, you may find it easier to begin the project by cutting the aluminum to fit the different shapes of the wood pieces, rather than by sawing wood to fit the aluminum

FIGURE 2–31. Chandra has removed the tape that preserved a border and is nailing her panel to a block of wood.

panel after it has been made. Rub the completed counter-repoussé panel with very fine steel wool to bring it to a high polish.

FIGURE 2–32 *a, b, c, d.* Four counter-repoussé aluminum panels made with discarded offset printing plates, by sixth-grade students. *(a) Lion,* by Chandra, *(b) Pelican,* by Meg, *(c) Tree* by Polly, and *(d) Elephant* by Paul.

MASKS AND SCULPTURE

In our museums, we see masks and sculpture from West Africa and consider them works of art. However, all these pieces were created for a particular purpose, most often for a religious or magical rite. Children in Western society think of a mask as a disguise or as a chance to play the role of another

FIGURE 2–33. An antelope dance mask, worn by the Zamle Society, Guro, Ivory Coast; and a highly abstract Kplekple mask, commonly called "moon mask," Baule (bä-ōō-lee), Ivory Coast. Courtesy of the Plymouth House Galleries, Plymouth, Michigan.

FIGURE 2–34. Chi Wara headdress, depicting a mythical antelope, Bambara, Mali. Collection of Charles and Julie Steedman.

person or animal at Halloween. In Africa, masks are created and used for a number of very different reasons—usually as a link with the supernatural. They are only part of a more complete costume, and the accompanying music and dance are equally important in the ceremony.

Many West Africans believe that when a dancer puts on a mask, he becomes the spirit he is portraying. The masks are used for many different purposes. They are used in administering justice and in teaching young people the laws, history, and traditions of their society. Some of the ceremonies are an attempt to influence the forces of nature, such as to ensure a good harvest. In the mythology of the Bambara people of Mali, the Creator sent an antelope, Chi Wara, to earth to teach the people how to raise corn. Every year, in celebration of the birth of agriculture and to ensure a good harvest, the Bambara hold a dance. A male and a female dancer each wear-

FIGURE 2–35. A sixth-grade class has the opportunity to visit a gallery that has an African art collection. The students are sketching from a display that shows a variety of masks including two Dan masks from the Ivory Coast (upper left), a Bambara antelope mask from Mali (center), and a large round Baule kplekple mask, commonly called "moon mask," from the Ivory Coast. Courtesy of the Plymouth House Galleries, Plymouth, Michigan.

FIGURE 2–36. John makes a sketch of a Bambara antelope headdress from Mali (on the shelf). It is flanked by two Ashanti statues from Ghana. Behind them on the wall is a Bobo butterfly mask from Upper Volta. Other masks from the Ivory Coast, Guinea, and Nigeria are on the floor. Courtesy of the Plymouth House Galleries, Plymouth, Michigan.

ing a beautiful headdress depicting Chi Wara, gracefully imitate the motions of the antelope. (Figure 2–34 shows a male Chi Wara headdress; a female Chi Wara headdress is in the form of a doe with a fawn on her back.)

Some sculptures are made to ensure health. The Ashanti women of Ghana carry small sculptures resembling dolls to ensure the birth of healthy children. (Examples of these akua'ba statues can be seen flanking the antelope headdress in Figure 2–36.)

Sometimes sculptures are made to embody spirits. In some cultural groups it is believed that when a person dies the spirit wanders until it finds a suitable home. An ancestor figure is created to make a home for the spirit.

Masks are carved by specially trained artists, often after long apprenticeship in the art. The very tools the artist uses are sacred, and the artist uses all his skill to create a unique and powerful mask that is still within the traditions of his people. He works alone, in a special hut, with simple tools—an adze, a curved knife, and perhaps a chisel and hammer—carving in new, unseasoned wood.

African masks are created in an astonishing variety of forms, sizes, and styles. Some masks go over the head; some rest on the shoulders. Others are worn as high headdresses. Such materials as shells, seeds, beads, and sheet metal are sometimes added to the wood to suggest hair and ornamentation. In some masks, the surface is incised or painted with geometric designs. The colors are derived from native materials—white kaolin, black charcoal, and other earth and vegetable colors (see color plate 4). Artists rub oil or mud into some masks to darken the wood, which is polished to a satiny sheen; in other masks the wood is not treated or polished. Long straw or raffia fringes are frequently attached around the base of the mask to hide the identity of the person wearing it.

Although some masks are representational, most are not copies of nature but are highly stylized and symbolic. This increases the psychological impact on the viewer. Aspects of the figure are exaggerated to emphasize strength and awesome qualities. The human and animal forms are translated into geometric shapes often highly abstracted from reality. They are symbolic of the *qualities* of the animal or spirit being portrayed.

Papier Mâché Masks and Sculptures

If it is possible to arrange a visit to a museum or art gallery that has a collection of African sculpture, such a trip would be a great inspiration to the students. Make arrangements ahead of time with the people in charge so that they can be prepared to explain the items in the collection, answer questions, and help make the visit a valuable learning experience. Students should take paper and pencils and drawing boards (squares of corrugated cardboard work well) to make sketches of the pieces that most interest them.

If a museum experience is not practical, most li-

FIGURE 2-37. The framework for a sculpture of an antelope is created of half an egg carton (base), toilet paper rolls (legs), two juice cans (body), and a roll and wad of newspaper (neck and head). Later, tubes from clothes hangers will be inserted in the head for horns. The base for a mask is made by clipping a strip of cardboard into a circle and filling it in with crumpled newspaper.

FIGURE 2-38. John applies torn pieces of newspaper dipped in wheat paste to his sculpture of an antelope, inspired by a Bambara headdress.

braries have excellent books on African art, and students should have a chance to study them.

Making large wood sculpture would be an overwhelming project for most young students, but sculpture built of papier mâché is a fine substitute. This technique can be used in many other art projects as well.

First, a basic form or framework for the sculpture is built by taping or tying together boxes, tubes, other containers, or rolled newspaper. (See Figure 2–37). Then pieces of torn newspaper are covered on both sides with wheat paste and applied to the basic form, as shown in Figure 2–38. (See appendix for directions for making and using wheat paste.) At least four layers of paper should be applied for a strong sculpture. If one alternates between torn newspaper and torn paper toweling, it is easier to make sure each layer is complete.

To make a mask that can be worn, use the following procedure: fold one opened sheet of newspaper into a strip of paper 2 x 29 inches, or use a strip of flexible cardboard. Clip the ends of this folded paper or cardboard strip together to form a circle, or collar, a little larger around than your face. In masks based on animal figures the collar is not round but taped into a different shape, as was done in the

FIGURE 2–39. Nick applies a final layer of paper to his face mask, and Scott covers the twine-wrapped horns of his antelope mask with a layer of paper. The twine will give the horns the appearance of being carved in ridges.

FIGURE 2–40. After painting a base coat of black, Tamar paints the eyes and geometric designs on her mask, which is based on her drawing of the Baule mask in the gallery.

antelope mask in Figure 2–41. Scrunch up newspaper and fill in this collar. The stuffing should not be packed in flat; it should rise in a gentle curve up from the sides (see Figure 2–37). After applying one or two layers of papier mâché to this form and letting it dry, tape on tubes or cut cardboard shapes to create horns, noses, ears, eyes, mouths, or other protuberances. These are secured and integrated with the rest of the sculpture by adding two more layers of papier mâché. In Figure 2–39, one student is adding the final layers of papier mâché to his face mask, and another is working on an antelope mask. For the antelope mask, the tubes have been wrapped with twine to form ridges on the horns, which will still be visible under one layer of papier mâché if it is smoothed down carefully. After the mask is dry, the paper stuffing is removed from the collar. Eye and mouth holes can be cut into the mask with sharp scissors or a mat knife.

When the papier mâché mask or sculpture is dry, it may be painted with tempera paint. Apply a basic

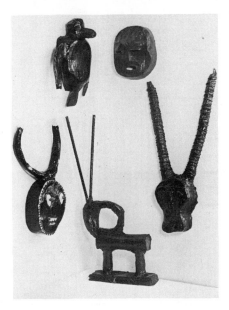

FIGURE 2-41. Five papier mâché sculptures based on drawings made in the art gallery by sixth-grade students. Clockwise from top left: sculpture based on a Senufo flying bird, by Monique; interpretation of a Dan mask, by David; antelope mask, based on a Bambara mask, by Alex; antelope sculpture based on a Bambara headdress, by John; mask based on a Baule mask, by Tamar.

coat of one color. Geometric designs or other color areas can be added after the basic coat is dry. (See Figure 2-40). If desired, other materials may be added for hair or decorations: yarn, grasses, shells, twine, stones, metal, beads, seeds. The mask or sculpture will be more durable if given a protective coat of shellac.

You can get ideas for many other art projects based on African arts by looking through the books listed in the bibliography, or by visiting art import shops or galleries. Jewelry, pottery, basketry, and weaving are all possible creative projects for the home or classroom.

3
ARTS OF
THE MIDDLE EAST

The rich cultural heritage of the Middle East is represented by arts that cover a time span of 4,000 years: twenty-fifth-century B.C. hieroglyphs carved in sunken relief on an ancient Egyptian tomb; sixth-century mosaic floors from recently excavated temples in Israel; the Persian miniature paintings of the fifteenth century; and finally, in twentieth-century Egypt, the contemporary tapestry weaving by the children of Harrania.

EGYPTIAN ARTS

Five thousand years ago a civilization grew up along the Nile River, developing and flowering over a span of three thousand years. It was a peaceful culture, living on a narrow strip of very fertile land and protected from invasion by deserts on either side. Over these many centuries, a great range of magnificent art and architecture was created, and because of the dry climate and the Egyptian desire to preserve everything for the afterlife, we are still able to enjoy many examples of these arts.

Most of the art that survives from ancient Egypt was created to provide continuity between life and death. The name for sculptor means "he who makes to live." The Egyptians believed that earthly life was merely a step people took before entering a spirit world. In that world a person would need his body, which was carefully preserved, and would want all the things he had enjoyed in life. Therefore, sculptors and craftsmen were set to work reproducing servants, animals, and domestic furniture. Ancient Egyptians believed that by magic these things would become real in the spirit world. Portrait sculptures of the kings and persons of high rank were also made, so that the spirit would have a place to go if it could not inhabit its own body. By the same token, the beautiful wall paintings on the tombs depicting hunting along the Nile, servants dancing, and other domestic scenes were to provide after death the things loved in life. Much that we know about ancient Egypt today comes from the sculpture and paintings and artifacts left in the few tombs that escaped the plunder of later years.

Beautiful objects were also created for the living, however: jewelry, vases, small sculptures, elegant hand mirrors, cosmetic containers, fine furniture. All these things were created by well-trained, anonymous craftsmen. There is no evidence that individuals became known as "artists" in their own right.

This high civilization came to an end with the occupation of a succession of invaders after 300 B.C. Many tombs were plundered, and temples were destroyed. Eventually the language was no longer spoken, and the ancient writing could no longer be read.

Hieroglyphs

For many centuries the meaning of the ancient Egyptian hieroglyphs was a mystery. Then in 1799, French soldiers, digging trenches at Rosetta after Napoleon's conquest of Egypt, came upon a stone with three different styles of writing engraved on the surface: hieroglyphic; demotic, a popular handwritten form of hieroglyphic; and Greek. It was realized that all three might say the same thing and that the inscription in Greek might provide clues to the two forms of the Egyptian language. Napoleon recognized the importance of the discovery and set scholars to work on it. Two years later the French were defeated. The stone was surrendered to the English and taken to the British Museum in London. Scholars there went to work on the problem immediately. The task was difficult, because part of the text was missing, and it was hard to match words. Many scientists, working on the deciphering, began to unravel 1,500 years of mystery. In England, Thomas Young made out three royal names, which gave clues to a few hieroglyphs; but the most brilliant work was done by a French scientist, Jean Francois Champollion. He had decided at the age of ten that he wanted to decipher the Rosetta Stone and pursued studies that would help him toward that end.

FIGURE 3–1. Egyptian sunken relief of the Courtier Biu, Sakkarah, Egypt, circa 2500 B.C. Courtesy of the Oriental Institute, The University of Chicago. The hieroglyphs, part of a speech by the noble, were cut into limestone in the chapel of his tomb. The vertical lines are the speech, and the horizontal line at the bottom serves as a label and reads, "The sole companion (of the Pharoah), Biu." Guided by the sounds given for hieroglyphs in Figure 3–2, can you find the name Biu?

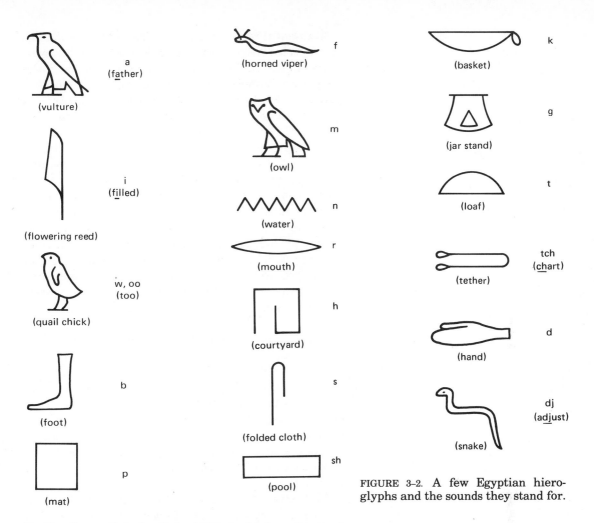

a (f**a**ther) (vulture)

i (f**i**lled) (flowering reed)

w, oo (too) (quail chick)

b (foot)

p (mat)

f (horned viper)

m (owl)

n (water)

r (mouth)

h (courtyard)

s (folded cloth)

sh (pool)

k (basket)

g (jar stand)

t (loaf)

tch (**ch**art) (tether)

d (hand)

dj (ad**j**ust) (snake)

FIGURE 3–2. A few Egyptian hieroglyphs and the sounds they stand for.

By the time of his death in 1832, he had made great progress in understanding the hieroglyphs and Egyptian grammar. The work of studying Egyptian writing is a continuing thing, however, and words are still being added to the known vocabulary.

Some hieroglyphs represent a single sound. For instance, an owl represents the sound *M* because an owl's name begins with that sound. However, some hieroglyphs represent a group of sounds, and some stand for an entire word. There are many hundreds of hieroglyphs. In ancient Egypt, the average person did not read or write. Scribes trained for many years to do the writing and record keeping.

There are two forms of hieroglyphic writing: the

monumental form used on statues and in paintings and the cursive script form used for keeping records. Viewed entirely from an artistic point of view, the former are sometimes a beautiful fine art, enjoyable just for the skill of execution, grace of form, and balance. They were carved and written so they would fill the space properly, not just to follow the necessary sequence. For instance, instead of simply stringing hieroglyphs in a line, one low symbol might be placed on top of another to balance a tall one next to them. The hieroglyphs usually read from right to left (in the direction they face), but sometimes for the sake of symmetry they read from left to right. The hieroglyphs, whether on flat surfaces or engraved in stone, were usually colored. Often the colors were the same as that of the object they represented, but sometimes hieroglyphs were painted a single color.

Carving Egyptian Hieroglyphs

Plaster is a perfect medium for carving hieroglyphs. (The directions for mixing the plaster are given in the appendix.) Pour it into styrofoam meat trays or small shallow boxes. The styrofoam works nicely because it is easily removed when the plaster dries. Other containers will need a coat of petroleum jelly before the plaster is poured in, so that the plaster can be removed when it is dry. Pour in enough to produce a ½-inch thick slab of plaster. Set it to dry overnight.

First draw the hieroglyphs on the plaster with a pencil. They are then cut into the plaster with linoleum cutting tools. Be sure that the hand holding the plaster is *behind* the one that is using the cutting tool. (After use, wash the tools; the plaster is corrosive to metal.) Figure 3–2 shows how some of the ancient hieroglyphs looked and sounded. Students may want to combine them to make an approximation of their own names. Although there were no symbols for vowel sounds as we know them, some sounds came close. A few more hieroglyphs, some of those commonly used in Egyptian jewelry, are shown in Figure 3–6.

If the hieroglyphs are to be used for making beads, be sure that they are engraved deep enough in the plaster to give a good impression to the clay.

FIGURE 3–3. Debbie, age ten, cuts hieroglyphs into plaster, with a linoleum cutting tool after drawing them first with a pencil.

FIGURE 3–4. Debbie's hieroglyphic tablet.

No jewelry has ever surpassed that made by the ancient Egyptians. Its beauty is breathtaking—and what has survived the milleniums is only a small fraction of what was created. Jewelry was perhaps the most valuable property of the royal families and the wealthy. It was enjoyed in life and then put in the grave with the deceased so that it could be enjoyed in the afterlife. Unfortunately, grave robbers were active throughout ancient Egypt's history, and after its decline very little went unplundered. A few tombs escaped the thieves, however, and from these we have a glimpse at what was made and how it was worn. Both men and women wore jewelry: necklaces, pendants, bracelets, crowns, anklets, rings, and pectorals (ornaments worn on the chest by men). The earliest jewelry, from prehistoric times, was made of stones, ivory, bone, shell, and clay. Around 4000 B.C., gold and silver had begun to be used. Faience (a glazed clay-like material) in shades of green and blue, and sometimes red and yellow, was also used in jewelry. Throughout the span of Egyptian culture, not only these materials but also lapis lazuli, carnelian (a red stone), turquoise, and many

Jewelry

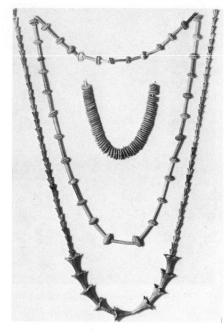

FIGURE 3–5. Blue and blue-green Egyptian faience beads from the New Kingdom, circa 1580–525 B.C. These have been restrung based on examples in which the original arrangement was preserved. Outside string is of lotus flowers, small and large; the next string alternates cylinder beads with fluted half-round beads; inner string is of lentil-shaped beads. Courtesy of the Oriental Institute, The University of Chicago.

other semiprecious stones and colored glass were used in jewelry.

Jewelry was made in workshops by artisans, whose families had been employed at the craft for generations. Beads were strung in many designs, perhaps the most well known being the intricate, broad collars. Pendants were sometimes made in animal forms: lions, crocodiles, frogs, flies, hawks, ibis, vultures. These were usually symbolic in nature. Serpents were frequent motifs, and so were flowers, especially lotus buds and papyrus. The scarab, the sacred beetle associated with the sun and worn as a protective amulet symbolizing immortality, was frequently used in rings, pectorals, and other settings. See color plate 5.

Hieroglyphs were used as design elements on jewelry. Figure 3–6 shows some that were commonly used: ankh, symbol of life; the udjat or Horus eye, source of health and happiness; and nefer, symbol of goodness, beauty, and joy. But hieroglyphs of stars, animals, birds, lizards, and fish were also used.

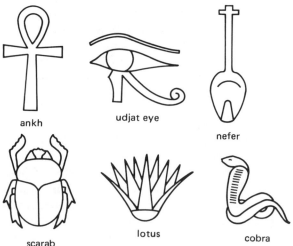

ankh   udjat eye   nefer   scarab   lotus   cobra

FIGURE 3–6. Hieroglyphs and designs commonly used in jewelry.

Making Clay Beads

A trip to a museum to see ancient Egyptian beads, scarabs, and other jewelry would be a great inspiration to students. Most of the jewelry found in the tombs is made of gold; the blue stone, lapis lazuli; turquoise; red carnelian stones; and glass beads. Fa-

40 Arts of the Middle East

ience, with a blue or blue-green glaze, was also used extensively. We don't know exactly how it was made, but many believe that it was a paste of ground quartz and some kind of adhesive, with a glaze containing copper. Students can use clay, which handles very much like the ancient paste. If the students make their beads of a clay that fires to a white or buff color, they can paint the beads to approximate a turquoise or blue faience. Fired red clay can approximate the color of carnelian.

Beads of clay may be rolled or patted into many shapes. To make cylindrical beads, form long rolls of clay about ¼-inch in diameter and cut in equal sections. Round beads are rolled between the palms of the hands. Lentil-shaped beads can be made by rolling a round shape and then flattening it. Many Egyptian beads follow a pattern of alternating shapes or sizes, small and large or cylindrical and round. The beads will have more interest if students use at least two different shapes. Pass a finishing nail (one without a head) completely through the bead and out the other side to form a hole for stringing. (If the nail is merely poked in and then removed from the same side, the hole tends to close up.) The hole must be made while the beads are still soft. Use a nail of eight penny size or larger. This may seem large, but the holes shrink during firing.

If the students have first made the plaster hieroglyphic slabs, they can create beads with fine raised designs. Roll out a marble-sized sphere in the palm of the hands, and then press this ball of clay into the hieroglyph. When it is lifted, an impression of the hieroglyph remains in the clay. Any number of impressions may be taken. The Egyptians made faience beads uniform by pressing the material into pottery molds in a very similar manner. If the bead is to lie flat when strung, be sure the hole is run through parallel to the flattened surface of the bead. This means that the bead cannot be pressed too thin, or there will not be room for the hole.

The beads should be fired in a kiln. The easiest way to keep students' beads separate from each other's is to make very simple clay pots to fire them in. Roll and pat a fist-sized portion of clay into a round ball. Then hold the ball of clay in the left

FIGURE 3–7. Kathy presses a round ball of clay into a hieroglyph carved in her plaster tablet to make a raised design on her bead. She has made a simple clay pot to hold the beads during firing in the kiln.

FIGURE 3–8. Kathy passes a finishing nail through the top of her clay bead. If it is put through parallel to the surface, the bead will lie flat when strung.

FIGURE 3-9. Clay beads by (from top) Kathy, nine, Debbie, ten, and Alec, ten.

hand, press into the top with the right thumb, and pinch in against the clay with the fingers. (Reverse if left-handed.) Keep turning the clay against the left hand and pinching the sides until it opens up into a bowl shape. Write the student's name on the bottom of the pot with a pencil or nail so that it can be identified after firing. If the pots are made first, the students can store their beads while they are making them. The pot will be fragile before firing, so handle it with care.

After firing, the beads may be left in natural clay colors, usually white or brick red. If the clay is white, the beads may be painted with water colors: a turquoise blue tint looks very much like Egyptian faience. If the painted bead has a raised hieroglyph on it, children can bring out the design by wiping some of the color off the raised figure with a damp cloth, creating a little more contrast with the rest of the bead. If painted, the beads should be protected with a coat of shellac or lacquer.

Nylon fishing line makes a very strong material for stringing beads. Because it is stiff, it can be pushed through the bead holes easily. Although heavy thread can be used, the holes may not be straight enough for a needle, and thread alone is not stiff enough to push through. Make strings of beads long enough to go over the head (remembering when you make them that with firing they will shrink in size), or make a catch by forming a loop in one end of the nylon line and tying a paper clip to the other. You can make better looking catches by twisting heavy copper wire into hook and eye shapes with hognosed pliers, or you can buy inexpensive commercial catches.

The Tapestry Weaving of Harrania

In the little village of Harrania, fifteen miles from Cairo, the children make very beautiful tapestry weavings that are now known and valued as far away as Europe and America. Work in this craft began thirty years ago, when Professor Ramses Wissa Wassef and his wife, hoping to revive crafts in the area, introduced the young children to the art of tapestry weaving. The Wassefs supplied the looms and wool and taught the techniques of weaving to the children, who were about eight years old.

Tapestry weaving involves working a picture into the design (unlike a rug of solid colors or stripes, for instance). It is done on a simple frame loom about which the warp (vertical threads) can be stretched in a way that keeps them taut. The weaver creates the picture by weaving colored wools over and under alternate threads of the warp.

The children of Harrania learned to weave directly on the loom without first making a drawing of their idea. Through long hours of practice (for even a small tapestry takes many hours of work), the children became excellent weavers. They learned to make their ideas visible and to keep very complex designs in their minds. The Wassefs, who had strong faith in the innate artistic abilities of children, were careful not to influence their designs. Their faith was well rewarded, for the tapestries are fresh and original. They often reveal close observation of natural surroundings: marvelous tree designs, animals, birds, fish, and the life of the people in the village. Sometimes the subject matter is portrayed realistically, and sometimes it is transformed by a whimsical imagination. The tapestries show a fine sense of balance and rhythm. Each is an individual expression. Copying is discouraged, and the work of each weaver can be distinguished quite easily from that of the others.

Using natural dyes, the weavers themselves dye the wool for the tapestries. The slight variations of hue in batches of hand-dyed wool add richness to the very colorful designs. See color plate 6.

There is no set time for weaving. The children attend school for part of the day and weave when they wish in their free time. Trips to such places as the Mediterranean, the banks of the Nile, or a zoo are arranged to give the children new experiences that often provide inspiration for their weavings.

Professor Wassef died in 1974, but the creative work continues in Harrania under the direction of his wife, Sophie Wissa Wassef. Some of the first "children" are still weaving, and have children of their own, who are beginning to weave also. There are currently twelve adults and about thirty children weaving at the Ramses Wissa Wassef Centre.

FIGURE 3–10. A tapestry woven by Reda Ahmed, fourteen years old. She has been weaving at the Ramsis Wissa Wassef Centre, Harrania, Egypt, for four years. Courtesy of the Middle Earth, Ann Arbor, Michigan, with the permission of the Ramsis Wissa Wassef Centre.

FIGURE 3–11. A young weaver at the Ramsis Wissa Wassef Centre brings her own ideas to life with colorful wool. Photo by Gretchen Whitman.

Their fine work is much sought after by museums and art collectors in Europe and America.

Making a Tapestry Weaving

Children in public school do not have time to weave large individual tapestries. However, a community project can both result in a large tapestry and introduce the art to many people.

One school decided to make a large tapestry to install permanently in the auditorium of their building. This was a cooperative art project, and parents, teachers, and children worked together. Because many people were to work on it, the tapestry's design had to be made first. The students saw photographs of the Harrania tapestries and of designs from other countries so they could understand the range of possibilities. They were encouraged, however, to use their own ideas. A great variety of designs was submitted, and it was difficult to make a choice, but a committee of parents selected one that they thought would work well. (They looked for bright color areas and not too many fine lines that would be difficult to execute.) A simple loom was constructed of 2 x

FIGURE 3–12. A simple tapestry loom of 2 x 2-inch wood, screwed together at the corners. It may be made any length or height desired. The brace in the center is simply wedged in, without screws or nails, after the loom has been warped.

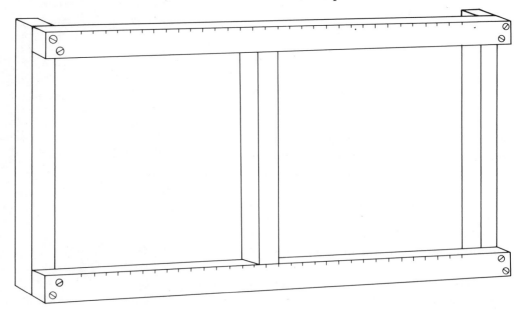

2 inch wood, screwed at the corners, measuring 3 x 5 feet. A 2 x 2 inch brace was inserted in the middle of the loom to keep it from sagging with the weight of the tapestry. The loom was marked off every ½ inch, top and bottom, as a guide to warping (see Figure 3–12).

The warp was tied to the frame. For this size loom, a piece of yarn ten feet long was doubled. The doubled end was wrapped around the bottom of the frame, and the two single ends were pulled through the loop (see Figure 3–13a). The ends were carried up and around the top frame and tied in a bow knot over the warp (see Figure 3–13b). This formed two warp threads, and the procedure was repeated until the whole frame was filled all the way across, with two warp threads every ½ inch. Since very young children were going to learn to weave on the loom, every other warp thread was dyed red to help them pick up every other thread as they wove the weft into the warp. (This was an afterthought. It would be much easier, in tying on the warp, to use two colors instead of one. Tie two pieces, one of each color and each five feet long, together. Place the knot at the bottom of the loom and proceed to tie on as before.)

Before weaving began, the original drawing was enlarged to the size of the loom (in this case into a half-circle shape to fit the contours of an area in the auditorium) and placed underneath the warp on a flat surface. The outlines of the design were transferred to the warp with a black magic marker. (This is somewhat difficult. Because the warp may turn during weaving, each thread must be separately marked completely around the strand.) An inch or so of extra heavy yearn was woven in at the bottom to space out the warp threads, which start out clumped together in twos. This was to be turned under when the tapestry was finished. The drawing was left taped to the back of the loom as a color guide.

The loom was placed in a hallway. The school was fortunate in having several parents who were weavers. A schedule was set up, and most afternoons found parents and children weaving together. The parent-teacher organization had voted a sum of

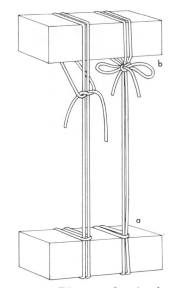

FIGURE 3–13. Diagram showing how to tie the warp to the upper and lower beams of the frame.

FIGURE 3–14. Lois Kane, parent and weaver, supervises second-grade students working on a tapestry. This tapestry, "A Sea of Fish" was designed by Sarah, age ten.

FIGURE 3–15. Fifth-grade students Jon, Julie, John, and Angie take a turn at weaving on a tapestry.

Some Weaving Procedures

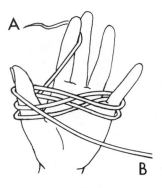

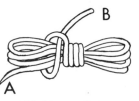

FIGURE 3–16. Making a "butterfly" of yarn.

money for wool, and this was supplemented by left-over wool brought from the students' homes. The original weavers taught other parents, who also supervised. Children who had completed their classroom assignments took turns weaving. The loom was big enough for four people to weave at the same time.

Altogether more than 100 parents and children worked on the tapestry for three months, watching it grow into a beautiful addition to their school environment. Through this work they gained a great appreciation of the much more complex work of the children of Harrania. Many children, from six years old through eleven, were introduced to a new art form. A companion piece to the first tapestry was completed the next year.

A heavy four-ply yarn is best for tapestry weaving. If the yarn comes in skeins, it must first be rolled into balls. The yarn is then twined into "butterflies" to be used in weaving. Figure 3–16 shows how to make a butterfly. Hold the end of the yarn (A) between the first two fingers. Wrap the yarn into a figure eight around the thumb and little finger. After you have made two or three dozen turns, cut the yarn from the ball, remove the yarn from the thumb and little finger, and wrap end (B) around the middle of the figure eight. Tie by putting end (B) through the last turn around. Take it around once more and tie again in the same way. While weaving with the butterfly pull yarn out at end A.

Pick up a group of warp threads of one color (every other one). Holding them in one hand, pass the "butterfly" of wool through the "shed." Do not pull the yarn straight across, but leave a "hill." This is very important. Because the wool goes over and under each warp thread, it requires a longer piece of yarn than just the distance across the weaving. Pat the hill down flat with a fork (see Figure 3–17A). At the end of the row, the yarn circles the last warp thread and comes back, this time going under every thread it went over on the previous row (and over every thread it went under).

When starting a new color area, pull weft that is ending through to the back, and let it dangle there.

You do not need to tie any knots. Start the new yarn in the same place, letting the end hang in the back also. This allows the tapestry to be woven face forward so the children can see the work as it progresses. Traditional tapestries are sometimes woven with the back facing the weaver.

When one color area meets another, the weft can turn around and go back, building up that area, so long as there is always solid weaving underneath to beat against with the fork. (In other words, a pyramid area could be woven in the warp to completion without weaving surrounding areas of a different color until later, but a funnel shape could not be done until surrounding areas were done first.)

There are several different ways to weave adjacent color areas. The easiest for beginners is for each color to turn and go back, as is shown in Figure

FIGURE 3–17. The yarn should not be pulled straight across but left in "hills," which are then beaten down with a fork (A). When one color reaches another color area it turns around and goes back (B).

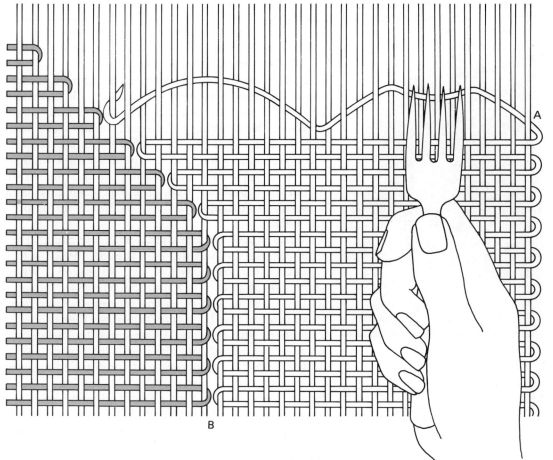

FIGURE 3–18. Overhand knot. Push the knot up close to the weaving.

FIGURE 3–20. A detail of the tapestry. A few fine lines—such as the birds' feet—were embroidered on after the weaving was done.

FIGURE 3–19. A finished tapestry, "Tree of Animals," designed by Jenny, eight years old, and woven by over 100 parents and students. Because it was designed to fit an alcove in the auditorium, it is mounted on semicircular, heavy cardboard, with warp ends tied and stapled to the back.

3–17*B*. Although this forms a vertical slit in the tapestry, unless the slit is very long, it does not cause a problem and is commonly seen in tapestries. If it does cause a gap, it can be sewn together on the back after the tapestry is completed.

As the weaving progresses, the warp may become loose. If it does, the knots at the top should be untied one by one and the warp pulled tighter and retied.

When the weaving is finished, tie the warp with the overhand knot (see Figure 3–18). Cut two strands loose from the loom and tie them up close against the weaving before progressing to the next two. When the tapestry is hung, the tied warp may hang down as a fringe, or it may be taped up against the back.

Many tapestries are woven with the design running parallel to the warp—on the loom it looks like a picture turned sideways, or "up ended." When such a piece is off the loom, the fringe will appear at the sides instead of at the top and bottom (this is shown in the Harrania tapestry, Figure 3–10). Beginners find it easier to weave with the design parallel to the weft, just as it will look when taken off the loom. The fringes are at the top and bottom.

THE ANCIENT MOSAICS OF ISRAEL

Israel is rich in arts that reflect the many religious and cultural groups that have lived in this tiny but ancient land. Judaism, Christianity, and Islam have their roots in this area, and synagogues, churches, and mosques have been carefully preserved over many centuries. History is piled upon history, and the architecture and arts of early times are continually being brought to light. Sometimes this is by accident, and sometimes it happens through the efforts of archeologists.

In the early twentieth century collective settlements *(kibbutzim)* were begun in many parts of the country, which at that time was called Palestine. The people worked very hard to raise crops and dug irrigation ditches to bring water to the arid land. In 1928, while digging such a ditch, people from a settlement at Hefzibah in the valley of Jezreel unearthed some ruins. They realized they had made an important discovery. The site was carefully excavated by Professor E. L. Sukenik, an archaeologist from the Hebrew University in Jerusalem. When the earth was removed, the foundations of an ancient synagogue named Beth Alpha were revealed. The synagogue had a beautiful mosaic floor, the most complete to be discovered in Israel. An inscription in Aramaic (a Semitic language) states that the floor was laid down in the reign of the Roman Emperor Justinian, who ruled from 518 to 527 A.D.

The art of making mosaic floors was developed by the Greeks in the Mediterranean area as early as the fourth century B.C. In Greek and Roman times, it was widely used in public and private buildings. However, the design of the floor at Beth Alpha is very unusual, because it is unrelated to classical art styles of the time. It is signed by two craftsmen, Marianos and his son Hanina, and is a refreshingly original and touching expression of these two craftsmen, about whom we know little else. A childlike directness and simplicity embues the mosaic with a spirit of joy and reverence. It is believed that the craftsmen were not trained in mosaic work but were unusually gifted folk artists of that rural area.

The floor is divided into three panels that include designs relating to religious services, signs of the zodiac adapted from Greek figures, and a depiction of the Biblical story of Abraham and Isaac. Archaeologists think that the synagogue was probably destroyed by one of the earthquakes that devastated

FIGURE 3–21. Detail of a servant from the panel of Abraham and Isaac, part of the mosaic pavement of Beth-Alpha Synagogue, Hefzibah, Israel. Early sixth century. Photograph by Palphot-Holyviews Ltd., Jerusalem, Israel.

the area in ancient times.

Another beautiful mosaic floor from the fifth-century synagogue of Ma'on was discovered at Nirim, a kibbutz founded in southern Israel in the Negev Desert in 1946. This mosaic, which includes brightly colored birds and animals in its design, was discovered during the ploughing of a field. It was excavated in 1958. A detail is shown in Figure 3–22.

Mosaics were often used on floors and walls in ancient times. They made a decorative and durable surface in homes and public buildings. Small cubes of stone, called tesserae, were cut and set in cement mortar. The range of colors was usually limited to the limestones available locally. These ranged from white and cream to red-brown, browns, and black. In some areas craftsmen used marble and brick. Sometimes blue, yellow, and green glass cubes added to the colors. See color plate 7.

Since the color range was limited, the designs depended on value for effectiveness. Value is the range from light to dark. Usually, a craftsman set off a figure from the background by composing it of dark colors against a light background, occasionally by using light colors against a dark background. Another common way to make the design stand out was to outline the shapes in a very dark color. The small square shapes that make up the mosaics create a very pleasing pattern and give unity to the designs.

In all, over 500 mosaic floors have been found in Israel. Discovered in ancient churches, synagogues, Roman palaces, villas, and baths, they reflect the long history of the area and the many peoples who have lived there.

In many places, archaeologists working at "digs" are finding other arts from the past: prehistoric stone tools from 300,000 years ago, sculpture, bits of household pottery, oil lamps, and coins from early civilizations. In 1947 a Bedouin shepherd boy looking for a stray goat found jars containing ancient manuscripts in a cave at Khirbet Qumran near the Dead Sea. They were Biblical and sectarian texts of great importance, estimated to be 2,000 years old and now known as the Dead Sea Scrolls. They are housed in a special building, the Shrine of the Book, at the Israel Museum. Since then archaeologists ex-

FIGURE 3–22. Detail of a leopard from the pavement of the Synagogue of Ma'on at Nirim, Israel. Late sixth century. From *Israel: Ancient Mosaics,* produced by the New York Graphic Society and published by Little, Brown and Company. Photograph courtesy of UNESCO.

50   Arts of the Middle East

ploring these caves have found other written materials and artifacts dating from the second century.

All these items made by hand so long ago tell us about the people who lived in those times. Archaeologists, in studying their finds, are working to put a puzzle together, seeking clues about earlier ways of living. It is surprising how much we can learn about ancient civilizations from the arts that have survived them.

Lower elementary students can make very lovely mosaic designs using paper tiles. Cut ½-inch strips of construction paper in many colors (including white), and then cut these strips into ½-inch squares. Make the mosaic designs on pieces of 9 x 12-inch colored construction paper. Brown and dark blue make good backgrounds.

Paper Mosaics

FIGURE 3–23. Becky, six, works on a paper mosaic design.

FIGURE 3–24. *Flower,* paper mosaic by Rachel, age eight years.

At each table, put trays of tiles sorted out by color (aluminum TV dinner trays that have separate compartments are excellent for this). Students select their colors and work directly on the background paper, pasting each tile down with white paste. The best method is to make one large central figure and then fill in the background with a contrasting color. The spacing is difficult for young children—explain that the tiles should not touch but should not be too far apart either. Make a sample to show them.

When the mosaic design is finished and dry, you can much enhance it by brushing on a coat of shellac or polymer medium. This gives a glazelike sheen to the paper tiles. Glue or staple the mosaic design to a slightly larger piece of colored construction paper (that repeats one of the colors used in the design) and then to a larger piece of black or dark brown paper that extends 2½ inches beyond the design. See Figure 3–24.

Making Tile Mosaics

Older elementary students can use ceramic tiles in place of the stone and glass cubes used in ancient mosaics. Tile can be purchased from ceramic tile dealers or building contractors. Occasionally tiles left over from jobs or in discontinued colors will be donated to a school. Tiles are available in two thicknesses. It does not matter which thickness you use, as long as you don't mix them in one mosaic (irregular height makes the final step of grouting very difficult). Small one-inch square tiles are a little easier

FIGURE 3–25. Diagram of a tray for a tile mosaic. *(a)* Top view. The screen molding is glued around the outside of a plywood base. *(b)* Although the two shorter pieces of molding are the same length as the sides of the base, the other two pieces must be longer in order to overlap them.

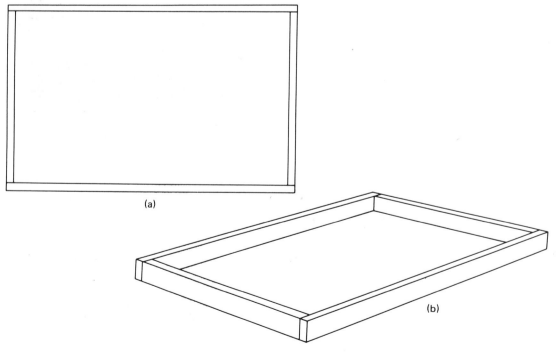

(a)

(b)

to handle. The color range of ceramic tiles is somewhat limited (just as it was in ancient times, although for different reasons)—they tend to be quiet, muted colors. In selecting tiles, think more of value than of color. Be sure that there are some very light and some very dark colors. Imported glass tiles (tesserae) are made especially for mosaic work and can be purchased at art supply stores and some tile supply stores. They come in a wider range of colors, but these can be expensive if you have a large group of students.

First make a wooden tray to hold and frame the mosaic. Quarter-inch plywood works well. A size of approximately 7 x 10 inches is ample for a sixth-grade student. Junior high students may have the patience for a larger piece. Frame the plywood with ¼ x ¾-inch pine molding. A common mistake is to cut all the pieces the same size as the sides. Two must be longer so they can overlap adjacent strips (see Figure 3–25). Glue the strips to the plywood with white glue, applying glue to the plywood edge and the corners where the molding joins.

Work out a design with charcoal on a piece of paper cut to the size of the plywood. The charcoal will help the students think in terms of bold designs with thick lines and solid color areas. Very fine lines and details cannot be made in an area this size with tile fragments.

It is very important to explain the concepts of color and value before students begin. They often find the concept difficult because they are used to thinking only in terms of color. You may have tiles in several different values of the same color, for instance, from light blue to dark blue. Because a mosaic design is disconnected (made up of pieces), a design does not show up unless it contains contrasting values. For example, if a figure is made of light blue tiles and the background is made of light green tiles, the figure will tend to disappear into the background. No matter what the color, if the figure is to stand out from the background, it must be very different in value—either much lighter or much darker.

The tiles must be broken up into smaller pieces. It would be too time-consuming for a large group

FIGURE 3–26. Tamar, eleven, breaks tiles into smaller pieces for her mosaic. She places the tiles between a folded newspaper and hits them with a hammer. It is important to wear goggles as a protection against flying fragments.

FIGURE 3–27. Tamar puts white glue on a piece of tile with a brush. She will then fit the tile into her mosaic design.

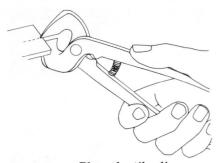

FIGURE 3–28. Place the tile clippers so that the blades just nip the edge of the tile. The dotted line shows where a cleavage will form when the handles are pressed together.

of students to cut the tiles into many smaller square shapes like the ancient cubes. Fortunately, fine mosaics can be made from irregular pieces. (Even the small 1-inch tiles should be broken up. They are not only too large for this size mosaic; they are too mechanical and regular in appearance. All ancient mosaic stones were hand-cut and quite uneven.) To break up the tiles, place them between several layers of newspaper or between the pages of an old magazine and hit them hard with a hammer. Always wear protective goggles, because the newspaper often tears and the fragments of tile can fly a good distance. Replace torn papers immediately with new papers.

The design, which has been worked out in charcoal, is drawn directly on the plywood. Small pieces of tile are then glued to the plywood, filling in the design. Use a white glue. Leave a space of approximately ⅛ inch between pieces. Occasionally it may be difficult to fill a space with the accidental shapes created by breaking the tiles. In this case, shapes can be cut to fit with tile clippers. Tile clippers look a bit like pliers, but the cutting blades do not come completely together. Place the clipper blades so that they just nip the *edge* of the tile and press the handles together. A cleavage will form straight across the tile from the point of pressure (see Figure 3-28). When you cut tiles, always keep both the tile and the hand holding the clippers inside a clear plastic bag. This prevents fragments from flying all over the room and still allows you to see what you are doing.

When the tile pieces have all been glued to the plywood, let the mosaic dry overnight before filling it with grout. Grout is available at art supply stores and wherever tiles are sold. Mix the grout to a thick, creamy consistency and spread it over the mosaic, forcing it down into all the cracks with a straight piece of cardboard. Scrape the surface as clean as possible and wipe it gently with a damp sponge. After the grout has dried, clean the surface more thoroughly with the sponge. Clean the wood frame, too. When the frame is dry, use fine sandpaper to remove any remaining traces of grout and make a smooth surface.

(a)

(c)

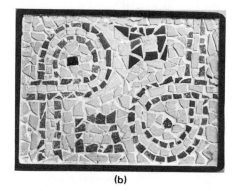

(b)

FIGURE 3–29 *a, b, c, d.* Tile mosaics by sixth-grade students. *(a) Duck on Pond* by Ellen, *(b) Abstract Design* by Steve, *(c) Pot of Plants* by Elizabeth, and *(d) Whale* by Marie.

(d)

The mosaic will look more finished if the frame is stained. A walnut stain goes well with most colors. Place masking tape on the mosaic surface around the edge where it meets the frame to protect the mosaic from the stain. Apply the stain with a brush to the inside and outside of the frame. Wipe off any excess, and let it dry before removing the masking tape. If some stain has seeped under the tape it can be scraped off the grout with a knife, and it can be removed from the tile surface with turpentine or paint thinner.

The sizes suggested for the mosaic panels are for

individual student projects. Several students working together might want to make a large mosaic for permanent display in their school, public library, or other civic center.

PERSIAN MINIATURE PAINTINGS OF IRAN

Persia was the ancient civilization in which present-day Iran has its roots. The miniature paintings for which it is so well known were a late development. Much of the early art was on a very grand scale—great carvings in rock and huge wall paintings. There was also work in bronze, other metals, and fine ceramics with decorative brush work. In the early thirteenth century, the Mongol invasions of Persia opened the way for Chinese influence on painting styles. By the late thirteenth century, this influence combined with Persian concepts to give

FIGURE 3–30. *Asfandiyar Slays a Dragon,* from a manuscript of the *Shah-Nameh* by Firdausi. Iranian Timurid School, mid-fifteenth century. Courtesy of The University of Michigan Museum of Art.

new impetus to Persian artists. For a period of over 300 years, they created manuscripts illustrated with small paintings of great purity of color and fine detail.

Schools of manuscript painting developed under the patronage of the shahs, the rulers of Persia. Fine books were traditionally held in great respect. Because they were meticulously made by hand with expensive materials, only the very wealthy could afford them. Workshops were set up, and specialists were hired for every aspect of book making. Very fine paper was made of linen and brought to a glossy finish by careful burnishing. Calligraphers, who did the writing, were held in very high esteem. Some craftsmen specialized in sewing the pages together and others made elaborate leather covers for the books.

Artists trained for years to become painters. To begin with, there were long hours of lessons in drawing. Before they used color, they had to learn to make their own brushes. They raised white Persian cats just for this purpose and plucked especially fine hairs. These they bound together to a pigeon quill. At first they filled in the colors after a master had drawn the outlines. Gradually, if they showed talent, they were given more responsibility, until they too held positions of honor. Artists of exceptional ability could rise to a high position in the shah's court, even though they were of humble birth.

The paintings illustrate traditional stories of action, both historic and romantic. Because the painters used contemporary settings (rather than setting the stories in their actual earlier historical period), the paintings show life in the Persian courts of the time. They are so detailed that we can learn much about the clothing, customs, and occupations of the people in those days. They are not realistic, however. The people and their surroundings are arranged to make a flat, balanced design in a mosaic of bright color and decoration. Gardens bloom; every surface of wall and courtyard is decorated with geometric or floral designs; and clothing, saddles, and tents are richly patterned. Gold was used lavishly—it was often used for the sky or for mountains and in clothing and ornaments. Silver was used for pools and

FIGURE 3–31. *Siyawush Displays His Prowess Before Afrasiyab,* from a manuscript of the *Shah-Nameh* by Firdausi. Iranian, Timurid School, mid-fifteenth century. In this polo game, a test of strength and skill, Siyawush drove the ball "out of sight, to see the moon," which pleased King Afrasiyab. Courtesy of The University of Michigan Museum of Art.

streams (although it now looks black, having oxidized over the centuries).

The brilliance of the Persian pigments has never been rivaled for its purity and intensity of color. Such minerals as lapis lazuli, for blue, were pulverized and mixed with special binding materials. Some minerals were brought by camel from thousands of miles away. The workshops kept their formulas secret, and we still do not know the exact methods that produced the paints. Brilliant reds, pure yellows, many shades of green, and intense blues glow like jewels on the paper.

The paintings were bordered in gold, and the page was often further embellished with a wide margin that was flecked with gold or painted with decorative birds and animals or golden arabesques (flowing flower and vine designs).

These great manuscripts are treasured and kept in museums in many parts of the world. We are fortunate that present-day methods of reproduction can bring some of their beauty within everyone's reach.

Figures 3–30, and 3–31 and color plate 8 are paintings that were made to illustrate the *Shah-Nameh* (the *History of Kings*). This great Persian epic poem of some 60,000 verses was written by the poet Firdausi, who finished it in 1010 after working on it for thirty years. It is a legendary history of the Persian people, full of heroic adventures and the rise and fall of empires and leaders. Many illustrated editions of the *Shah-Nameh* were commissioned by princely patrons of the arts.

Miniature Painting

Most students have been told in painting classes for so many years to "make it big" that they are delighted to work on a small, intimate scale and to paint tiny details to their heart's content. A piece of white drawing or construction paper about 7 x 10 inches is a good size. Draw a ¼-inch border around the edge with a ruler.

If the painting is to have the feeling of the Persian miniatures, there needs to be an emphasis on three things: action, color, and surface decoration. Although there were a few ancient portraits and animal paintings, most told a story. The Persian miniatures seem to come from a land of eternal spring, with flowers always blooming amidst scenes of battles, dragon slayings, and duels. Students may want to paint a scene typical of a Persian painting, or they may want to use subject matter with which they are familiar. They may want to illustrate historical stories, legends, or narrative poems from their own heritage. Longfellow's *Hiawatha,* the story of Daniel Boone, and the legend of Paul Bunyan are only a few of many possible inspirations to the student.

Have students make a careful drawing in pencil before they begin painting. Surfaces in the miniatures are richly patterned. A tree is not just an expanse of green; it has leaf patterns in great profusion painted in different shades of green or gold. The ground is decorated with tiny flowers. Our buildings do not have the elaborate surface designs found in these paintings, but a pattern of bricks or shingles can add a design quality. If an area of grass or a wall or clothing is to be embellished with flowers or a pattern, first outline the area, *omitting the de-*

FIGURE 3–32. Miniature paintings by sixth-grade students. Clockwise from top left: *Man Playing a Lute,* by Fred; *Hunting by Horseback,* by Saskia; *Unicorn,* by Eileen; and *Deer,* by Chris.

tails, and paint it with a background color (say, green for the grass). Let the paint dry, and then draw the flowers or patterns that will be painted on top of this basic color. Paint with a fine detail brush, using tempera paints in bright reds, yellows, blues, greens, and gold. White, too, plays an important part in most of the paintings. Everything should be kept on a small scale. Although some of the Persian paintings illustrated rather large books, they are still miniature, because the figures are small and the paintings filled with action and detail.

The border should be painted gold. Mount the painting by first gluing it to a white or cream-colored piece of paper that is ⅛-inch larger all around than the painting. Then mount these two pieces on a mat of decorative paper that extends an inch or more beyond the painting. Wallpaper sample books often contain many gold designs—flecked, flowered, or marbleized—that are very much in keeping with the Persian miniatures. (The artists who painted the miniatures did not usually make the page margins themselves; they were painted by students who were trained to do only that.)

4

EUROPEAN ARTS

Although this book associates a particular art with one country, the art may not be unique to that country. This is particularly true of the arts and crafts of Europe. Cookie stamps, here associated with Sweden, are made in many parts of Europe for decorating cakes and sweets. The art of pressing and arranging flowers is probably just as common in Switzerland as it is in Germany. Although craftspeople in Poland excel in the art of wycinanki, or cut paper designs, artists in Germany also create intricate cutouts, which are called Scherenschnitte. In several European countries it is the custom to decorate eggs for the holidays, although many different methods are used. Straw decorations in great variety are created in rural areas throughout the continent.

However, although the general idea may be the same and similar materials used, arts and crafts are usually distinctive to a particular cultural area. Traditional designs, patterns, and styles that de-

61

velop in one country, or in regions within a country, set them apart from items of a similar kind made elsewhere.

SWEDISH COOKIE STAMPS

In the old days, the interiors of Swedish farm houses were brightened with many decorative arts. During the long, dark winters people spent a lot of time indoors, and they passed the time making clothing, furniture, tools, and decorations for the home. Fine linen wall hangings were woven to hang from the rafters on special occasions; clothing, cushions, and coverlets were embroidered; mittens were knitted in fancy patterns; wooden boxes and kitchen utensils were richly carved; chests, boxes, and bedsteads were painted in floral patterns. Gifts of beautifully carved spoons and other household implements often showed a young man's serious attentions to his beloved. If they married, the implements were used and treasured throughout their married life. A young girl began filling a chest with her handwoven and embroidered linens long before her marriage took place.

One of the items made for cooking was the cake or cookie stamp. It was the custom for each family to have a set of beautifully carved stamps to use for special holiday celebrations, weddings, and funerals. Guests were given small cakes stamped with their host's designs to take home. At Christmas piles of little cakes or cookies were made for all the members of the family, each cake impressed with its own special stamp. The stamps were round, square, or diamond shaped, and cut into them were geometric patterns or figures of birds, animals, or hearts. Some designs became traditional to a particular province, especially if it was isolated from other areas.

A girl's fiancé would carve a stamp and give it to her as a token of his love, and she in turn would make him some cookies, decorating them with the stamp. These were called fiancé buns. There were several different cookie recipes. One favorite cookie still being made is called the pepparkaka. It is a spice cookie much like a gingersnap.

The custom of making cookie stamps is believed to have begun sometime in the early sixteenth century, and it reached its height during the eighteenth

FIGURE 4–1. Carved wooden cookie stamps from Småland, Sweden. Nineteenth century. Courtesy of the Nordiska Museet, Stockholm, Sweden.

and nineteenth centuries. In some rural families, stamps handed down for generations are still being used in Sweden today.

With industralization home crafts began dying out, but when this trend became apparent, Sweden made an effort to foster the work of its country craftsmen. Organizations were formed to market products, and linen, wooden articles, baskets, and rugs were commissioned. The heritage of fine craft work has not been lost. Sweden is famous for its contemporary arts and crafts as well as its traditional home crafts.

Swedish cookie stamps were made of clay or carved in wood. Clay is an easier and safer medium for young children. Make a ball of clay by rolling a walnut-sized piece around between the palms of your hands. Then place the ball on the table and flatten it to a disk about ½ inch thick—no thinner, or there will not be room to carve in designs. If you make several of these, you will have a set. Stamp bases may also be formed in square and triangular shapes. Next roll out some clay under the fingers and palms in a back and forth motion against the table. This makes a long "snake." A ½-inch-thick roll is about right. Cut this roll into sections about 1½ to 2 inches long. Each section will be a handle. Place the handle in the center of a disk and join by smoothing away

Making Cookie Stamps

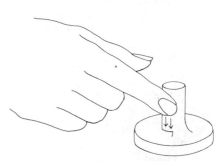

FIGURE 4–2. Push a little clay down the handle to fill in the crack at the base.

the crack where the handle joins the base. This may be easier to do if you slide your finger down the side of the handle, bringing a little clay with it, to fill the crack at the base (see Figure 4–2). Rotate the stamp, smoothing all the way around the handle until the joining is complete.

FIGURE 4–3. The classroom teacher joins Megan, Rachel, and Jane in stamping cookies for the party.

Before the design can be cut into the bottom of the stamp, the clay must dry to the leather-hard stage. This is dry enough to be firm and hold its shape but still damp to the touch. (If the clay reaches this stage before you have a chance to cut the design, place it in a tightly closed plastic bag to prevent further drying out.) Cut a design into the bottom of the disk, using linoleum cutting tools. Geometric patterns, flowers, snowflakes, heart shapes, animals, leaves, birds, and holiday symbols are all good designs. Thin lines will not show up when stamped on the cookies. A simple design cut in deep, wide lines is most effective. Stamping reverses images, so initials or words must be carved in "mirror image" (reversed in both order and direction) if they are to read correctly. The stamps must dry thoroughly for several days before being fired in a kiln.

After firing, the stamps are ready to be used, although they will look fancier if the handle and the top side of the disk are glazed. Commercial glazes come in powdered form. Mix to a creamy consistency and apply with a brush. *Do not glaze the part that presses into the cookie dough.* Fire again at the specified temperature.

FIGURE 4–4. Cookie stamps made by fourth-grade students and the decorated cookies.

Now all is ready for a cookie stamping party! The two recipes below work well.

SWEDISH PEPPARKAKA

⅔ cup brown sugar	½ tsp cloves
⅔ cup dark syrup	¾ Tbls baking soda
(Karo or molasses)	⅔ cup butter or margarine
1½ tsp ginger	1 egg
1½ tsp cinnamon	5 cups flour

Heat the sugar, syrup, and spices to the boiling point. Add baking soda, and then pour the heated mixture over the butter and stir well until the butter melts. Add the egg and flour and mix well. Chill an hour, roll out, and cut into rounds with a small juice glass. Press with a stamp. Bake for 8 to 10 minutes at 325°. (If dough is handled too much, it gets tough.) Makes 5 dozen cookies.

ALMOND BUTTER COOKIES[1]

1 cup butter or margarine	2 cups flour
½ cup sugar	¼ tsp salt
1 tsp almond extract	

Cream the butter and sugar. Add almond extract. Add salt and flour. Chill the dough. Form one-inch balls and roll them in sugar. Stamp with cookie stamps. Bake at 350° for 12 to 15 minutes. Makes about 3 dozen cookies.

POLISH WYCINANKI: PAPER CUTOUTS

In the early nineteenth century in Poland, the farming families decorated their homes with beautiful cut paper designs called wycinanki (pronounced vĭ-chee non-key). Each spring, just before Easter, people put new whitewash on the walls of their homes and glued colorful wycinanki designs to them for decorations. These intricate cutouts show how a distinctive new art can develop from the most basic materials. The designs were cut out with the best tool available—sheep shears. It seems incredible that such lacelike designs could be created with these mammoth scissors. They are cut out freehand with no preliminary sketching.

[1] From Eleanor and Carroll Rycraft, *Rycraft Scandinavian Cookie Stamp Recipes* (Corvallis, Oregon: Rycraft, 4205 S. W. 53rd St., 97330, 1971).

FIGURE 4–5. Kurpie leluja wycinanki design from Poland, early twentieth century. Signed by Czeslawa Konpka. Originally a bright color, it has faded with age to almost white. Collection of the author.

FIGURE 4–6. Contemporary Kurpie gwiazdy design. Collection of the author.

Traditionally in Poland, men did the heavy craft work (carpentry, pottery, and blacksmithing); women decorated the men's work with painted designs and did such lighter craft work as weaving and embroidery. Although men now cut wycinanki too, the designs were originally created by women, who would sometimes gather together, young and old, to make them. This work was done not for money but for the satisfaction of making the home beautiful and for the pleasure of excelling in an art form.

The wycinanki are cut from folded paper, so that when the paper is opened up and spread flat, the design is symmetrical. The subject matter reflects the countryside: trees, flowers, roosters, birds, stars, and sometimes, men, women, and religious symbols.

Many different regional styles developed. The Kurpie (koorpy-eh) designs from the area around Ostroleka (north of Warsaw) are cut from a single color, glossy paper. There are two main types, the leluja (le-lu-ya), which is cut from a piece of paper folded lengthwise, and the gwiazdy (g-vee-azda, meaning star), which is a circular design. Leluja designs usually include a central treelike form and one or more pairs of roosters or birds, although each design is different. Gwiazdy designs, cut from a round piece of paper, are folded to make patterns that repeat eight, sixteen, or sometimes even thirty-two times. They are often incredibly intricate and lacelike.

From the Lowicz area west of Warsaw come very colorful wycinanki made from layers of symmetrical paper cutouts. Basic shapes of peacocks, roosters, and flowers are first cut out and opened up. Then different colored smaller shapes are cut out and glued one on top of another, each added color smaller than the preceding one. There are two types of Lowicz cutouts. One is a collage of birds, flowers, and leaves. The other, with the same subject matter, is cut in black from a folded circle, and additional colors are pasted to this base. (See Figure 4–7.)

Other regions have also developed distinctive styles. In Opoczno they specialize in tree designs; in Lublin the wycinanki resemble embroidery. The Sanniki area specializes in peacocks and wedding scenes.

All the cutouts show a fine and joyous sense of design. The birds, trees, and plant forms are all decorative rather than realistic, and they show the individual style and ideas of each craftsperson. The unique beauty of these designs soon created a demand for them outside the home. Although in some rural villages wycinanki are still pasted directly on the walls of farmhouses, they are more frequently made now to be framed. Many are sold to people living in the cities and in other countries. The high level of skill in the cutouts is still maintained. In both Poland and America exhibitions and competitions are held in which people display their wycinanki. Prizes are given for originality and fine craftsmanship.

There are many other folk arts in Poland: wood carving (especially of religious figures), decorated Easter eggs, straw designs, painting on glass and walls, pottery, weaving, and elaborate embroidery on clothing. All these arts brightened and enriched the lives of rural people in days gone by and are engaged in today by many Polish craftspeople who decorate their homes for special occasions.

FIGURE 4-7. Lowicz wycinanki, circular design. Collection of Mrs. Andrew S. Ehrenkreutz.

Making Kurpie Wycinanki

The Kurpie wycinanki are made in two forms, leluja and gwiazdy (see color plate 9). Both designs are made by folding and cutting single sheets of brightly colored paper. The colored craft paper that comes in large rolls, which is used by some schools, works well. You can also use fadeless colored papers, gumbacked papers and origami papers. All are available at art supply stores. Solid color wrapping papers are excellent, but construction paper is too thick for this project. Whatever the paper, choose the deepest colors, which look most effective when set off against a white background.

To make leluja wycinanki, fold a piece of 12 x 18-inch paper lengthwise (this is a little larger than most Polish designs but easier for beginning students to handle). Draw one-half of the design on the folded paper, so that when it is cut out and opened up it will form a symmetrical design. Keep in mind that the folded edge will form the center of the design (see example in Figure 4–8). In the most common leluja design, a pair of birds or roost-

FIGURE 4–8. The wycinanki design is drawn on folded paper (color inside). Shading in the areas to be cut away helps make the design stand out. Cut on the solid lines. The fringe (dotted line) need not be drawn. It is cut in after the basic tree form has been cut out.

FIGURE 4–9. Masashi has drawn his design on folded paper and is cutting it out.

ers is near the bottom and an abstract treelike form is in the center. This form may also include another pair of birds. The design is enhanced with fanciful flower and leaf shapes and some purely geometric patterns. The decorative edge to the tree form need not be drawn in. It is cut into the edge after the basic shape has been cut out. The entire design must be one connected piece. The penciled outline should be one continuous line that never crosses over itself or cuts across the fold. If students shade in the part that is to be cut away, they'll be able to make sure that the design consists of only one piece. The fold must be kept intact.

Small pointed scissors are the easiest to use in cutting out the wycinanki. It is best to do the cutting in stages. First cut the lower part and the outline of the tree form. Next, cut a decorative fringe into the border of the tree. When students think of "fringe," they usually think of a series of parallel cuts. This type of fringe will close up when it is pressed flat. Pieces of paper must be *removed* by curved or wedge-shaped cuts. (See examples in Figure 4–10.) Lastly, cut the designs within the tree. Occasionally an extra fold is made to do this. In the leluja wycinanki (Figure 4–5), you can see that while the paper was still folded, the two large leaves at the bottom and the two at the top were folded again along a center line, and the vein patterns were cut into them.

FIGURE 4–10. Examples of fringe designs used in leluja wycinanki.

FIGURE 4–11 *a, b, c.* Wycinanki designs. *(a.)* by Masashi, age eight, (*b*, page 70) by Jennifer, age nine, (*c*, page 70) by Amy, age nine.

(a)

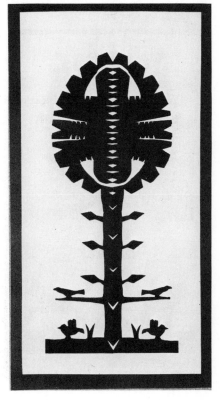

When the cutting is finished, open up the wycinanki and glue it with a white glue to white paper or another color paper that contrasts with the wycinanki. The wycinanki makes an especially nice display if the white paper is then glued to an even larger piece of construction paper that repeats the color of the cutout design.

Gwiazdy, the "star" designs, are cut from a round piece of colored paper. Draw a circle (6 to 7 inches in diameter for small designs, 12 to 14 inches for large) on the paper with a compass, or draw around a bowl or other round object. Cut out the circle. Fold it in half with the colored side *inside*. Fold it in half again, and then fold it in half again. This will give a pattern of eight repeats. When students are more experienced (and if the paper is quite thin), they may want to fold once more for a pattern of sixteen repeats. In either case the folding will create a wedge-shaped piece with folds on both sides (see Figure 4–12.)

Before using the colored paper, however, students should probably cut some practice designs from newsprint or newspaper. The design is created by

European Arts **69**

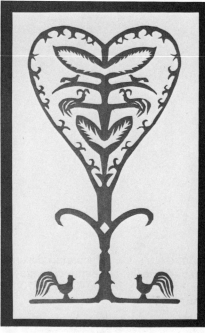

(b)

(c)

cutting into both edges and the curved outer edge. Students may cut freehand, or they may wish to make a pencil drawing as a guide, based on their experiments with the newsprint. In most gwiazdy, the basic roundness of the edge is maintained—it is not turned into starlike points, for instance.

When the gwiazdy are completed, they look especially nice framed. Glue them to a larger square of white paper with a margin of at least ¾ inch at the sides and 1¼ inches at the top and bottom. Place this on a piece of thin cardboard cut to the same size. The wycinanki should be protected with a sheet of acetate. The least expensive is a thin sheet that comes on a roll. It can be drawn around to the back of the cardboard and held in place with tape. A thicker acetate, which is still pliable but stiffer, can be cut the same size as the cardboard and used like a sheet of glass.

You can make wood frames similar to that in Figure 4–6 with ¼ x ¾-inch flat screen molding. Saw the strip of wood with a fine-toothed saw into sections and glue them to the top and bottom edges of the acetate. When the glue is dry, staple the design and the cardboard backing (shirt or posterboard thickness) into the wood from the back. See Figure 4–13*a*.

The small gwiazdy student work illustrated in Figure 4–14 was framed with plastic tubes that are used for packaging integrated circuits. These tubes are discarded by manufacturers of computer-related equipment. (You might find such a company by calling businesses listed under data processing equipment, electronic equipment and supplies, or electronic research and development in the yellow pages of the telephone book.) The tubes measure eighteen inches long. In cross-section they are hollow, but a notch pushes into the center, giving the tube an angular *C* shape. The tubes can be cut with a very fine-toothed saw. The wycinanki is mounted on white paper, backed with *corregated* cardboard, and protected with sheet acetate. Spread white glue along the top edge of the mounted wycinanki and push it into the notch or slot of the tube, which has been cut to fit. Do the same on the bottom edge. When the frame has dried overnight, you can thread

70   European Arts

FIGURE 4–12. To make a gwiazdy (star) wycinanki, fold the round piece of paper, colored side inside, three (or in this case, four) times, and draw a design on the pie-shaped piece. Shaded areas in the diagram are cut away to produce the design shown at the right. This design is based on a wycinanki by Rachel, age eleven.

FIGURE 4–14. Small framed gwiazdy designs by Brian, age eleven, and Alison, age ten.

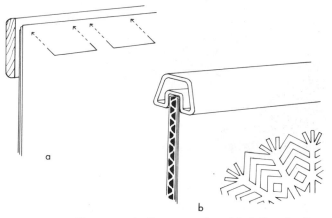

FIGURE 4–13. Two ways to frame wycinanki: (a) by stapling the design to screen molding, and (b) by using plastic packaging tubes.

FIGURE 4–15. A display of large gwiazdy designs by fifth- and sixth-grade students. In the center is a round design like those from the Lowicz region in Poland.

a piece of yarn through the top tube to form a hanger. See Figure 4–13b.

You can also frame wycinanki by holding the cutout, acetate, and cardboard together with a border of Mystik tape (see Figure 4–7, page 67).

European Arts **71**

UKRAINIAN PYSANKY: DECORATED EGGS

A few weeks before Easter every year, Ukrainian women make decorated eggs called pysanky. The eggs glow with bright colors, and the intricate designs are made with traditional symbols handed down for generations. Although associated with Easter, this custom began long before Christianity came to the Ukraine in 988. In neolithic times, people worshipped the sun. The egg was a symbol of the life-giving sun. Every spring, when the sun's warmth returned and things began to grow again, people decorated eggs in celebration. Using dyes made from plants, bark, and berries, they gave the eggs the brightest colors they could find.

FIGURE 4–16. Ukrainian pysanky, from the collection of Mrs. Cyril Miles.

With the coming of Christianity, the custom continued. Many of the same designs were used, but they were assigned new meanings. The egg, pagan symbol of the life force, of rebirth in the spring, became the Christian symbol of spiritual rebirth. The villagers made two kinds of decorated eggs at Easter: the pysanky, which were too beautiful to be eaten, and the krashanky, which were dyed bright solid colors and hard-boiled for later eating.

On Easter morning villagers put both kinds of eggs in a basket with other foods, especially a particular round bread called paska (a work of art in itself), and the baskets were blessed at the church. Then they were taken home, and the krashanky and other foods were shared for breakfast.

Many ancient traditions were associated with the colored eggs in these farming villages. They were thought to have special powers and were used to heal, to assure a good harvest, to bring children to a childless couple, and to protect the home from fire. According to an ancient legend, making pysanky kept the world from destruction: evil, which took the form of a creature in chains, had the power to destroy the world. In years when few pysanky were made, the chains became dangerously loose; when many pysanky were made, the chains tightened, and love conquered evil.

The pysanky are now exchanged by family members and friends as a sign of love on Easter morning. Symbols are often appropriate to the person the eggs are made for: a chicken or bird, a fertility symbol, may be drawn on an egg that is given to a young married couple; a rake and wheat symbolize a good harvest for a farmer. A young woman might make pysanky with flowers, symbolic of love, for her fiancé. The designs suggest these objects rather than depicting them exactly. There are geometric patterns and plant and animal designs.

Each egg is unique—the same exact design is never used twice—but the Ukrainians follow a particular framework and use traditional symbols. Thus the eggs have an overall design quality that is easily identified as Ukrainian, even though many countries in central Europe have egg-decorating customs. This framework is created by first dividing the egg into geometric areas. This makes wide bands, triangles, or ovals in which further designs are made.

The tools and materials are simple. A smooth, unblemished, fresh egg; a candle; a lump of beeswax; a kistka (a tool that draws with melted wax); and dye. The kistka, a tiny metal spout or funnel attached to a handle, is heated over a candle. The hot spout is pressed into the beeswax, and melted wax is scooped up into it. Designs are drawn on the

FIGURE 4–17. Some traditional pysanky designs and what they symbolize: the sun (life and growth), evergreens (eternal youth and health), hen (fertility), another sun or star design, butterfly, wheat (good health and bountiful harvest), fish (Christianity), flower (love and good will), deer (good will, wealth), ram, and pussywillows.

egg with the kistka, which lets out a fine line of melted wax. (The word *pysanky* comes from the verb *pysaty,* "to write.") The egg is then dipped into a dye, usually yellow; the beeswax lines resist the dye, which preserves the white color underneath. After the egg has dried, more areas are covered with beeswax, this time preserving the yellow. The egg is dipped in a darker color, perhaps orange, and then waxed again, and so on, until the final color of black or red is used. Then the egg is warmed until the wax melts. The wax is wiped off, and the many-colored design is revealed. The eggs are usually lacquered, which strengthens them and makes them glossy.

The psyanky are made with skill and pride in a tradition that has passed from mother to daughter over so many generations. A gift of a pysanky is truly meaningful. The psyanky are not only beautiful works of art but a remembrance of someone's love, and they are kept and treasured for a lifetime. (See color plate 10.)

Making Pysanky

It is difficult to give adequate instructions for making pysanky in the space available here. There are excellent, inexpensive booklets that are available (some are listed in the bibliography of this book); or better yet, find out if your community has a Ukrainian family that carries on this tradition and can demonstrate pysanky making. It's much easier for children to understand the art if they can watch a demonstration, and it is an exciting experience to see the design grow under the hands of a skilled person. In many cities international organizations can help you contact people of different ethnic backgrounds.

Because this project uses candles to heat the kistkas, it must be done under careful supervision. Long hair should be tied back, and the candles should be in secure holders on metal sheets or pans. Because the short, squat casserole warmer candles cannot tip over, they are the best to use.

Use fresh, white eggs that are free from bumps or blemishes. Clean and rinse them with a vinegar solution to remove any grease. (Greasy fingers will also make spots that will resist dye, so be sure hands are clean.) Check to see that there are no cracks in the eggs. Traditional pysanky are usually made with fresh eggs. As the egg dries inside, gases build up, and if there are weak places in the shell it will burst. To ensure against bursting, some Ukrainians use blown eggs. Moreover, some people may be concerned about wasting food. In that case the eggs should be blown before beginning the project, and the yolk and white should be saved for cooking. (The eggs should be blown *before* dyeing, because the dyes, which are not edible, may seep inside.) Make small holes about $\frac{1}{16}$-inch diameter at both ends of the egg by poking briskly with the point of one blade of a sharp pair of scissors. A large needle can be used to make the holes, but it is harder to break the shell with it. Be sure to break the membrane inside with a needle. Blow through one end; the yolk and white will come out the other. It's easiest to do this if you use an ear syringe to blow the air; hold the nozzle against one hole, and squeeze the bulb. (Syringes are available at drugstores for about $1.50.) Eggs should be at room temperature when you apply the wax (cold eggs will "sweat" when they are taken from the refrigerator, and the wax will not adhere).

Kits that have dyes, kistkas, and beeswax can be obtained quite inexpensively at the sources mentioned in the bibliography. If this is not practical, substitute other materials. You can use strong solutions of fabric dyes, or you can make excellent dyes by soaking colored crepe paper in hot water. Any dye will be brighter if one tablespoon of vinegar is added to it. Put the dyes in wide-mouthed jars (such as peanut butter or mayonnaise jars), and have a separate spoon for each dye. If you use the same spoon to put the eggs in all the colors, they will soon be mixed. Well-covered dyes can be stored for many months. (If you don't use them for a while, add more vinegar.) Red, blue, yellow, and black will give you all the colors you need. If the dye has been prepared with hot water, wait until it is cold before using it, or it will melt the wax on the egg.

You must use beeswax for making the designs. Paraffin and candle wax flake off too easily and expose the shell to the dye. A very small cake of bees-

FIGURE 4–18. Marianna Liss demonstrating Ukrainian egg decorating to fifth-grade students. First she heats the wax in the kistka over the candle flame, then she draws with the hot wax on the egg.

FIGURE 4–19. Marianna alternates waxing and dyeing the egg. When it is finished, she heats the egg beside the candle flame and wipes the melted wax off with a paper towel to reveal the brightly colored egg.

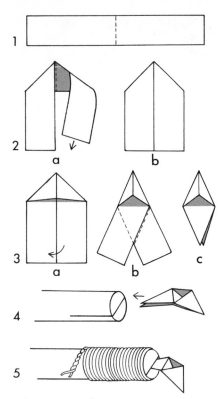

FIGURE 4-20. One way to make a kistka.

FIGURE 4-21. A few basic ways to divide the egg into geometric areas.

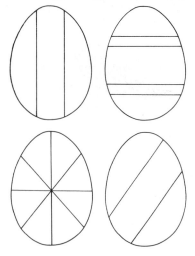

wax, which you can buy at some sewing supply stores and art stores, will make many eggs.

Kistkas can be made in several ways; each craftsperson has her favorite. Figure 4–20 shows one way of making them. The directions are as follows:

1. Cut a strip of brass shim (0.005 inches thick) in a strip ¼ inch wide by 1½ inches long. Fold it in half, and open it up again to get a center line.

2. (a) Fold sides in and down along the center line, creating shape *b*.

3. (a) Turn the folded piece of brass over and cross one end over the other. This raises the spout. (b) Trim ends to a point by cutting along dotted lines, resulting in spout *c*.

4. Take a piece of ¼-inch dowel, 4½ inches long, and cut a slit in the end of it. Make the slit by placing a mat knife on the end of the dowel and tapping it with a hammer. Adults should do this step, but *do not hold the dowel in your hand and force the knife in.* Insert the brass spout and bend it down.

5. Wrap the end of the dowel tightly with copper wire, covering ½ inch of the dowel, and twist the ends of the wire together.

To prepare the kistka for drawing with the hot wax, hold the point over the tip of a candle flame for about ten seconds. Be careful that the wood handle does not burn. Quickly scoop up a little wax into the larger part of the funnel. The wax will melt and flow into the point. Heat again if necessary. Applied to the egg, the wax will flow out in a dark line. Draw on a practice egg until you can control the flow of wax.

Most pysanky have some formal design framework, rather than designs drawn freely on the surface. This framework usually consists of lines that go around the egg to create geometric areas. Although a practiced pysanky maker can do this freehand, it is a great help for a beginner to use ½-inch tape or a rubber band as a guide. Put a wide rubber band around the egg and draw *light* pencil lines on either side of it as a guide for the kistka. Do not make erasures; they will cause smudges. The

FIGURE 4-22. Some traditional ribbon designs for narrow bands around the egg.

band can run around the middle, or it can run lengthwise. It can also go both ways, dividing the egg into quarters. The quarters may be further divided into triangular-shaped eighths. One design usually runs around inside this band (which is also often bordered with smaller bands called ribbon designs), and other designs are repeated inside each geometric area (flowers, stars, birds, deer, and the like). This is a great simplification of pysanky designs, which are extremely elaborate and have many fine details.

Here are the steps in making a pysanky design. The design is not meant to be copied—substitute your own variations—but it will take you through the whole process. (See Figure 4–23 a-e.)

a. This looks complicated but is really quite easy taken step by step. The egg is still white, and everything covered with wax (black lines and areas in this figure) will remain white. First divide the egg in the middle with a wide band. Run two narrow bands above and below it. Draw a small circle at each end of the egg and draw lines down to the band, creating eight sections. Draw a sunflower petal in each section. Divide the wide band into four sections with four narrow columns. Alternate deer and pine trees in each section, or use some other figure of your choice. Draw a triangle design in the narrow

FIGURE 4–23 a, b.

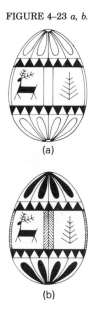

(a)

(b)

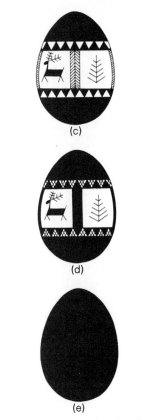

(c)

(d)

(e)

FIGURE 4–23. (continued) *c, d, e.*

FIGURE 4–24. The finished pysanky.

ribbon bands. Fill in one line of triangles, as shown. When all this is done, dye the egg yellow. Put the egg in a spoon and lower it gently into the dye. (If the egg is blown, the holes should be sealed with wax first to keep dye out of the inside. It will have to be held under the dye, because it will tend to float.) Remove the egg with the spoon and blot it dry with paper toweling. The lines that were drawn with the kistka will look black from the burnt wax, but they will actually stay white because the wax will have protected them from the dye. (Remember, however, that none of the wax is removed until the end of the decorating process.)

b. Cover with wax the parts to remain yellow: the sunflower center and petals and a design drawn in the upright columns. Then dye the egg orange. (In dyeing the eggs, you will notice that successive dyes will be affected by the color previously used. A yellow egg dipped in a red dye will become orange at first. The longer it stays in the dye, the redder it will get. A yellow egg given a quick dip in blue will turn green and then deepen to blue-green. Purple can be made by combining blue and red.)

c. Cover with wax the parts to remain orange: the area around the sunflower. Then dye the egg red.

d. Wax the parts to remain red: cross-hatch the triangles in the ribbon bands, and wax the columns between the deer and the tree. Next, dye the egg black. It may have to stay in the dye for some time for you to get a good solid black.

e. The whole egg will be almost completely black with wax and dye; only a suggestion of color will show through the wax. Let it dry thoroughly. Remove the wax to reveal the finished egg, restored to brilliant color. (Figure 4–24 shows the finished egg.)

You can remove wax by holding the egg close to the *side* of the candle flame until the wax begins to melt. (If it is held above the flame, smoke will discolor the egg.) Wipe off the melted wax with a tissue or soft cloth. Melt only one small area at a time. Now for the first time you will see the design revealed in full color.

You can soften wax from many eggs at once by

placing them in a warm oven. Make an egg holder by pounding into a board three nails about an inch apart in the form of a triangle. Place each egg in a triangle of nails and put the board in a slightly warm oven for ten to fifteen minutes. Leave the door open and watch the eggs. When the wax begins to soften and get shiny, remove them. Wipe them clean with a soft cloth or tissue. The holes in the ends of blown eggs may be sealed again with a spot of wax.

The eggs will be somewhat strengthened and the colors more brilliant if they are given several coats of clear lacquer or varnish. Between coats, the eggs should be set to dry in the egg holder.

In many parts of the world, decorative items are made from straw. It is a mark of the creative human spirit that farming people, who labor so hard in the fields, can see the aesthetic potential of what they raise as well as its value for food and profit.

In Byelorussia, for generations folk artists have made items of bright golden rye straw: dolls were fashioned from it, and straw birds and spiders were hung from the ceiling beams for good luck. Many useful items were also woven and plaited from straw: boxes, baskets, and chests.

In the city of Zhlobin in the 1950s, a group of craftspeople formed an artel, or art guild, to make straw inlay designs for sale. Each item they produced was a unique, original design, although all were based on the traditional folk arts of the area. The artel sold its work in the cities of Byelorussia. Two of the first people in the artel were Mikhail Vasilyevich Degtyarenko and Vera Nikofimovna Degtyarenko, a married couple. Although they are now retired, they continue to create inspiring original inlays.

The demand for this work became so great that the small number of craftspeople working at the artel could not produce enough to fill the orders. In 1960, to meet the demand, the government constructed a factory in Zhlobin to make the decorative straw inlays. Many artists specializing in applied folk arts were employed. Using traditional folk motifs, senior artists developed designs, which were

FIGURE 4–25. Pysanky by sixth-grade students.

BYELORUSSIAN STRAW DESIGNS

FIGURE 4–26. Deer and birds. Straw inlay panel, Zhlobin, Byelorussia. Collection of the author.

FIGURE 4–27. Motherhood. Straw inlay panel, Zhlobin, Byelorussia. Collection of the author.

then used as patterns. In this way many inlays are made of the same design, although they are all made by hand. This work requires considerable skill. Several hundred men and women work at the factory, and others are enlisted to make designs but do the work at home. The art of straw inlay is taught in shop classes in the secondary schools, and especially talented students work in the factory after school or during summer vacations.

The straw designs decorate both boxes and panels. The wooden article is first sanded smooth and then covered with a black dye and warmed joiners glue. When this covering is dry, the artist cuts dampened rye straw into pieces according to the design to be made and glues it to the surface of the box or panel. Sometimes the designs are composed only of the natural gold-colored straw, and sometimes they include straw that is dyed bright red, green, or yellow. (See color plate 11.) The finished design is given two coats of lacquer.

The panels usually show village scenes, people in native costume working at domestic chores, birds, or animals. The boxes are covered with a mosaic of small bits of straw that form intricate geometric designs. On both the panels and the boxes, the bright straw glows against the black background.

The straw inlays of Zhlobin, which were first created for sale by a small group of artists, are now found in museum shops and import stores in the United States and other countries.

Making Straw Designs

Straw is available in most cities because it is used as insulation, for bedding in kennels, and for mulching. For this project you will need new straw that has not been lying exposed to the weather for long (under those conditions it turns dull). You can buy it very inexpensively by the bale at farming and garden supply stores. It is also available at farms outlying the cities. If you cannot find a source, ask the parks department of your town where their supply comes from—they use it to protect newly sown grassy areas. Although the Byelorussian designs are made with rye straw, oat and wheat straws can also be used. Oat straw is brighter in color, and broader, which makes it easier to handle than wheat.

Use ¼-inch plywood for this project. Cut a rectangle approximately 5½ x 8 inches. Sand this piece of wood until it is very smooth. Then apply a coat of black tempera paint or India ink to the board. When the paint is thoroughly dry, apply two coats of lacquer. Allow the first to dry before applying the second.

While the panel is drying between coats of paint and lacquer, the students can plan their designs. Give them pieces of black paper the same size as their panel and strips of yellow paper ⅛ inch to ¼ inch wide. The students can experiment, cutting the paper into small squares, triangles, and various lengths and gluing them to the paper to form geometric designs, animals, flowers, people, houses, or other subject matter. They should look at illustrations to see how the artists build up solid areas by gluing straws side by side, and how they create patterns by using square shapes. This was done in the deer's horns and the woman's dress in Figures 4–26 and 4–27.

FIGURE 4–28. Nora first worked out a design with paper. After preparing the panel, she made a frame near the edge with narrow strips of straw. Now she is beginning to make her design, cutting the straw with scissors and gluing it in place.

FIGURE 4–29. David uses a mat knife to even the edges of the straw before the glue is completely dry.

FIGURE 4–30. Fifth-grade straw designs. Clockwise from top: *Horse* by Nora, *Outdoor Scene* by Peter, *Dragon* by David, *Design* by Liz, and *House* by Katie.

When the second coat of lacquer has dried, the students can begin their straw designs. To prepare the straw, peel off the dull outer covering from the larger stalks. Soak these stalks in water until they are pliable. Slit the damp straw along one side with scissors or your thumbnail so that it can be opened up and flattened out. Then cut shapes from these pieces and glue them with white glue to the panel.

It is a good idea to make a frame for the design first. Glue a thin strip of straw close to the edge on all four sides of the panel. Then proceed with the design, referring to the plan you created earlier with paper strips. In most cases the straw is cut with scissors before being glued to the panel. However, some large areas of straw can be glued on and then cut to shape with an X-acto knife, or mat knife, before the glue sets (see Figure 4–29). As work proceeds, wipe any glue that seeps under the straw off the surface of the panel. After it has dried, the finished design is given a final coat of lacquer.

FLOWER-RELATED ARTS OF GERMANY

FIGURE 4–31. *Great Piece of Turf,* by Albrecht Dürer, watercolor and gouache, 1503. Courtesy of Graphische Sammlung Albertina, Vienna, Austria.

Germany has a long history of flower-related arts. Pressed flower collections and flower drawings, paintings, and prints have been made for centuries.

During the Renaissance, the artists who painted flowers as an incidental part of a larger painting were so careful that particular species can be identified by botanists today. Albrecht Dürer (1471–1528), the famous German painter, engraver, and woodcut artist, often studied plants. For one of his watercolor paintings he dug up a piece of turf and brought it to his studio. He made a painting of every detail of the dandelions, plantain, yarrow, and grasses growing in the soil. His painting (Figure 4–31) shows a reverence for natural things and captures the freshness and beauty of even a common patch of ground on a summer's day.

Starting about the same time (the late fifteenth century), books describing medicinal plants and herbs were printed in Germany and other parts of Europe. Called herbals, these books were illustrated with woodcuts so readers could identify plants used in the treatment of illness. Herbals had been compiled since antiquity, but with the advent of the printing press they could be made for the general public. The woodcuts were printed only in black ink, but the purchaser of the herbal frequently painted them with watercolors. Although the woodcuts were made for purposes of identification, not aesthetics, it is obvious that the often unknown artists took pleasure in their task. The woodcuts have a simple, strong beauty. (See Figure 4–32.)

Many flowers in Germany have symbolic meanings. Folk stories explain the origins of others. One of these is the edelweiss, a particularly treasured flower that grows in the Alps. In German, the name means "noble white." A small, star-shaped flower with white, velvety leaves, it is associated with immortality, purity, and courage. The edelweiss grows very high up, at the snow line, in almost inaccessible places. It often took an act of daring to return with one from the heights, so bringing one to a loved one was regarded as proof of a young man's affections. It would be carefully pressed between the pages of a book and regarded as a treasured keepsake. Unfortunately, if the plant is disturbed it often will not grow again, and strict regulations against picking the edelweiss now protect it from extinction.

The origin of the edelweiss is explained by a folk story. An angel wanted to visit the earth again and was allowed to take her human form and descend to the Alps. When a mountain climber discovered her and fell in love with her beauty, God transformed her into the edelweiss.

Another folk story concerns the origin of the wild chicory flowers that grow in profusion along the country lanes. A young girl waited for her lover by the roadside for a very long time. When he did not come, she turned into the chicory plant, her eyes the dancing blue flowers, forever watching.

No one knows when flowers were first pressed in Germany as a way of preserving them. For many years it has been the custom to press flowers under heavy books and then to put them under the glass around the border of religious pictures.

In 1735 a Swedish botanist, Carolus Linnaeus, published *Systema Naturae,* a system of plant classification that is still used today. During his work Linnaeus amassed a large botanical collection,

FIGURE 4–32. Woodcut of the wild iris, or water-flag, from *Hortus Sanitatus Deutsch (The German Herbarius),* published by Peter Schöffer, Mainz, 1485. From a facsimile printed in 1924 by Mandruck A.-G. in München, W. Germany for Verlag der Münchner Drucke Zu München. Courtesy of The University of Michigan Library.

FIGURE 4–33. A pressed edelweiss from the collection of Karin Douthit.

FIGURE 4-34. Left: a framed pressed flower arrangement from East Germany with gentians, primulas, wild geraniums, clover, sedge, and grasses. Right: a bookmark from West Germany with buttercups, clover, wild geraniums, and sedge. Collection of the author.

called a herbarium, of pressed and classified flowers and plants. The method of pressing flowers between sheets of paper had been developed in Italy in the sixth century. This method became the basis of all herbaria. (Most major universities with botany departments still use herbaria in the study of plants.) Linnaeus's work in classification inspired many amateur botanists. By the nineteenth century, it had become a fashionable leisure time activity for young people in Europe and America to start a herbarium of their locality. Many flower collections were made in Germany at this time. Flowers and plants were gathered, very carefully pressed and dried, and then mounted on paper. The plants were identified and the Latin name written down, along with the date of collection and the location where the plant was found. Although herbaria were meant to be primarily a learning experience, some of these very carefully pressed flowers were beautiful from an artistic point of view. Perhaps this is how the art of making pressed flower arrangements began.

Wild flowers grow in rural areas throughout Germany, but the high Alpine meadows of southern Germany are especially rich in many different and very colorful flowers. Among them are blue gentians, rhododendron, wild geraniums, yellow and pink primroses, buttercups, pink and white and yellow clovers, violets, Queen Anne's lace, cyclamen, snowdrops, and bluets. The flowers are collected and pressed and made into lovely flower arrangements. Sometimes school children make bookmarks from their pressed flowers. Framed pressed flowers can be found in craft shops and are exported to other countries. These arrangements combine the delicate bright flowers with grasses, sedges, and mosses in a natural way that brings to the imagination a glimpse of the fresh mountain meadows where they were gathered. See color plate 12.

Making Pressed Flower Arrangements

In gathering flowers to be pressed, several things must be taken into consideration: the places to find them, the time of day, the weather, and the kinds of flowers most suited to pressing.

Before setting out to collect flowers, contact your state agricultural department's Division of Natural

Resources for a list of protected flowers. Some wild flowers are so near extinction that they must never be picked (unless you cultivate them in your own garden). Others are so common that they can be picked freely. Get a wild flower identification book from the library, or go with someone who knows the flowers so that you are sure of what you are picking.

Most parks forbid all flower picking. Fortunately, some of the most common wildflowers make the nicest pressed arrangements, and they can be found in vacant lots and along sidewalks and roadways. The buttercup, found almost everywhere, is one of the few flowers that will keep its color a long time. Daisies, asters, clover, yarrow, Queen Anne's lace, and goldenrod are very common and can be freely picked. Even so, they are beautiful and enjoyed by other passers-by, so follow these rules: always ask permission if the flower is growing on private property, and when you do pick always leave some for others to enjoy. Do as little damage to the plant as possible so that it will bloom again.

The smaller cultivated flowers, such as violets, lilies-of-the-valley, grape hyacinth, and small marigolds, also make good arrangements. If they are not growing in your own yard be sure and get permission before you pick them. Gardeners are often very willing to share their bounty—especially if you explain your project.

Gather plants, if possible, in the late morning or late afternoon when they are dry. If they are picked in the middle of the day, the plants may wilt from the heat. Never pick after a rain because the flowers will mold when they are pressed. If possible, take a can or jar of water; if you put the stems in, the flowers will stay fresh. If this is not practical, put them in a plastic bag as they are cut. You will want a 3 to 4-inch length of stem below the flower and, if the stem does not include leaves, a sample or two of leaves. Be careful not to pull the plant up by the roots; take along a little pair of scissors so you can cut the flower.

Choose small flowers, all on the same scale. One large flower will so dominate an arrangement that the smaller flowers will be overlooked. A large flower, such as Queen Anne's lace, can be taken apart and used as smaller florets. Unfortunately, very thick flowers, such as dandelions, do not press well, nor do those that have a very thick middle, such as large daisies. Look for interesting shapes as well as for color. The graceful line of little bells in a spray of lily-of-the-valley is very pleasing. Many of the colors will fade in time anyway, and when that happens you will still enjoy the arrangement if you have a variety of shapes.

Do not forget to pick interesting grasses and small leaves. Yarrow leaves look like miniature ferns, are delightful in an arrangement, and can be found almost anywhere. Small bits of moss, which grow in poor soil in both city and country, help make the arrangement look more natural.

Try to press the flowers on the same day you gather them. If there is a delay, keep the flowers in water. Professional flower pressers usually use blotting paper, but old newspaper works very well, too. If the papers are at least a week old, there is no danger of ink being transferred to the petals.

Take one sheet of newspaper and fold it once down the middle along the fold that is already there, and then fold once more (as it is usually folded on the newsstand). This folded piece now measures 11 x 14 inches. Open up the last fold and place the flowers on one side of this fold. (If the stems have been kept in water, wipe them dry first.) Try to keep the leaves and petals spread out flat. Do not overlap the flowers. Press the leaves and moss, too. Insert a long tab at the edge of the newspaper to identify the student's work. Fold over the other half of the newspaper on top of the flowers. Place the first section of newspaper with the flowers inside on a flat board. Pile the other sections on top, lining up edges and corners exactly. Place another board on top of the pile and weight it down with very heavy books or bricks. This press should be in a dry location.

Now forget what you have done for four to six weeks! It takes time for the flowers to become completely dry, and they can be spoiled by impatient exploring to find out how they are progressing.

When at least a month has gone by, the press can be opened. Meanwhile you can be gathering ma-

FIGURE 4–35. A flower press made of two boards, folded newspapers, and bricks.

terials for mounting the flowers. If you like to make use of scrap materials and have the time to find them, this can be a very inexpensive project. Companies that do framing work often throw away great quantities of old or miscut mat board. These boards are frequently in 3½ to 4-inch wide strips, which are perfect for this project. Glass companies also throw away leftover strips of glass in similar dimensions. They will often set aside a box for their scrap pieces if you promise to pick it up at a designated time. Cut appropriate sizes of glass from the scraps (see appendix on how to cut glass) and then cut mat board to fit each piece of glass. You will have a variety of sizes, which should measure in the range of 3 ½ to 4 inches wide by 5 ½ to 7 inches long. The examples of student work in this book were made from scrap materials. You can, of course, purchase a large sheet of glass and have the shop owner cut it into smaller pieces for you.

When the flowers are dry, they are very fragile. Handle them gently. Look them over and decide which ones would make a nice arrangement. Place these on a piece of mat board that has been cut to fit a piece of glass. Arrange them so that they seem to be growing—not all spaced out in a row, but with stems somewhat grouped at the bottom. Flowers should be at different heights, usually with the tallest in a central position. Occasionally a single spray of one flower is most effective. Interesting leaves or small pieces of moss can cover the awkwardness of bare stems at the bottom of the arrangement.

When you are pleased with your composition, lift each flower or leaf gently, one at a time, and put very small spots of white glue on the back of the stem with a toothpick. Also glue behind the thickest parts of the flowers. Replace them on the mat board.

There may be oil on the glass from the glass cutting tool, so before placing the glass over the arrangement be sure that it has been washed and dried thoroughly. Bind the glass to the mat board with ¾-inch tape. Most colored tapes overpower the delicate hues of the plants, so white usually looks the best. If you extend the glass and mat board over the edge of the table by the exact width to be taped, it is easier to apply the tape in a straight line (see

FIGURE 4–36. Jeannie, age nine, demonstrates how to get the tape on in a straight line by using the table edge as a guide.

FIGURE 4–37. Pressed flower arrangements by fourth-grade students. Clockwise from upper right: by Geordie, Robin, John, and Naomi. Flowers include lilies-of-the-valley, buttercups, Virginia bluebells, violets, and grape hyacinths. Moss covers the stem ends.

Figure 4–36). Apply the tape to the glass first and then pull the tape around to the back of the mat.

Do not display the pressed flowers in direct sunlight, or the colors will soon be gone. Blues and purples (except for delphinium) fade especially quickly; yellows and oranges are more long-lived.

Making Bookmarks

Bookmarks are easy to make. Cut a strip of white paper 2 x 7 inches. Any heavy drawing paper will do. A slightly textured handmade Japanese paper makes an especially nice background.

Glue the flower arrangement to the paper (see previous project) and let it dry. Cut a piece of clear, self-sticking plastic film (available at hardware stores) so that it is ¼ inch larger all around than the paper. Peel off the protective backing from the plastic film. Starting at the bottom front of the arrangement, smooth the film down over it, letting the film down gradually with the left hand as the right thumb and forefinger press out any air pockets. It has to be placed correctly the first time; the flowers cannot be moved once they have made contact with the plastic film. Apply film to the back also. Press the edges firmly again and then trim off excess plastic. Since this marker will be kept closed in a book, the colors will remain fresh a long time.

Making Herbals and Botanical Drawings

If gathering flowers is impractical, students may wish to make their own herbals, each student researching a plant, writing a description of it and its uses, and making a woodcut or linoleum cut as an illustration. (See Chapter 5 for instructions on making woodcuts.) Or a few flowers could be brought to school by the teacher and the students could make careful botanical drawings and watercolors in the manner of Dürer.

ITALIAN MARIONETTES

Puppets of many kinds have been known the world over from ancient times. But Italy especially comes to mind when people think of marionettes (puppets manipulated with strings). Perhaps this is because of the tale of Pinocchio, which was written by an Italian author, Carlo Collodi, in 1880. Gepetto, the poor marionette maker, and his wayward marionette, Pinocchio, are familiar to children all over the world. On the surface, *Pinocchio* is a warning to children about the dangers of skipping school and telling lies. The book urges a life of honesty, hard work, and obedience to parents. But the real theme is close to the hearts of all puppeteers and puppet lovers. It is set forth in the first chapter, when Mastro Cherry, the carpenter, finds a piece of wood that "weeps and laughs like a child." The wood, glue, and cloth that make up a marionette can create an illusion of life. The way inanimate materials become alive through the skillful manipulation of the strings forever teases the mind.

Puppetry has long been a tradition in Italy. Marionettes of terra-cotta have been found in ancient Roman ruins, and the tradition has been carried on without much break over the centuries. In the fifteenth century, traveling troupes of Italian puppeteers took the buffoonery of the Pulcinello dramas to England. Over many years, Pulcinello changed to Punchinello and finally to Punch, of the Punch and Judy shows.

In the sixteenth century an Italian poet, Ludovico Ariosto, wrote *Orlando Furioso,* a long epic poem of knighthood and chivalry. It was based on legends that revolve around the eighth-century Frankish knight Roland, who served as a commander under Charlemagne. Although based in fact, over the centuries the stories have become embroidered with romantic tales, magic, and pure fantasy. Marionettes were developed to dramatize this epic in France and Belgium, but most of all in Sicily, which has become famous for its Orlando Furioso marionette shows.

Although the Orlando Furioso marionettes are the same type as those used in ancient Roman times, they are much larger—some as big as four to five feet tall—and they are dressed in shining metal armor. They weigh up to eighty pounds and are held and manipulated from above by an iron rod that runs through the head and into a loop of iron in the body. Another rod manipulates the sword arm, and strings run to the arm carrying the shield and to the visor. The knights frequently engage in battle as they go about their chivalrous deeds, and there is much clanging of swords against armor and heavy feet marching across the stage boards (legs are

FIGURE 4–38. An Orlando Furioso marionette from Sicily, from the collection of Mrs. Cyril Miles. This is a small model of the original marionettes, some of which were five feet tall.

hinged at the hip). There are 500 plays based on the epic, which has over 300 characters. A real aficionado knows them all and follows play after play of intrigues, battles, dragons, and romantic adventures. Immigrants from Sicily brought Orlando plays to America in the late nineteenth century, and for many years the Orlando Furioso plays were performed in several of America's big cities.

Making Marionettes

Puppet is an all-inclusive term for any figure manipulated by a person to entertain an audience. Marionettes are jointed puppets controlled with wires and strings from above. The Orlando marionettes are too heavy to be supported by strings, although some strings are involved. They fall part way between the classifications of rod puppets and marionettes. Pinocchio was constructed as a marionette, a jointed lightweight wooden figure designed to be controlled with strings, and this is the type described here.

A marionette is not a doll. It is made for a performance; that is part of the definition. There are two ways to go about deciding what to perform. A play can be chosen or written by the students first, and students can choose or be assigned a character. Or students may make the characters they dream up, and then get together and write a play that includes them all (or write several short plays involving groups of three or four marionettes each). This latter approach is a great deal of fun and generates a lot of enthusiasm, because it involves each student in every part of the production, including writing the script. It is an especially good project for allowing students freedom to create their own characters. As in dressing up for Halloween, students can be someone they always wanted to be: a magician, a giant, a dancer, a hero, a clown. One class chose to make animals—horses, giraffes, even rabbits. Children identify easily with animals.

Another group came up with a compromise between performing a familiar story and writing their own. When the marionettes were finished they found they had one very large male marionette, a very small male marionette, assorted ladies, and a turtle. They put on a hilarious performance of the familiar "Jack and the Beanstalk," in which the giant, in lieu of a golden goose, had a turtle that laid emerald eggs.

For a different approach to performing a play, in which the students learn to identify with another culture's heroes, see the project describing Indonesian shadow plays. Using this approach for marionettes, students could study *Orlando Furioso* and perform a play based on one adventure in the epic.

Although they look complicated, marionettes are really quite easy to make. Follow the diagrams. Lengths are not given, because these should vary with the size of the puppet. An average size might be approximately 1½ feet high. Start with the body

FIGURE 4–40. Linda, nine, assembles her marionette. A screw eye is put in the shoulder to join the arms to the body.

FIGURE 4–39. Diagram of a marionette.

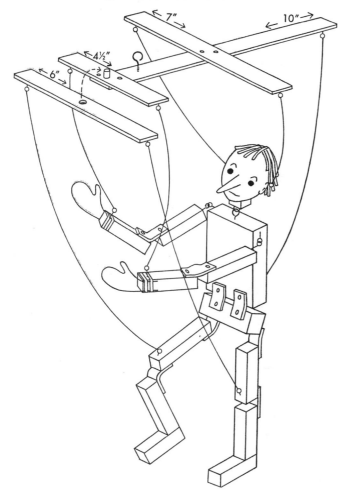

FIGURE 4–41. Hinges are glued on the backs of the legs. A piece sawed out at the neck hides the screw eyes that will join the head to the body. (This is not necessary. Screw eyes can instead be covered with scarves, neckties, and so forth.)

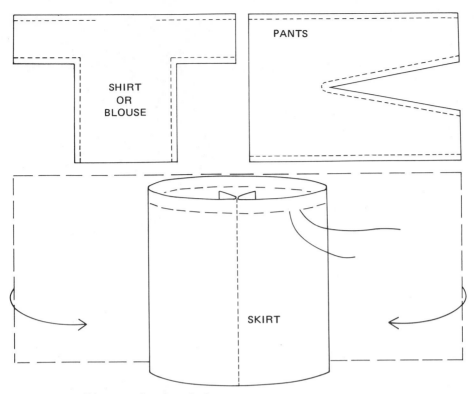

FIGURE 4-42. Diagram showing clothes patterns.

FIGURE 4-43. Chuck, ten, pins a newspaper pattern to two layers of cloth and cuts out a pair of pants for his marionette.

piece. It should measure ⅓ the total height desired. Use scrap pieces of 1-inch thick pine boards. Although a neck hole (as in Figure 4-41) can be cut out with a coping saw, this is not absolutely necessary and so is not included in the diagram. To make the hip joint, saw off the bottom 1½ inches of the body piece, and then attach it to the body again with two hinges cut from soft scrap leather or strong canvas. Align the wood pieces about ⅛-inch apart, put glue on the hinges, and tack them in place on the front of the body.

The arms and legs are constructed of ¾-inch square pine baluster, available at a lumber yard. The upper arm and forearm together should extend from the shoulder to slightly below the bottom of the body-hip piece. The upper arm is slightly longer than the forearm. The arms are attached with ¼-inch screw eyes at the shoulder. Insert screw eyes in the shoulder and in the end of the upper arm

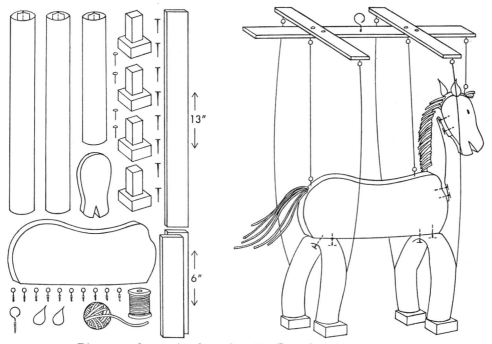

FIGURE 4-44. Diagram of an animal marionette. (I am in-debted to Paul P. Smith of *People Puppets* for this method of constructing animal marionettes.)

piece. Open one screw eye slightly with pliers or a small screwdriver, insert the other screw eye, and clamp the first screw eye closed again with pliers. Glue and tack leather hinges on the top side of the elbow joint so that the arms bend *forward*.

Hip to knee length is slightly longer than knee to ankle length. Turn the marionette over and at-tach leather hinges to the *back* of the hip and upper leg pieces, leaving a ½-inch space between them. Apply hinges to the *back* of the knee joint. (This joint may be closer together.) Glue two short (1½-to 2-inch pieces of baluster wood to the ankles for feet.

To make the head, prepare a mash of sawdust and wheat paste. (See appendix for mixing wheat paste.) Mix sawdust into wheat paste until the mash holds together and can be molded like clay. Mold a head around a piece of baluster wood, leaving ½ inch of wood exposed for the neck. Marionettes are to be seen from some distance, and it is sometimes effective to exaggerate important facial features (the

FIGURE 4-45. Peter holds the controls while Abbot ties the strings.

FIGURE 4-46. Jenny, nine, puts a screw eye in her giraffe prior to stringing it to the controls.

FIGURE 4-47. Finished marionettes: *Lady*, by Dana, nine, and *Giant*, by Charlie, ten.

eyes, the nose, or the shape of the mouth), depending on the character to be portrayed. Place on wax paper to dry.

After a day of drying, re-form the back of the head (which may have flattened where it rested on the table). Then turn the head occasionally as it dries to let air circulate around it. When the head is completely dry, which may take several days, insert ½-inch screw eyes in the neck (baluster wood) and in the top of the body piece. Join the screw eyes in the manner already described. The head should be painted with tempera paints. Apply a basic skin color, let it dry, and then paint features. Hair, mustaches, and beards made of yarn, cotton, or fleece can be glued to the head after the paint is dry.

Hands may be made by twisting wire into mitten shapes and wrapping this form with masking tape. Tack or tape the long ends of the wires to the forearms. This way of making hands is good because they can be bent to hold objects. Hands can also be cut from felt or cardboard and glued on.

Lay the puppet out on a piece of newspaper and draw shirt or pants patterns to the dimensions of the marionette (see Figure 4–42). They must be cut to fit very loosely, or they will prevent the action of the limbs. Cut out the newspaper patterns, pin them to doubled cloth, and cut out around them. Place the two pieces of cloth right sides together and sew with a running stitch on the dotted lines. Turn right side out. Gather pants at the top with a running stitch and tie the ends of the thread together around the upper body piece.

A skirt is merely a long rectangle, sewn into a cylinder and gathered at the top with a draw string, just like the pants top.

If a student wishes to make an Orlando marionette, the chest should be padded out in front with rags bound to the body with string. Make a shirt and a knee-length kilt. Cut pieces of aluminum (from pie plates and aluminum trays) to make armor. Put the armor on over the shirt and kilt, tacking it to the body at the sides. The helmet and visor are nailed to the head at the temples (the visor can be raised or lowered). Armor can also be tacked to feet, lower legs, and upper arms, and cuffs can be tacked to the wrists. Be sure to keep joints free to move. Most Orlando marionettes have a feather in the helmet and a flowing cape attached at the shoulders. A shield should be made for the left hand. Emboss the shield by pressing in designs with a pencil.

A diagram of an animal marionette is shown in Figure 4–44. By varying the length of the tubes, students can make the proportions of many different animals. Saw out the bodies and heads from one-inch thick pine board scraps with a coping saw or adult-operated power saw. Sand the pieces smooth. The tubes are made from long strips of cloth, about four inches wide and double the length of one leg (each tube will make two legs). Fold the strip of cloth with the right side in and sew a seam down the edge. (This sewing is best done on a machine by a parent or teacher.) Then turn the tube right side out and stuff *lightly* with cotton or soft foam pieces to fill them out a bit. Fold each tube into two legs and tack it to the bottom of the body. The neck, which is made in the same way, is attached to the back of the head and the front of the body piece. Put a touch of glue on the cloth where it is tacked against the wood. Wooden feet are made from ¾-inch pine baluster and wood scraps. (See the diagram.) Insert, with glue, into the bottom of each leg.

Controls should be made of 1⅜-inch lattice wood. Follow the diagrams. Note that the knees on people marionettes are worked from a separate bar of wood. Glue a short piece of dowel to the center of the front cross piece, drill a hole in the center of the knee control, and slip it over the dowel when not in use. Place ¼-inch screw eyes in the upper knee pieces, wrists, and just above the ears in the head. Dip the ends of the screw eyes in white glue before screwing them into the head.

Use heavy carpet thread or fishing line for the controls. Three people should work together to begin stringing the marionette. While one holds the marionette so it is standing erect on the floor, the person who is going to use the marionette holds the controls at a height that will be comfortable during a performance (slightly lower than shoulder height). The third person ties strings to the screw eyes in the

FIGURE 4–48. *Tiger,* by Ronald, eleven, and *Mortimer,* by Peter, ten.

FIGURE 4–49. *Turtle,* by Fred, ten.

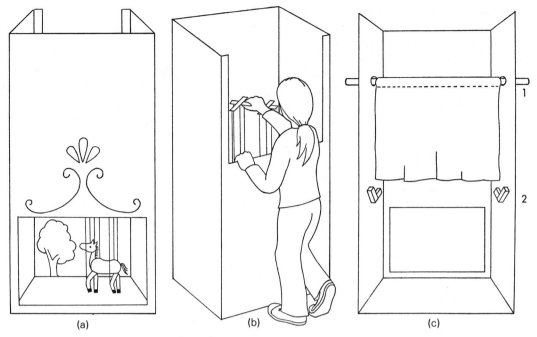

FIGURE 4-50. Diagram of a cardboard carton stage.

(a)   (b)   (c)

head, carries them up, and ties them to the middle cross piece. After this is done, two people can do the rest of the stringing; one holds the controls and the other ties the strings. Tie the knee controls to the bar next. If the screw eye is under the clothing, tie the thread to the screw eye, and then with a needle bring the thread through the clothing. Tie the controls for the hands, which should be in the resting (down) position, to the front cross piece.

Put a screw hook in the top of the control. *Always* hang up the marionette when it is not in use, or it will get hopelessly scrambled. If the threads do get tangled it is sometimes easier to cut them at the controls, untangle them, and retie them than to try to set them right without cutting them.

See the diagram for controls and screw eye locations on animal marionettes and string them up using the same methods. The first screw eyes to attach to the controls are those on the animal's back.

A simple theater can be constructed from a refrigerator carton. Figure 4-50a shows how to cut the opening for the theater. Use the widest side of the box if it is not square. Do not cut all the way to the corners but leave at least two inches around the opening to keep the box strong. For most cartons, the opening will be approximately 27 x 22 inches.

Cut the opening for the puppeteer in the back, as in Figure 4-50*b*, again leaving two-inch edges to keep the corners strong.

Figure 4-50*c* shows an inside view of the front and interior sides of the theater as the puppeteer sees it when performing. Two methods of hanging the curtain are shown. (Since these methods require different length rods, be consistent and use only *one method* for *both* upper and lower holders. The curtain is removed from the lower holders at the beginning of a scene and placed above, being returned to the lower holders at the end of the scene.) For method 1, make four holes (a pair below and another pair above) and insert a dowel which extends well beyond the sides. This is the easiest, but the rod is also easily knocked down from the outside. For method 2, glue two pieces of wood to the interior sides in a *V* shape to hold the rod. The rod is cut to the exact width of the box and rests on the *V*s (one pair below and one pair above).

Dampness quickly weakens cardboard. The carton will be protected and strengthened by a coat

FIGURE 4–51. Diagram of a plywood or hardboard stage.

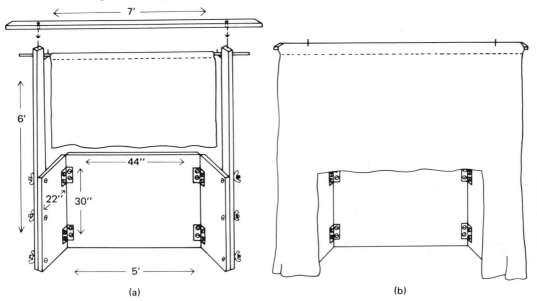

(a)   (b)

FIGURE 4–52. Behind the scenes at a performance put on for other classes in the auditorium. The theatre is on the stage. Charlie walks his marionette, holding the knee control in one hand and the main control in the other.

FIGURE 4–53. An original marionette play is put on for the first grade. The theater is placed on two tables to raise it off the floor.

of latex or enamel paint. The theater will have to be put on a table to have the performance at a level where it can easily be seen by an audience. In that case, the puppeteers will have to work from chairs or another table behind the box.

Another more permanent theater can be made from plywood or hardboard (see Figure 4–51). This is not only durable but will accommodate several puppeteers at one time. It is surprisingly easy to construct and can be folded up for moving and easy storage. It is constructed from ¼-inch hardboard or ½-inch plywood. The hinges should be put on with nuts and bolts. The two uprights, of 1 x 2-inch wood, should be attached with wing nuts for easy removal. (Do not put wing nuts on the hinges; they will protrude against the puppeteers standing at the back.) The drop curtain in Figure 4-51*a* rests on two *L* screw hooks (or bent nails) during the performance and is put down directly on the theater sides at the close of a scene. Two headless nails (finishing nails) are hammered into the top of the uprights. A bar of 1 x 2-inch wood, with two holes drilled at the proper places, rests on the uprights and is held in place by the nails. Figure 4-51*b* shows a permanent curtain of lightweight material (but not so light as to be transparent), which hides the puppeteers from view and covers the rough edges of the theater. The top of the curtain is folded back and sewn, forming a hem, and the 1 x 2-inch rod is slipped through it. The curtain and rod are then pushed down over the nails on the uprights.

This theater also rests directly on the floor. It should be placed on a heavy table (the performers standing on benches behind it) or on an auditorium stage.

In both types of theaters, scenery should be painted on paper and tacked or taped to the back of the stage. Students can make props from all kinds of scrap and natural materials. Appropriate background music should accompany the performance. Use either live music (piano, guitar, recorder, or harmonica) or music from a record player or tape recorder.

5
ASIAN ARTS

As was noted concerning the European art projects, many of the arts described in this chapter are not unique to one country but are also found in some form in other Asian countries. For instance, shadow puppets are made in India and China as well as throughout much of Southeast Asia, and they are expressive of differing traditions in those countries. Several countries are known for their lacquerware, among them China, Japan, Thailand, and Burma. Although the art probably originated in China, each country has developed its own styles and methods. Kite making and flying, of which the Japanese fish banner presented in this chapter is one form, are enjoyed as an art and a pastime in many Asian countries.

Sometimes an art reaches its highest form in a country other than that in which it originated. Woodblock prints were invented in China, primarily as a method of making available multiple copies of illustrated texts. Later, in Japan, the woodcut came to be appreciated as an art form in itself and is now associated more with that country. A method of decorating cloth first begun in India was developed to such a high degree after spreading to Java that it is known by a Javanese name—batik—and is identified around the world with that culture.

CHINESE ARTS

Fine artwork has been a tradition in China from as early as 4000 B.C. The development of the arts was not interrupted by invasions or the rise and fall of dynasties. China has always revered its past; early skills were not lost but carried on and developed to great heights. The earliest surviving work is in bronze, clay, stone, jade, and turquoise. The art of pottery reached perfection in the porcelain vases and bowls of the Sung Dynasty. By this time, too, a new art had developed: pure landscape painting. The brush work in these paintings shows a very close observation of nature and great skill in setting down its forms and moods. These two arts, ceramics and painting, are perhaps those best known by the Western world, but in recent years, especially with new archaeological finds, the great sculptures of the past have become widely known as well.

Three projects have been chosen for this book: calligraphy, a unique combination of art and writing; the making of paper; and woodblock printing. Paper making and woodblock printing were Chinese inventions that have greatly affected the rest of the world.

Calligraphy

The first writing in China, in the middle of the second millenium B.C., was in the form of pictographs (simplified depictions of objects) on bones and turtle shells. There were 5,000 different pictographs representing animals, plants, people, and objects. They were arranged in verticle columns placed in order, usually from right to left. As the language developed, the pictographs evolved into abstract characters. See Figure 5–1.

FIGURE 5–1.

These three sets of figures show an early pictograph (on the left) and the character that developed from it (on the right).

Two or more characters are often combined into one character to make a new symbol representing an object, idea, or feeling. For example, the character for east is made by combining the character for sun and the one for tree to symbolize the direction you would face in seeing the sun rise up behind a tree in the morning. Figure 5–2 shows some examples of combined characters.

日 月 明　木 木 林　日 木 東
sun + moon = bright　tree + tree = forest　sun + tree = east

FIGURE 5–2.

There are 40,000 characters in the Chinese language. A well-educated person needs to know 3,000 to 4,000 of them.

Chinese characters are frequently used as designs on art objects in bronze, clay, and stone and in textiles. Four of the characters in Figure 5–3 are frequently used in decorative arts. They are the characters for good luck, happiness, long life, and rice. Figure 5–5 shows a common tea cup decorated with the character for long life.

仁　平　吉

kindness

peace

good luck

喜　愛　米　壽

happiness　love　rice　long life

FIGURE 5–3.

The Chinese language is used not only to communicate ideas but also as an art form known as calligraphy. The word *calligraphy* comes from the Greek and means "beautiful writing." In Chinese calligra-

FIGURE 5–4. Calligraphy by Chiang Shao-shen, An-hwei, China, 1971. 2 feet, 9 inches x 13 feet. The four characters in translation read, "The Sound of the River Carries the Rain." Collection of Mr. and Mrs. James P. Wong.

FIGURE 5–5. A porcelain tea cup for everyday use decorated with the character for long life.

Introducing Calligraphy

FIGURE 5–6. Vee-Ling Edwards shows several different styles of calligraphy to a fifth-grade class.

FIGURE 5–7. Vee has written Hal's name in Chinese characters. She invites him to try his hand with the brush.

phy, art and language are combined in a manner unknown in the Western world. To many, calligraphy is more exalted than painting, because it is a more complete abstraction of form. One of the early calligraphers was Wang Hsi-Chih (303–79). A later emperor compared his work to "a dragon leaping over the Heavenly Gate"[1] From this remark, you can understand that his brush work conveyed tension and vigor and spirit. The meaning of the characters, therefore, fuses with the art of setting them down. The beauty of the forms themselves and the energy instilled in them by the artist are as important as the message.

A calligrapher spends a lifetime studying and copying master calligraphers and developing skill with his brush. It is a difficult art to convey in a book. If you live in a large city, chances are there is someone in the community who can demonstrate calligraphy. If a demonstration cannot be arranged, the lesson in Figure 5–9 can give the student a feeling for the art. The characters in the column on the left read (from top to bottom): "Ancient For Today Use." Before beginning, discuss the meaning of these words with the class. Two possible interpretations are: "Don't discard the past as there are lessons to learn from history," and "We build on our heritage, using what others have learned before us."

Use a one-inch brush that comes to a fine point. The brush should be held straight up and down, as in Figure 5–8. Dip the brush in India ink and practice drawing thin or heavy lines by applying more or less pressure on the tip of the brush. The lines in each character are always made in a certain order and direction. The students begin with the character at the top. The progression of strokes and the direction in which each stroke is made are shown at the right of each character. A teacher should practice first and make a large chart on newsprint so that the students can see the steps clearly. The students should notice the variation in the thickness of the lines made possible only by using a brush. Try to put life into the strokes.

[1] Bradley Smith and Wan-go Weng, *China. A History in Art,* (N.Y.: Harper and Row, 1976), p. 101.

When the student has gained some skill by practicing on newsprint, he may want to make a final copy, either on newsprint or on rice paper from an art supply store. Chinese calligraphers and painters sign their work in calligraphy and with a seal bearing the characters of their name. The owner of a piece of art will also stamp the work, so that frequently an important scroll will carry several stamps (or seals, as they are usually called) of successive owners. The signatures are usually stamped in red ink. Students can make a seal by cutting a small cube of potato and incising their initials in it with

FIGURE 5–8. Vee corrects Nora's calligraphy. She demonstrates the correct way to hold the brush.

FIGURE 5–9. The calligraphy in the column at the left reads, "Ancient For Today Use." The steps for making each character are given at the right. They are always made in a certain order and direction. Calligraphy for this chart, and elsewhere in this project, by Vee-Ling Edwards.

a knife or linoleum cutting tool. Printing reverses characters, so the letters must be made backwards and in reverse order to come out correctly when printed. Brush the seal with red watercolor and press it on the paper.

The calligraphy should be mounted on a scroll. Scrolls are the Chinese way of framing a work of art. They can be rolled up for easy and safe carrying or storing. The student's best example of calligraphy can be mounted by pasting it on a longer piece of brown wrapping paper. If the school has long rolls of colored craft paper, the brown paper can be pasted on a piece of colored paper as well. The Chinese often use colored silk. In Western mounting, the custom is to leave a larger space at the bottom of a mat. In Eastern mounting, it is the opposite—the larger space is at the top. Glue ¼ x ¾-inch screen molding, painted black, to the top and the bottom of the scroll (Figure 5–11) and glue a hanger of string to the back of the top. Instead of molding, scrolls can also be glued around dowels at the top and bottom.

FIGURE 5–10. Calligraphy by Julie, age ten. She signed her name in Chinese and also with a stamp bearing her initials and mounted the calligraphy on a green scroll.

FIGURE 5–11. Julie and Angie glue wooden strips of screen molding to the top and bottom of their scrolls.

The Invention of Paper

It is hard to imagine a world without paper! Paper, as we know it, was first invented in China around the year 105 by Ts'ai Lun. The first paper was made by soaking rags, rope, bark, and other materials and adding glue to the mixture, which was then pressed into thick sheets. The knowledge of paper making

FIGURE 5-12. Hand-made paper, textured with grass, is the background for the character *Autumn*. Calligraphy by Cho-Yee To.

spread very gradually to other parts of the world, not reaching Italy until 1276. Mills were not established in England until 1495.

Although paper can be made from almost any fibrous material, most paper today is made from wood pulp. Chemicals are added that maintain whiteness, stick the fibers together, and size the paper so that ink will not spread.

Making paper from most raw fibers (cotton is an exception) requires the use of caustic acids and can prove dangerous. However, old used paper can be recycled into fresh new paper, and one can add new fibers to this base.

How to Make Recycled Paper

1.   Make a frame of ¾-inch square pine baluster wood the size of the piece of paper you wish to make. A comfortable size to handle is 7 x 10 inches. Nail the frame together, and nail or staple aluminum window screening to the frame. (See frame in Figure 5-13.)

2.   In a blender three-quarters full of water, reduce to a pulp old paper of any kind: computer print-

FIGURE 5-13. Dip the screen under the pulp and then, keeping it level, bring it straight up above the water, letting the water drain through.

FIGURE 5-14. Invert the screen on a paper towel and press the back with a sponge to remove the excess water. Then lift the screen off the new paper. On the left is a sheet of new paper that is dry and ready to be removed from the paper towel.

FIGURE 5-15. Linocut by Leah, age eleven, on hand-made recycled paper.

out, paper towels, newspaper, advertisements, old cards.

3. Put two or three blenders full of this pulp into a pan or tub of water three to four inches deep and several inches wider than the screen.

4. In the blender (filled with water) chop up new fibers: grass clippings, flowers, carrots, beets, or leaves. These ingredients, separately or in combination, add color and texture to the paper. Add this to the pulp.

5. Thoroughly mix the pulp and vegetable fibers with the water and then slip the frame into the bottom of the pan, with the flat screen side *up*. While holding it there with one hand, be sure that the pulp is equally distributed in the water by whisking it with your other hand. Then slowly, using both hands now, bring the screen straight up above the surface of the water. Keep it level so that the paper will not be thicker on one side than on the other. The water will drain through the screen, leaving a layer of pulp (see Figure 5–13).

6. Drain off any excess water and invert the screen onto a paper towel on a flat surface. With a sponge, press on the back of the screen to remove excess water (Figure 5–14). Then, slowly, lift the screen by pulling up on one edge of the frame. The new paper will stay on the paper toweling.

7. The paper can dry as it is and then be lifted off the toweling, or a second piece of toweling may be placed over it, and it can be ironed dry in a few minutes. Iron one side and then turn the sandwich of paper and toweling over and iron the other side. Be careful not to overiron it, or it may scorch. Peel off the toweling.

Experiment with different textures. If the paper is to be used for calligraphy or printing, it may be most effective with very subtle or no texture. (See Figure 5–12 for an example of calligraphy on handmade paper. Students could use one of the characters in Figure 5–4 on their paper.) If the paper is to be used as a decorative paper that is beautiful in itself, more textured fibers may be added.

Woodblock Printing

In the year 251 Wei Tan created an indelible ink by mixing lamp black with other ingredients. This, combined with the invention of paper, led to the invention of the woodblock for printing.

The Chinese made seals, little carved wooden or stone characters that people used to show ownership, as early as 1000 B.C. They were sometimes stamped in clay tiles. Probably from this, around the year 600, the woodblock was developed. Taoist

FIGURE 5–16. *Chrysanthemums and Bamboo,* color woodcut from the *Mustard Seed Garden Manual of Painting* by Wang Kai, nineteenth-century edition. Courtesy of The University of Michigan Museum of Art.

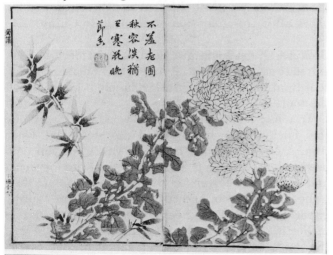

priests and Buddhist monks made impressions on paper from large seals to illustrate religious writings. In this way, they could reproduce drawings in quantity for the first time and make them available to many people. By the time of the Sung Dynasty (960) line prints were colored in by hand. Many woodblock books of very fine quality were being made. Histories, works of poets and philosophers, and a book on agriculture from this time are treasured to this day. Later, books for artists were also printed.

One book that became very famous was the *Mustard Seed Garden Manual of Painting,* a handbook of instruction in landscape painting produced in 1679 by Wang Kai. It used color woodcuts for illustrations. The manual, written in three parts, sets down general principles of Chinese painting and gives instructions for preparing brushes, colors, and inks. The woodcuts illustrate the brush strokes used in painting a great variety of subjects: trees, rocks, people, buildings, and clouds. There are even woodcuts of all kinds of insects and a section with the delightful title, "Book of Feathers-and-Fur and Flowering Plants." Figure 5–16, a color woodcut from a later edition of this manual (nineteenth century), illustrates how to paint bamboo and chrysanthemums. Color plate 13 is another illustration from the same book.

The art of printing with woodcuts was not widely used in Europe until the fourteenth century—900 years after the invention of printing in China.

Making Woodcuts

Because sharp tools are used, this project is best suited to students of fifth-grade level and older, when coordination and strength levels make handling of the tools safer.

To make a woodcut, use soft wood (such as pine) that is clear of knots. Cut the size block you want from a one-inch thick board. If you wish you can use linoleum, which is a modern substitute for wood and somewhat easier for the beginner to cut. Buy a sheet of linoleum and cut it into pieces on a large paper cutter or with heavy shears. A piece 6 x 9 inches is probably ample. It is not necessary to use the more expensive blocks in which linoleum has been glued to wood. A print made from linoleum is called a linocut.

Work out a design on paper the same size as the block. Transfer the design with carbon paper onto the block, and then go over the design on the block with a magic marker to strengthen the lines.

Using linoleum or woodcutting tools, cut away the wood or linoleum, leaving the inked design uncut and therefore raised. If you are using wood, you will find it easier to cut with the grain (in the direction of the grain). Linoleum cutting tools come in sets with round and V-shaped gouges and one flat blade. For woodcuts you will need to cut around the contours of the design with the flat tool or an X-acto knife and then remove wood with a gouge. For linoleum blocks only the gouges are used—round for large areas or wide lines and V-shaped for fine lines. *Always cut away from the hand holding the block.*

When the block has been cut it is time to print. Water-base printing ink is best for beginners because it is easy to clean up afterwards. Squeeze the ink out onto a smooth surface (tile or glass) and roll it out with a brayer until it stops being slippery and has a sticky texture. (It will make a faint crackly noise as the brayer runs over it.) Then transfer the ink to the block with the brayer, returning to the tile to pick up more ink until the block is covered. Next, move the block to a clean area and make a test print with newsprint. Carefully place the paper on top of the block and rub it well. It can be rubbed with the side of the hands or with a smooth, hard object such as a wooden spoon or drawer knob.

Lift up one corner of the paper while holding the rest down and check to see if the block was inked well and the print is evenly rubbed. It may be necessary to add a little more ink while someone holds the paper up for you. Replace that corner, rub it to keep it down, and lift up another portion. If it is rubbed well and the paper is not too thick, the design should be visible through the paper. A wood block absorbs ink at first, and it may take another inking to get a good print.

When you pull the test print from the block, check to see that all the areas have been cut correctly. Usually you will find areas that may need more cut-

FIGURE 5–17. Kristin, age eleven, demonstrates how to cut a linoleum block. The hand holding the linoleum is always *behind* the cutting tool.

FIGURE 5–18. *Curlew,* linocut by Ellen, age eleven.

FIGURE 5–19. Four prints by sixth-grade students. Clockwise from top right: *Seagull,* linoprint by Annette; *Fish,* woodcut on blue paper by Myles; *Tree,* linocut by Eileen; *Mountains,* linocut on handmade paper by Chris.

ting to get the impression you want. You can make your design totally free of ink in background areas by carefully removing all wood or linoleum that is surface height, or you can get a textured background by letting the cutting tools leave ridges.

After the block has been corrected make prints on more permanent papers: your own recycled paper, imported rice papers, or colored construction papers. Use a variety of ink colors, too, until you find a combination of ink and paper that pleases you.

JAPANESE ARTS

Perhaps in no other culture has art been more integrated with daily life than in Japan. This may be changing with increased industrialization and Westernization. But for many, art was and is a way of life; the utensils used, their manner of use, and the design and order of the home are often seen in an aesthetic or spiritual light. Daily sights and occurrences are still recorded in poetry and painting by many Japanese, the object being to try and express the essence of a sight or an idea in the most succinct manner possible. This is not a shorthand but a distillation; the essence is not lost but made more compelling.

Haiku (hi-cōō) is a short Japanese poem with a traditional form and content. Sumi-e (sōō-mē-ā) is the art of painting with ink (*sumi* means Chinese ink, and *e* means painting). Both these arts, writing haiku and sumi painting, take many hours of practice—in the case of the masters, a lifetime of training. Many subtleties in haiku are lost in translation, and without knowing the Japanese language one can never fully appreciate haiku. Sumi-e is not attempted by most children in Japan, as it is thought to be successful only if the artist's mind is mature. However, students can gain a beginning appreciation of haiku and sumi-e by reading the poems, trying to write them, making ink paintings, and putting together a booklet of their own work. Some eighteenth-century haiku writers, such as Buson, combined sumi-e and poetry on one scroll. Figure 5–20 is such a combination by the poet-painter, Bashitso, who lived from 1768 to 1852. A little book of one's own poems and ink paintings can be a record of one's feelings to be treasured and shared for a long time.

Haiku were being written over 700 years ago and reached a peak in the seventeenth century. They have continued to be a part of Japanese life to this day and are written by many people, young and old. Haiku are short, have a definite pattern, and are intended primarily to express an emotion. They usually sketch a poignant moment in nature that stirred an emotional response in the observer, although the emotion is suggested and not stated in the poem. Haiku record meaningful but perhaps very brief events that are good to remember because they set ones mind to thinking. They also include some reference to a season, usually in the form of some part of nature associated with a particular season (such as chrysanthemums, which bring fall to mind).

The Haiku Society of America has defined haiku as an "unrhymed poem, recording the essence of a moment, keenly perceived, in which nature is linked to human nature." The poems contain seventeen syllables: five to the first line, seven to the second, and five again in the third. (Although in the Japanese language most haiku have this 5–7–5 syllabic count, it cannot always be successfully retained in translation.) Although haiku are not rhymed in Japanese, some translations to English are rhymed in an attempt to give a feeling for the rhythm of the original language. Here are translations of haiku by two of Japan's most well-known poets.

What a huge one, how splendid it was,—
The chestnut
I couldn't get at![2]

ISSA

On the temple bell
has settled, and is fast asleep,
a butterfly.[3]

BUSON

[2] From R. H. Blyth, *Haiku*, vol. IV, p. 140. Copyright 1952. Reprinted by kind permission from the Hokuseido Press, Tokyo.

[3] From Harold G. Henderson, *An Introduction to Haiku* (Copyright © 1958 by Harold G. Henderson. Reprinted by permission of Doubleday & Company, Inc.), p. 104.

Haiku

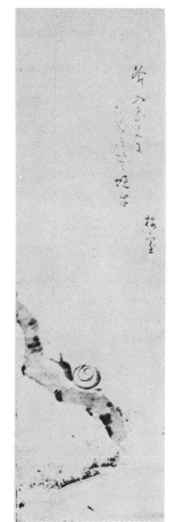

FIGURE 5–20. *Snail* by Baishitsu. Reprinted from *Haiku* by R. H. Blyth, vol. III, p. 245. Copyright 1952, by kind permission from the Hokuseido Press, Tokyo. The haiku inscribed on the painting reads:

The axe bites into the tree,
But the snail
Is calm and serene.

Issa describes a situation familiar to us all: an elusive perfection just beyond one's grasp. Sometimes haiku are inspired by other haiku or by sumi-e, like the one by Oguri Sokyu of a squirrel in a chestnut tree (see Figure 5–21). Just above him is a splendid chestnut. Could Issa have seen and been thinking of this painting (which was done 300 years before his birth)? We do not know.

Buson's poem first forms a lovely picture in the mind: massive, ancient bronze versus a delicate, ephemeral butterfly. The poem causes the reader to wonder: what will happen when the bell rings? Perhaps the priest cannot bring himself to ring it. A haiku should always set one's mind to seeing and thinking.

Many different levels of meaning arise from studying a haiku by a master, and some of them are not immediately apparent in translation. For instance, read this poem by Kikaku:

A tree frog, clinging
to a banana leaf—
and swinging, swinging.[4]

One sees the small frog getting a ride on the enormous banana leaf that is tossing in the wind. Is he enjoying it? Or is he holding on for dear life? Can he change his situation? This is thought to be Kikaku's comment on human life. It may also be a pun on his own poetic career. He was a student of Basho, one of the earliest and perhaps the most famous of haiku writers, and Basho means "banana leaf" in Japanese! Many haiku have these associations to the Japanese, subtleties that Westerners, unfamiliar with many of the symbols used, are unable to appreciate fully. Although we can understand part of the haiku in translation, some of the intended meanings are lost.

Student Poetry Inspired by Haiku

In helping students write poetry for their own books, remember that haiku always include some reference to a season. It is, however, rarely necessary to use a seasonal name; the poem should be more reserved, only hinting at the season. For instance, leaves turn-

4 Ibid., p. 58.

ing color and pumpkins both suggest fall immediately without using the word *fall*. Adjectives like *beautiful* or *sad* also depreciate the quality of the haiku. This feeling should arise from the image suggested by the words but not be stated outright.

Some haiku do not attempt to give much more meaning than a clear picture of a beautiful moment. Students should start with the idea of expressing such a moment, without trying to put too many levels of meaning into it. The image and ideas are more important than the 5–7–5 syllabic counts, and students can take some liberties to preserve a particular feeling.

Here are some examples of poems by fifth-grade American school children that contain some of the principles of haiku:

The caterpillar
walking slowly through the grass—
baby butterfly.

MAREN

This expresses the wonder of transformation from a pedestrian life to flight.

Seagulls flying high
way above the roaring sea
descending slowly down.

TAMAR

This is suggestive of contrast—delicate controlled flight, destructive power below.

Praying mantis eat the fly
then stand unaware
of a lizard hunger.

JASON

The snow falls lightly.
Try to catch it on your tongue.
No luck, try again.

ADAM

These poems give the feeling of the transitory nature of life and beauty.

Sumi-e

Although ink painting began in China, Japanese painters adapted it to their own style of painting. Sumi-e is the visual equivalent of haiku. The aim of the artist is to express emotion through the beauty of the forms rather than merely to reproduce objects. Through observation and practice, the artist distills the essence of the subject matter into a minimum number of brush strokes. Usually only black ink is used and, when water is added to the ink, many gradations of gray. In this way a whole range of color and texture is suggested. Sometimes a color is added as well, but the painting is kept to the bare essence of the object. The white space of the paper is a very important part of the painting. It takes on a positive meaning in relation to the ink strokes, becoming in the imagination sky or water, wooded hill or snow.

From early childhood, the Japanese learn to use a brush in writing their language characters. Even so, if they wish to pursue sumi-e as adults, they

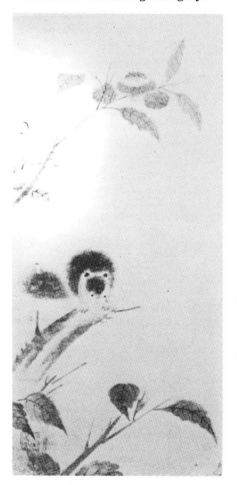

FIGURE 5–21. *Squirrel on a Chestnut Tree* by Oguri Sokyu, 1398–1464. Reprinted from *Haiku* by R. H. Blyth, by kind permission from The Hokuseido Press, Tokyo. Notice the variety of brush strokes from fine fur and twig lines to broad leaves. The central point of interest (the squirrel) is darkest, and distance (the highest branch) is indicated with the lightest gray.

FIGURE 5–22. Mr. Saburo Ikeuchi prepares to demonstrate sumi-e to a fifth-grade class. Seiichi Sasaki, his interpreter, stands by his side. Mr. Ikeuchi first arranges his materials carefully on a mat and then spends a few moments in quiet contemplation.

must spend countless hours learning to control the brush so they can express exactly what they wish. Usually they work with a master and learn stroke by stroke the way he does a sparrow, a fish, plum blossoms, and so on. Like practicing a musical instrument, one does it by rote until one is sure enough to put one's own interpretation into it. Sumi-e are not painted outdoors while looking at a scene, although a master painter may have spent many hours observing and sketching from life. From these observations he devises brush strokes that will simplify while keeping the essence of the object. These are the set brush strokes that are then taught to his students. In sumi-e many traditions are followed, even the way one arranges materials before oneself and prepares one's mind to be quiet and contemplative before beginning (see Figure 5–22).

By far the best way for students to gain an appreciation of sumi-e is to have them watch a demonstration by a Japanese painter. In our larger cities this is frequently possible if one contacts international organizations, universities with Asian studies departments, or import shops that sell Japanese art supplies. If a demonstration cannot be arranged, there are now books available in English that explain the steps in sumi-e. They are sometimes available at art museums and import shops as well as bookstores.

The Japanese use a hard cake of ink, which is rubbed on a stone with water to make the liquid ink. Students may use India ink. There should also be water for diluting the ink to make gray and a cloth to wipe the brush with. Newsprint is fine for practicing sumi-e. Paintings to be kept may be made on imported Japanese papers prepared especially for sumi-e, and these are often available in art supply stores.

The Japanese use several different brushes, most of which are not available outside Japan. However, the most important is a large brush (at least one inch) that comes to a fine point when wet. Brushes like this are available at art supply stores. With this one brush, students can draw many different lines. The brush is held between the thumb and the fingertips in a vertical position, and brush strokes

Teaching Ink Painting to Students

FIGURE 5-23. With the brush held in a vertical position, Mr. Ikeuchi uses the fine tip to draw delicate plum blossoms. They contrast with the rugged branch. Part of the branch is drawn with a dry brush, which creates a texture suggesting bark.

are made by moving the entire arm. Fine lines are drawn with the tip of the brush (see the plum blossoms in Figure 5-23). With more pressure down, the artist can draw wider lines.

By holding the brush in a slanting position (as opposed to vertical), the artist makes a wide, soft line. (See hand position in Figure 5-24.)

The student should experiment with adding water to the ink to create a variety of grays. To get a single stroke that is graded from dark to light, immerse the brush in water and then wipe out excess moisture. Put the tip of the brush lightly into the ink and then press it up and down on a plate to mix the ink into the interior of the brush. Then dip just the tip into the ink again. When applied with the brush handle almost parallel to the paper, this will give a wide line with a gradation from dark to light, as in the trunk of the tree in Figure 5–27. This gives the impression of roundness to a form.

Students should also practice making brush strokes with wet versus almost dry brushes to see the different effects this makes. In Figure 5–23 the plum branches were painted with an almost dry brush. This creates a texture suited to bark or to fur. To obtain a dry brush, after dipping it in ink, scrub it lightly on newspaper until most of the ink is gone and the brush hairs no longer come to a point but are separated.

After practicing the brush strokes described above, the students should try painting flowers, birds, animals, or other subject matter. They should be reminded of the importance of white space in their compositions and of keeping the brush strokes to the minimum necessary to get their ideas across. There should be a variety of gray tones as well as accents of pure black.

If the paintings are being made to illustrate poems they have written and are to be included in a booklet, they will have to be made on paper that measures 5½ x 8½ inches.

FIGURE 5-24. Mr. Ikeuchi creates a wider line by holding the brush in a slanting position.

Making a Booklet for Poems and Ink Paintings

A traditional Japanese way to make a book is by folding paper accordian style. This requires a roll of paper. White, nonglazed shelf lining paper works well. Cut the paper nine inches wide, and fold the paper accordian style every six inches. A piece of paper 96 inches long will make a book of seven pages with two extra leaves to glue to the covers. (See Figure 5–26a.) The folding must be done *very* accurately if the pages are to be even, and this is surprisingly difficult for many students. If it proves too difficult, students may fold five 9 x 12-inch sheets in half, creating the middle pages of the book, and two sheets 9 x 18 inches into thirds. These last two sheets will be the first and last pages because they have an extra leaf to glue to the cover (see Figure 5–26b).

The first step in making a cover is to decorate two pieces of construction paper, 11½ x 8½ inches.

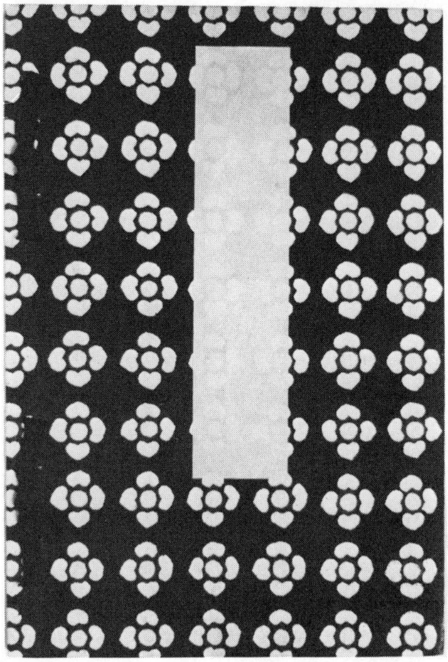

FIGURE 5-25. A Japanese notebook with folded pages and decorative cover.

The Japanese make fine decorative papers by many methods: by incorporating pressed leaves in the paper when it is made, by using a batik-like method with paste and stencils, by folding the paper and dipping it in dye to create patterns, and also by printing. Students may decorate their cover papers by printing with objects: forks, spools, container tops, and so forth, or by printing with shapes cut from slices of potato. Heather's book covers (Figure 5-27) were decorated by printing fish shapes cut from a piece of potato and overlaying a water design made with a fork. The fish are printed in goldfish colors—red, orange, and yellow—and the wave lines are blue. In printing, an object is pressed into a pad of soft styrofoam or paper toweling that is saturated with tempera paint. It is then pressed onto the construction paper in a pattern or design. Be sure there is a thick pad of newspaper under the construction paper. This helps to get a good impression. Push the object into the paint again each time before you print with it.

When the paper has been printed and is dry, it is glued to cardboard covers. Cut two pieces of shirt cardboard (or cardboard of similar thickness) 9½ x 6½ inches. Glue them to the center of the non-printed side of the decorated paper with white glue. Cut off the corners at an angle. Fold the sides in and glue them to the cardboard (see Figure 5-26c).

To assemble the book, place the covers on either side of the folded paper. The spine of the paper insert should be even with the back edges of the covers. (In the front of the book, the covers protrude beyond the pages by ½ inch). Glue the first six inches of the folded paper down to the inside of the front cover and the last six inches to the back cover (Figure 5-26d). Next punch two holes ½ inch in from the spine of the book, one located two inches down from the top, and one located two inches up from the bottom. The hole punching must be done in three steps: punch the front cover first. Then mark the pages through the holes in the cover with a pencil. Punch the pages, mark again for the back cover, and punch again. Thread yarn through the holes and tie it with a bow knot (Figure 5-26e).

The student may copy his poems directly into the

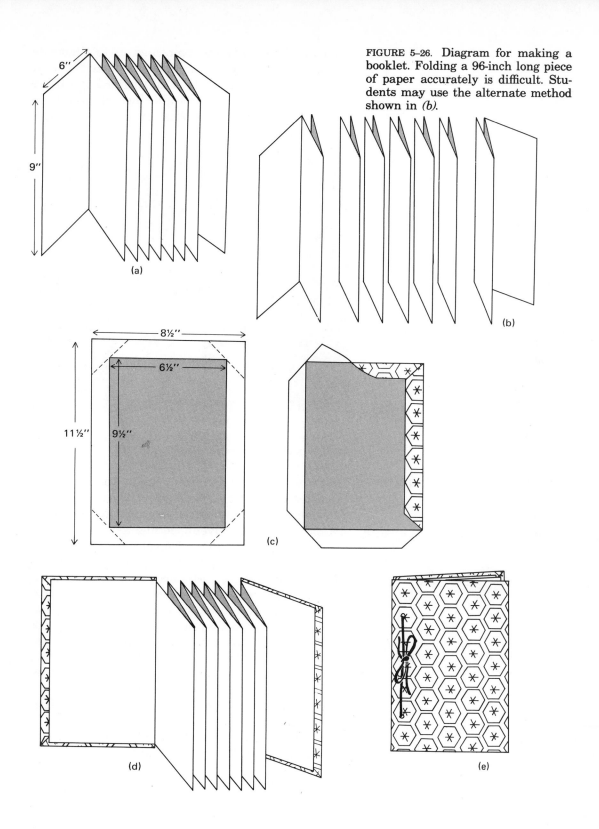

FIGURE 5-26. Diagram for making a booklet. Folding a 96-inch long piece of paper accurately is difficult. Students may use the alternate method shown in (b).

6″

9″

(a)

(b)

8½″

6½″

11½″

9½″

(c)

(d)

(e)

book and paste his ink paintings in to illustrate them. Traditionally, Japanese books started at what is to the Westerner the back of the book, with the pages turning from left to right. Increasingly, however, they are now made Western style with pages turning right to left.

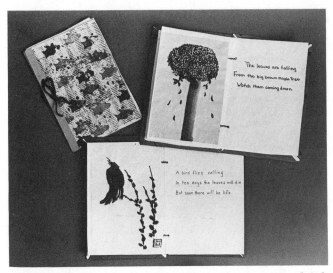

FIGURE 5–27. Booklets of Japanese-style poems and ink paintings by fifth-grade students Heather, Tamar, and Paul (clockwise from upper left).

Fish Banners

FIGURE 5–28. Japanese fish banners fly from bamboo poles on the Children's Festival in May.

People who live in a country made up of many islands feel a great closeness with the sea and much dependence on it. With its teeming life, the ocean not only provides a livelihood and food for millions of people, but it figures in much of the art of Japan—in woodcuts, in paintings, in clay, and in fabric design. Japan also has streams and ponds in abundance, and raising goldfish has become an art form: they are bred for beauty and for pleasure. These goldfish, or carp, as they are commonly called, reach upwards of 1½ feet in length. Many homes and apartments, even with very small yards, include a pool in the garden for goldfish, which are prized for special colors and fancy fins and tails.

May 5th is a national holiday in Japan. It used to be called the Boys' Festival; now it is called Children's Day. As part of the festival, each family that has boy children flies banners in the shape of carp

120 Asian Arts

from a pole attached to the house. The carp is a symbol of masculinity, power, and determination. The carp banners are purchased by the family and friends on the first festival after the child's birth and are flown every year afterwards on the festival day. They are not made to fly free like a kite on a string. Being made of two pieces of cloth, they form a kind of "wind sock" and fill out into a tube when the wind blows through them. The action of the wind in the tube makes the banner look very much like a carp fighting hard to swim upstream against the current. Paper banners, made for the same purpose but less often flown outside because they are not as durable, can often be found in import shops and are painted in many different colors. They are used as decorations inside a home.

Making a Fish Banner

To make a fish banner, you need a large piece of paper, such as the 36-inch-wide craft paper that comes in large rolls of many colors. Fold the paper double in a long rectangle and draw the fish so that it fills one entire side. Then, keeping the paper doubled, cut out the fish. A staple or two will keep the

FIGURE 5–29. Rebecca, age seven, finds the floor a comfortable place for painting her big fish.

FIGURE 5–30. Fish banners by second-grade students Helen, Jonathan, and Tricia. Each banner is an expression of that individual.

two pieces from shifting as it is cut. This will give two identical fish shapes. Staple the pieces together all around the edge, but leave one gap large enough so the fish can later be stuffed with newspaper. The fish can now be painted.

The Japanese fish banners have a delightful pattern of scales, often painted in warm colors (red, pink, gold) or cool colors (blue, purple, gray). The children may want to make their own patterns, using stripes, dots, or shapes of their own devising. When one side is painted and dry, turn the fish over and paint the other side. When the painting is done, scrunch up a sheet of newspaper lightly (not into a tight wad, or it will become so heavy the fish will tear) and put it inside the fish to round it out as if the wind were filling it. Staple the opening together. The fish look very decorative hung up by a string indoors or outdoors on a sunny day. They can swim down the corridors of a school or make a colorful contribution to an art exhibition.

Gyotaku: Fish Prints

FIGURE 5–31. Gyotaku by Mr. Ogiso of Takebun-do, Toyoda, Japan. This print was made as a record of a fish Mr. Ogiso caught, an opaleye, which is found only in the Japan and China Seas. Its weight, length, place caught, and the year (1975) are also recorded. Collection of the author.

Gyotaku (gee-o-taku) is the art of taking prints directly from fish. The word comes from *gyo*, meaning fish, and *taku*, an abbreviation of the word for rubbings (a way of making prints from stone and wood reliefs by hand). Although now considered an art form, too, gyotaku was first done only as a matter of record keeping. As part of the training of Samurai warriors in Sakai Province, the men were required to record the fish they caught by inking them and pressing paper to the inked fish. There are archives with records of fish caught some 200 years ago.

In the past thirty years, after falling into disuse, there has been a revival of fish printing, both as a record by fishermen and also as an art in itself.

Two methods have developed. In the direct method, ink is painted on the fish and then paper is pressed carefully over it to receive an impression. In the second, or indirect method, moist paper is placed on the uninked fish and pressed to fit all its contours. When the paper is dry, ink is rubbed gently over it. The impression is made in the same way that rubbings can be taken from engraved stones.

Both methods require a great deal of skill if they are to achieve a print that is beautiful and true to the form of the fish. The aim is to record all the fine details of scales, fins, eyes, and tail. In 1957 a traveling exhibit of gyotaku was arranged by the Smithsonian Institution and toured the United States. A great variety of fish, large and small, were represented in the prints—salmon, carp, halibut, mackerel, and even squid, sea horses, shrimp, and octopus. The prints ranged from those using only black ink to those using soft subtle shades of rose, yellow, and gray. They all brought an awareness of the beautiful shapes, patterns, and lines in fish. The prints were mounted on patterned paper or silk and either framed or made into scrolls.

Beginning students will not be able to get the delicate, accurate prints made by practiced gyotaku artists, but they will be able to get satisfying results that introduce them to this art.

It is necessary to have a fish fresh from the market on the day of printing. Choose a fish that has a distinct scale pattern. Wipe the fish carefully to

Making Fish Prints

FIGURE 5–32. Serafim watches as Atsushi brushes India ink over a fish. Atsushi is careful to cover every part, including fins.

FIGURE 5–33. Tomoko presses newsprint over the fish after she has brushed it with ink. She will carefully smooth the paper down onto every part of the fish.

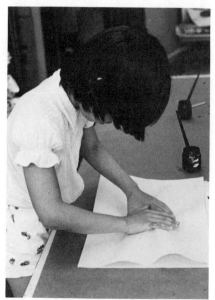

FIGURE 5–34. Tomoko signs her print.

FIGURE 5–35. A fish print by Jon, age seven.

remove any mucous or excess moisture and place it on a pad of newspaper. Before beginning to print, increase the students' awareness and perception of the fish by examining it with them. Explain how the fish breathes through its gills, how its shape is adapted to life in the water, how overlapping scales are smooth in one direction and rough in another—in sum, what a marvelous creature it is!

India ink makes the best prints for beginners, but it is indelible, so the students should protect their clothing with old shirts or smocks. For the classroom the direct method of printing is the most practical. Brush the ink over the fish lightly, being careful to cover every part of the fish, not forgetting the fins. Sometimes the fins tend to close up against the body. They can be fanned out and pinned to the newspaper in an open position. Place a sheet of thin paper over the fish and gently but firmly press it to the contours of the fish. Prints can be made with newsprint. However, imported papers from Japan make much better prints because they are more pliable and conform better to the contours of the fish. After pressing the paper onto every part of the fish, lift it off carefully and sign the print. Replace the newspaper under the fish frequently; ink that has spilled there will make spots on the paper used for printing the fish.

BURMESE LACQUERWARE

The Burmese nation includes over 100 different ethnic groups, the largest of which are the Burmans, the Shans, the Möns, and the Arakanese. Throughout this country there are many highly skilled artists and craftspeople working in many materials. Mandalay is noted for its fine silks; from the Shan state come brightly colored woven shoulder bags. There is artwork in gold and silver, carving in teakwood and ivory, and lacquerware in great variety.

The lacquerware made in Burma is of very fine quality. The area around Pagan is best known for this art, but it is done in many other places as well. The art probably originated in China centuries ago, but certain types, like that with reddish-orange finish, are unique to Burma. Lacquerware is often given as gifts, and most homes have some pieces.

It is used for bowls and dishes, covered betel nut boxes with interior trays, large shopping baskets, and containers of all sizes. Some lidded containers are made in the shapes of animals, ducks, fish, and owls (the owl is a symbol of good luck).

There are several steps in making lacquerware. First a basic shape is woven of very narrow bamboo strips, and the uneven surface is filled with a fine paste made with ashes. This is sanded very smooth. Then it is coated with lacquer (made from the sap of the thitsi tree), dried, and sanded. This is the first of many coats of lacquer. Some very fine pieces may be worked on for many months, as the successive coats are applied, dried slowly, and sanded.

The next step is to paint a design on the black lacquer with a vinegar and water solution. Lacquer is then patted on with a cotton ball and very fine gold leaf carefully pressed into the lacquer with the finger tips. (Gold leaf is real gold, which has been hammered and beaten by hand until it is very thin, sometimes an unbelievable $\frac{1}{200,000}$ of an inch!) The gold leaf will not adhere to the designs that were painted in vinegar and water. When the piece is washed, the gold leaf flakes off over those lines, revealing the black lacquer underneath. To the uninformed, it looks as though the designs had been drawn on with black ink.

The Burmese lacquerware is sometimes painted a reddish-orange inside the containers with a pigment made of cinnabar (mercury sulphide) mixed with oil. Sometimes a layer of dark green is applied under the black lacquer and then designs are incised through the lacquer to the green layer underneath.

Beautiful lacquerware baskets are made in Kengtung by the Khun, a branch of the Shan ethnic group. They are used much like large handbags and have intricate raised designs sculpted on the surface. Lacquer is thickened with ash until it can be rolled into fine threads. The threads are applied to the lacquered basket in floral and leafy patterns or in figures of men and women. Gold leaf is applied over this relief work to finish the richly ornate surface. A cloth handle is secured in two metal loops attached to the basket, and the interior is of either black lacquer or the orange finish (see Figure 5–36).

FIGURE 5–36. Gold-leafed lacquerware containers from Burma. Collection of the author.

Making Papier Mâché "Lacquerware" Containers in the Shapes of Animals

The steps in making a papier mâché container are illustrated in Figures 5–37 and 5–38. First, crumble newspaper into the form of a small animal. Make a very simple shape, suggestive of only head and body. The Burmese animals are simplified, and there is no attempt to be realistic. Hold the newspaper in this form with strips of masking tape. Apply four layers of newspaper dipped in wheat paste to this basic form. Work with small pieces to keep it smooth. (See appendix for general papier mâché instructions.)

Next, tear bits of facial tissue into a small con-

FIGURE 5–37. Steps in making a papier mâché container in the form of an animal. Newspaper is crumpled and taped into a basic form and then covered with papier mâché. Features are added with a papier mâché mash, and then another layer of papier mâché is applied to the whole figure.

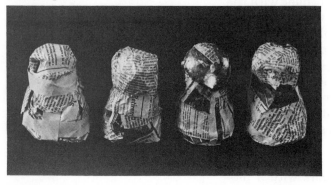

FIGURE 5–38. The papier mâché figure is sawed in half, the stuffing removed, and a flange glued to the inside top of the bottom piece. One layer of papier mâché is applied to the flange. When dry, the container is painted with gold paint and India ink designs.

tainer of wheat paste and mix together with your fingers, kneading and squeezing until you have a kind of mash that can be handled like clay. Of this mash form beaks or ears, the curve of a wing, or the suggestion of feet by molding them onto the basic shape.

Let the papier mâché dry thoroughly. Apply one more layer of newspaper dipped in wheat paste to the whole form. Use small pieces and smooth them down carefully, going over the entire piece, including the parts added with mash, and integrate them with the rest of the figure.

When the piece is thoroughly dry (after several days), smooth the surface with fine sandpaper. This will take out some of the ridges that are apt to form in papier mâché. Saw the papier mâché animal into two pieces so that it will make a container and a top. The best place is frequently at the neckline, but some figures may be sawed approximately halfway between top and bottom (see the turtle in Figure 5–36). It will be difficult to replace the top properly if the top piece narrows from the point where it is separated from the body. If this is the case, make the cut lower down in a more vertical area.

Remove the loose newspaper stuffing inside, leaving a papier mâché shell in the shape of an animal. With white glue, secure a cardboard flange to the inside of the bottom piece so that it stands up straight, about ¼ inch above the bottom piece (see Figure 5–38). The top piece will fit down over the flange, and the flange will hold the top in place, keeping it from slipping off. Apply a single layer of paper dipped in wheat paste to the flange. Smooth it down over the rough top edge where the figure was cut. Seal the cut edge of the top in the same way.

When the piece is dry it may be painted. The inside should be painted with black tempera paint, the outside with gold tempera or with gold polymer (the latter works especially well). After the gold paint has dried, make fine lines and fancy patterns with a tiny detail brush and India ink. (If the gold paint resists the ink, add a few drops of liquid soap to the ink.) The Burmese owl in Figure 5–36 has shiny black eyes, wings that look like flowers, a leaf pattern on its breast, and lots of little curved feather lines. See also color plate 14.

The black tempera on the inside should be given a coat of shellac. Shellac the eye spots, too, to make them shine. The little container is now ready to hold some special treasure.

FIGURE 5–39. Papier mâché containers in animal shapes, painted gold with inked designs. Left to right: *Cat*, by Dana, ten; *Owl*, by Jenny, nine; and *Owl*, by Linda, nine.

THE MARBLE INLAYS OF INDIA

In India today, skilled craftspeople do very fine artwork of many kinds. Carved ivory figures, brass sculpture, silver jewelry, pottery, woven fabrics of silk and cotton, paintings, wood carvings, and lacquerware are some of the many beautiful things made. The great variety of artwork reflects the diversity of India's 600 million people. Many different religious, cultural, and language groups make up the population of this vast subcontinent.

There have been 5,000 years of continuous civilization in India. Sculpture in clay, stone, and bronze has been found from as early as 2500 B.C. Over the centuries, the Indian culture has been based primarily on the Hindu religion and way of life, and many of the arts reflect this. Architecture and sculpture were integrated in the many richly carved stone temples built throughout India.

One art for which India has become well known is stone inlay work. Craftspeople in Agra make beautiful designs by cutting and shaping semiprecious stones and setting them in marble and soapstone.

This art goes back 400 years. Although the majority of Indians are Hindus, successive invasions over the centuries brought other religions and diversity of culture. One of the most important of these invasions was by Muslims from central Asia. The Moghul Empire, which they established, controlled vast areas of India from the sixteenth to the eighteenth centuries. Their rule brought a strong influence on the arts. Persian ideas combined with already established Indian painting traditions to form the Moghul school of miniature painting. Moghul architecture introduced the pointed arch and Persian decorative designs, including stone inlay work.

The Moghul capital alternated between Agra and Delhi. At Agra a large fort was built by Akbar, the greatest of these emperors. His son, Jahangir, and his grandson, Shah Jahan, in their successive reigns, made many additions to the fort. There were marble palaces, reception halls, baths, mosques, and formal gardens within the walls.

FIGURE 5–40. The Taj Mahal, Agra, India. Built as a monument to Mumtaz Mahal, beloved wife of Emperor Shah Jahan.

In Agra, also, is the Taj Mahal, built by the Emperor Shah Jahan in memory of his beloved wife, Mumtaz Mahal, who died giving birth to their fourteenth child. The Taj Mahal, a perfect synthesis of Hindu and Muslim arts, is so famous for its ethereal beauty and romantic origins that it has become for many a symbol of India. In this graceful memorial are combined the pointed arch of Muslim architec-

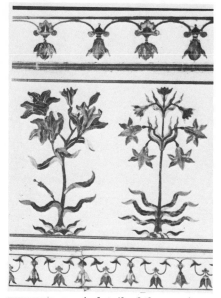

FIGURE 5-41. A detail of the semiprecious stones, in floral designs, that inlay the white marble cenotaph of Mumtaz Mahal. Photo courtesy of the Government of India Tourist Office, Agra.

FIGURE 5-42. Marble box inlaid with lapis lazuli, carnelian, jade, tiger eye, agate, and other semiprecious stones. Made in Agra, India. Collection of the author.

ture and the delicately perforated white marble grilles developed by Hindu architects for their temples. They give shade from the sun but allow breezes to flow through the building.

Artisans were imported from many lands, and 20,000 Indian craftsmen and laborers worked on it for seventeen years. The memorial was completed in 1647. Situated on the banks of the Jumna river, the Taj Mahal is made of white marble on a red sandstone base. A great dome rises from the center of the Taj. Inside, around the cenotaph (which is directly under the dome) is a marble screen, six feet high, carved into lacelike designs from a single block of marble. The actual burial crypt is down a flight of stairs and is directly under the cenotaph. Throughout the Taj Mahal, on the wall and screens and on the tombs, is inlay work of semiprecious stones in floral patterns. Jasper, lapis lazuli, agate, and cornelian stones were cut into leaf and flower shapes. Holes of the same size were chiseled into the marble and the pieces inlaid so carefully that no break can be detected between the stones—they are perfectly smooth to the touch. One flower, created in an area one-inch square, contains sixty different inlays. The colors glow against the white marble.

Shah Jahan originally planned to build a mausoleum of black marble for himself across the river. He expected this to be joined to the Taj Mahal by a silver bridge. However, these plans did not materialize, and he was buried in the Taj Mahal, beside his wife.

Inlay work is found in gateways and palaces constructed around this time in other parts of India, but none surpasses that done in Agra. The craftspeople working in Agra now are descendents of the artisans who worked on the Taj Mahal, and they are still carrying on the tradition of this beautiful art. See color plate 15.

In a related rural craft, many villagers in India decorate the interiors and exteriors of their homes with a kind of mosaic that resembles inlay work. Where the homes are constructed by plastering stone or brick walls with a smooth layer of a mud-clay mixture, broken glass (especially from the bright glass bangles that are worn in great numbers by women and young girls) and pieces of broken china cups and saucers are pressed into the mud before it dries. Intricate flower, leaf, and tree designs and sometimes words of welcome to the home are created in the brightly colored glass.

Stained glass inlaid in plaster has some of the same glow of color against a white background as do the marble inlays of India, although the method of working and materials used are very different. This process is perhaps closer to the rural art of glass and china mosaics.

Stained glass is rather expensive to purchase, but a small sheet will go a long way (it will be broken up into many much smaller pieces). Do not buy a textured glass for this project. If you explain your project, a glass company may be willing to save for you the scraps of colored glass left over from repair work.

It is not practical for students to try to cut small pieces of glass into predesignated shapes. Instead, the glass is broken into many very small pieces and a design is worked out using these irregular shapes. An adult should prepare the broken glass for the students.

There are two methods of breaking the glass safely. One method is to cut the glass into long, thin strips with a glass cutting tool. See the appendix for instructions on how to cut glass. Strips cut in this way should then be cut into small pieces with tile clippers. Tile clippers look a bit like pliers, but the blades do not come together completely. Place the clipper blades so that they just nip the edge of the strip of glass and press the handles together. A cleavage will form straight across the glass from the point of pressure. (See Figure 3–28.) Crude shapes may be formed in this manner, but it is difficult to control exactly where the crack will go. Always do the cutting with the hands and tool inside a clear plastic bag. Tiny fragments of glass will fly when you use these clippers. If you cut pieces inside a plastic bag, you can see what you are doing and be protected from the fragments. Safety glasses can be worn instead, but this does not protect other peo-

Making Inlaid Designs

ple nearby (the glass can travel a good distance), nor does it prevent glass fragments from falling over a wide area.

A second method for breaking glass is to place the sheet of glass between thick layers of newspaper and hit it with a hammer. There is less control over the resulting shapes, which tend to be sharply triangular. However, the pieces can be modified with tile clippers. A good working size for pieces is around ¼ to ½ inch in length.

In handling the glass, students may be cut if they are not carefully instructed. Separating the glass by color and storing it in flat trays helps minimize the amount of handling needed. The glass pieces should be picked up very gently, with light pressure. If they are not grabbed in haste, there should be no problem. Unused pieces should be carefully replaced in the tray, not dropped from a height.

When the glass is broken into small pieces, pick out the desired shapes and colors of glass and move them around until you have a pleasing design. The shapes themselves may suggest a design. The Moghul inlays were frequently floral and symmetrical, but geometric designs were also often used. Because of the nature of glass fragments, it is difficult to achieve symmetry in these designs. Also remember that this is an inlay design. It is not a mosaic in which the colored pieces cover the entire area. The design should leave plenty of white space as background.

A good way to work out a design is to wrap with masking tape a small piece of cardboard the size of the inlay to be made. Put the tape on sticky side *up* and slightly overlapping. Pieces of glass placed on this board will stay where they are put. (If you work on an untaped piece of cardboard or on the table a slight bump will cause the glass to shift and destroy the design in progress.) Pieces of glass can easily be removed from the taped cardboard and replaced until the design is completed to your satisfaction.

Next you will need a small, shallow container the size of the piece you wish to make. Little cardboard boxes, large wax paper cups (cut down to one inch from the bottom), aluminum containers, and

FIGURE 5-43. A piece of cardboard wrapped with masking tape, sticky side up, holds the glass fragments in place while Sara, eleven, works out a design for her glass inlay.

square sections of aluminum trays can all be used. Cut pieces of aluminum foil to fit the bottoms of the cardboard containers, being very careful to keep them unwrinkled and as smooth as possible. One by one, remove the bits of glass from the design on the taped cardboard and glue them in position with white glue on the aluminum foil or directly to the bottom of the waxed cup or aluminum container. Do not use too much glue; a spot in the center of the glass will be enough. Wipe up glue that oozes from underneath glass onto the bottom of the container, because otherwise it will make a hole when the plaster is poured. Let the design dry for several hours.

Mix plaster (see appendix) and pour it over the glass to a depth of ½ to ¾ of an inch in the container. Tap the edge of the container to eliminate bubbles. As the plaster is thickening, insert a loop of heavy string or copper wire (with the ends curled to make it hold better) into the plaster to use as a hanger for the inlay. It must be done before the plaster has become hard, and you must remember which is the top of your design. Let the plaster dry for two hours and then pull the container away from the inlay. The plaster will still be weak, so do this carefully (and do not pull by the hanger). In the case of glass that has been glued to aluminum, you will find that the glue is partially dissolved; the glass should be cleaned gently with a wet paper towel before it dries again. Glass that was glued to a paper cup will need a little more vigorous cleaning with a wet towel and some scraping with a table knife or flat linoleum cutting tool.

The glass should be nicely inlaid, level with the plaster. If there are imperfections in the plaster surface, a very small amount of plaster can be mixed and applied to the surface. Wet the inlay first, apply the plaster, and smooth it over with the straight edge of a piece of cardboard. When the plaster is thoroughly dry (this takes several days), it should be further smoothed if necessary with a fine grade of sandpaper. If sanding has dulled the glass, a touch of shellac or lacquer applied with a small brush will restore the surface (do not apply to the plaster). The sides of some aluminum containers are wrinkled.

FIGURE 5-44. A glass inlay of brightly colored butterflies by Annette, and one of a tree with a bird, by Monique, both sixth-grade students.

Since this imparts a wrinkle to the sides of the inlay, these should also be smoothed with a file or coarse sandpaper and then finished with a fine sandpaper. Plaster dust can create quite a mess. Work on newspapers, and roll them up with the dust inside when you carry them to the wastebasket.

INDONESIAN ARTS
Wayang Kulit: Javanese Shadow Plays

Shadow plays, one of the oldest forms of theater, have been performed in Java for over 1,000 years. Java is part of the string of more than 3,000 islands now known as Indonesia. They stretch from Sumatra, near the tip of Malaysia, down to West New Guinea, north of Australia.

No one knows when the plays were first performed, but it is believed that they originated in prehistoric times. The plays were probably an early expression of religious ideas. Hindu kingdoms were established in Java by the seventh century. During this time, the plays portrayed Hindu epics, especially the *Ramayana* and the *Mahabharata*. The legendary events and their original sequence were somewhat changed however, as Javanese characters and ideas were incorporated into these plays. Later, Muslim rule also had some influence on the plays, but they remain strongly Javanese.

The plays are called wayang kulit (wī-äng cōō lit), *wayang* meaning shadow and *kulit* meaning skin.

FIGURE 5-45. Wayangs from the plays based on the *Mahabarata* epic showing three types: Bagong, a clown; Arjuna, a prince; and a demon king. From the collection of A. L. Becker and Judith O. Becker.

The puppets, called wayangs, are made of thin buffalo hide with a fine, carefully smoothed surface.
There are over 600 distinct characters, their sizes
and shapes fixed by tradition. A single performance
may use as may as sixty. The puppet is traced from
a pattern and cut out with a hammer and small
chisels and punches. Some of these puppets are so
finely cut they look like filigree work. Arms are mov-
able, jointed at the elbows and shoulders, and are
manipulated with rods of buffalo horn. A large rod
runs the entire length of the puppet, supporting the
thin leather figure and ending in a handle at the
bottom.

The wayangs are brightly colored on both sides.

FIGURE 5-46. Some of the instruments used in a gamelan
(Javanese orchestra): gongs, bonang (pot gongs), and saron
(metallophones). Courtesy of the University of Michigan.

(See color plate 16.) The colors are often symbolic
and give clues to the puppet's character. The color
of the face, which may differ from that of the body,
is especially significant. A black face symbolizes inner calmness, maturity, and humility and also sometimes indicates physical strength. A gold or white
face indicates a person with good qualities. Gold also
often stands for youth. A red or pink face indicates
a crude, violent, and uncivilized nature. The shapes
of the wayangs and their clothing and jewelry also
give clues to character. The puppets are not meant
to look like ordinary people—they are stylized and
given shapes symbolic of certain personality types.
The spiritual wayang are slim and small. Their

Asian Arts **135**

heads are bent, and their faces look down in an attitude of humility. They have delicate noses and finely cut, inward-looking eyes. They are symbolic of the Javanese ideal character: introspective, intellectual, and refined.

The largest puppets, often portraying ogres, symbolize a violent nature and gross habits. They have heavy bodies, raised heads, big blunt noses, and round eyes. They symbolize great strength but lack spiritual power, and so they are always defeated by smaller but spiritually stronger heroes.

There is a third group of puppets whose nature is a mixture of these two. In general, the puppets portray humans, gods, and ogres. There are also wayang for deer, horses, armies, and such props as arrows and daggers.

All the puppets are manipulated by one man, the *dhalang* (dä läng), who speaks all the voices as well. The performance is accompanied by a gamelan (gämĕlän), which is a Javanese orchestra of twelve to forty instruments. The dhalang signals to the gamelan for tempo, mood, and piece changes. The shadows of the puppets are projected on a stretched white cloth screen by a flickering coconut oil lamp, which, added to the dexterous lifelike movements created by the dhalang, brings the shadows to life. Today, electric light bulbs are often substituted for the oil lamps.

The performances are held outdoors or on a porch. They begin at sundown and last until early morning. Before the performance, the puppets are stuck upright by their handles into a porous banana log that lies at the base of the screen and extends to either side. The performances begin and end with a tree-shaped wayang called a kayon (kä yōn) placed in the center of the screen. This represents all forms of life; during the play, it can also represent powers of nature: fire, water, and storms.

The plays are performed at births and marriages and at other religious rites. They are also given on many festival nights. Meant to be much more than entertainment, they preserve traditions and are a medium of instruction for both young and old. They deal with the forces of life, human nature, and its relationship to the natural and the supernatural order of the universe. People watching are believed to be protected from evil. Serious problems of good and evil are enacted, relieved occasionally with the humorous episodes of clown characters. There is no simple solution to the problems presented. Characters rarely are so bad that there is not some redeeming quality, and the "good" are prone to occasional mistakes or dilemas that force them into unfortunate actions.

The epics are long and very complicated. A brief synopsis of the *Rama Cycle* may give some idea of their content. Although based on the Hindu epic of the *Ramayana*, the Javanese play does not conform to it exactly:

FIGURE 5–47. Figures 5–47, 5–48, and 5–49 are from a sixth-grade shadow play based on the Ramayana epic. Here, a demon, disguised as a golden deer, leads Rama away into the forest, leaving his wife Sinta unprotected.

The aging King Dasarata, of Ngayoja, wants to abdicate and give his eldest son, Rama, the throne. However, through trickery, the king grants his second wife's wish to give the throne to her son, Barata.

Rama goes into exile with his faithful wife, Dewi Sinta, and his brother, Leksmana. They live in the Dandaka forest and fight the Raksasas, who are giants that trouble the ascetic hermits living there.

The king of the Raksasas, Rawana, abducts Sinta. (One of his demon servants changes himself into a golden deer to distract Rama, leaving Sinta unguarded; and Rawana, disguised as a hermit, seizes

FIGURE 5–48.   Sinta is abducted by the demon king Rawana. Jatayu, the vulture, fails to save her but tells Rama of her abduction.

FIGURE 5–49.   "There's a ghost behind you!" from a clown interlude.

her, and carries her off to his palace in a chariot.)

Rama allies himself with Hanoman, general of the white monkeys, and with the aid of the monkey armies they wage war on King Rawana. Rama wins the war, Sinta is rescued, and they return home. Barata gives up the throne, and Rama is crowned as rightful heir. (See Figures 5–47, 5–48, 5–49, and 5–56.)

This is the thread of one of the stories, which in reality is much more complicated. Only a small

138   Asian Arts

segment of the plot would be presented in one evening. The shadow plays have many levels of meaning, the subtleties of which are very difficult for a non-Javanese observer to comprehend; but the beauty of the shadows, the great skill of the dhalang, and the sounds of the gamelan combine into a very moving experience for anyone fortunate enough to attend a wayang kulit performance.

A wayang kulit performance can be a fine experience in integrated studies because it brings together art, music, theatre, literature, and cultural geography. A classroom teacher may enjoy working with the art and music departments in putting on a shadow play.

Students can write a play and create their own characters, or they may wish to read a translation of one of the Hindu epics and perform a simplified version of one episode. Whichever they choose to do, the basic construction of the puppets is the same. By performing one of the epics, students can identify with another country's villians and heroes and gain some understanding of a different culture. The wayangs, at first odd in appearance, become understandable when the symbolism of the different shapes is explained. They begin to convey to the students some of the meanings conveyed to the Javanese audiences. Students enjoy making the refined and gracious heroes, the rugged giants, and the inept clowns.

The brief clown interludes that relieve the serious epic are often original to the dhalang doing the performance. Dhalangs sometimes make wry comments on contemporary events. These parts will not be found in the Hindu stories and can be written by the students using puns and the slapstick comedy that is found the world over.

Several books listed in the bibliography can help students design wayangs like those made in Java. If the particular character they wish to portray is not illustrated, they can make one up by choosing body shapes, attitudes, and dress that symbolize the type of personality they want to portray.

A careful drawing should be made first on newsprint. Remember that size is important—heroes are usually *smaller* than more violent characters. A

Making Shadow Puppets and Performing a Play

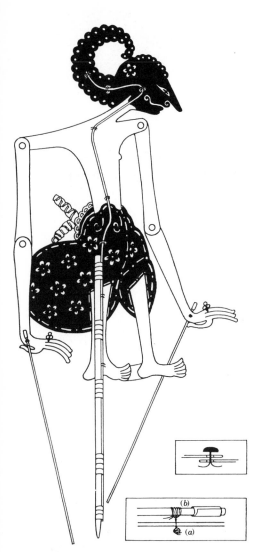

FIGURE 5–50. Diagram of a simplified wayang of Arjuna, made of poster board, jointed at elbow and shoulder with paper fasteners, and supported by coat hanger wire and a dowel. Details show a paper fastener joint and how rods are attached to hands.

kayon to begin and end the play and to be used as scenery should be made as well. Transfer the drawings to poster board with carbon paper. Cut out the figures with scissors. Use an X-acto knife or flat linocutting tool to cut out areas and designs within the figures, protecting the table with a pad of newspaper or piece of corrugated cardboard. The more details cut in, the more elaborate the shadows will be. A hole punch can be used for some of these patterns. The arms are cut out separately, in two sections, one piece being shoulder to elbow, the other elbow to hand.

The puppets should be colored appropriately, taking into account the symbolic meanings of the color. Clothing is multicolored. Magic markers work best. Although a water-based paint can be used, it might weaken the thin cardboard. The puppets will be more durable if they can be laminated on both sides. If not, two coats of shellac will also strengthen them somewhat. Test the shellac first on a scrap to be sure the colors do not run.

After cutting out the puppets, coloring them, and giving them a protective finish, assemble them. First the arms are hinged at the elbow and to the shoulder with paper fasteners (see Figure 5–50). A hole should be punched out first so that the joint will move smoothly. Spread the two fastener ends apart in a gentle curve, not hard against the cardboard. (See upper detail in Figure 5–50 for a cross-section of a paper fastener joint.) Then heavy wire rods are sewn to the hands so that the arms can be manipulated. Coat hangers, cut and straightened, work very well. See the enlarged detail in Figure 5–50 for a cross-section showing how to attach the rods. First double heavy carpet thread. Make a large knot in one end. Poke the thread through the thickest part of the hand (a) and twist the threads. Wrap the thread around near the end of the rod (b) and tie. Wrap tape around the end of the rod to prevent the rod from slipping out of the thread.

The central rod should run from the head down the body and one leg and extend for at least six inches below the foot for a handle. A very delicate figure needs only the wire, which is attached by sewing it to the cardboard at intervals. After the wire is sewn on, a heavier figure should be reinforced by taping a ¼-inch dowel to the lower half of the wire. The dowels should be sharpened on the end (with a pencil sharpener) so that the puppets can be stuck upright into styrofoam at the base of the screen when they are not in active use during the performance.

For a student production, it is better to let the students take the parts of their own puppets rather than have one be a "dhalang" and do all the performing.

There are many ways to make a shadow screen, the essence of which is a frame on which to stretch the cloth and a way of suspending a light behind it. Directions for many types, from simple to complex, are given in the book listed in the bibliography. The diagram given here (Figure 5–53) is for a screen built of heavy lumber and meant to last. It can be unbolted, if necessary, for moving and storage.

The frame can be made with either 2 x 4 or 2 x 6-inch boards. The foot pieces are cut from 2 x 10-inch boards. They are 8½ inches high and 2 feet long, with a 3½-inch-deep notch cut into them into which the lower beam is fitted and bolted with 9-inch carriage bolts.

The trough, which is to be stuffed with a stiff styrofoam slab, into which to poke the wayang handles, is made of 1 x 6-inch boards. Build it before attaching it to the frame. Notches 2 inches deep are cut into the bottom of the trough where it fits down over the feet. It is then bolted to the lower beam of the frame with 3-inch carriage bolts.

Notch the top beam to fit the 4-foot uprights and secure it to the uprights with screws as in the diagram. The uprights are then bolted to the trough with 3-inch carriage bolts.

A screen of white material is then stapled to the frame. Cotton or synthetic sheeting works very well.

A drawing board lamp that can be extended is clamped to the top middle of the frame. The screen should be elevated on a sturdy table when a performance is being given.

A performance will not have the right feeling without musical accompaniment. Almost every village in Java has its own gamelan. The village instru-

FIGURE 5-51. Brian cuts designs in his shadow puppet with a linoleum cutting tool. A hole puncher was used to make the hair designs.

FIGURE 5-52. Sara checks her ghost against the light.

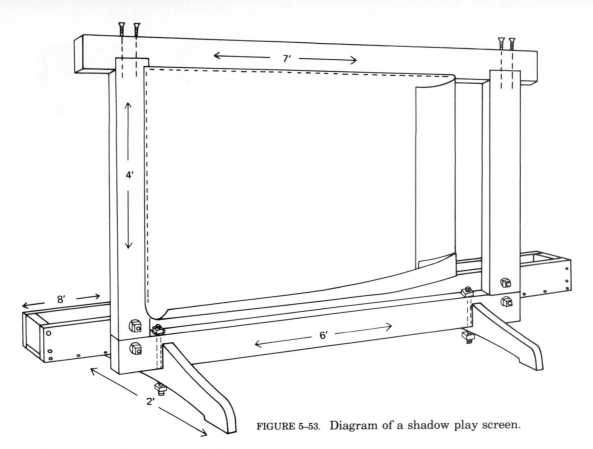

FIGURE 5–53. Diagram of a shadow play screen.

FIGURE 5–54. Putting on the shadow play. Behind the screen, Fred, Michael, and Keith manipulate the puppets.

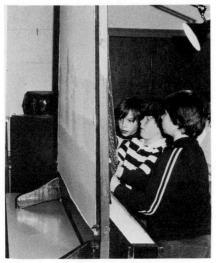

ments might be made of bamboo and iron; the large city gamelans have bronze instruments, primarily gongs and metallophones set in beautifully inlaid teakwood supports. The music is an integral part of the performance, each character and scene having its specific type of music. There are many layers of melodies going on at the same time.

The Javanese instruments are not easily available outside of Indonesia, but there is an excellent book (see bibliography) that introduces young students to the Javanese scales and rhythms, which are traditionally very different from those of the West. The book suggests western instruments that can approximate somewhat some of the sounds of the gamelan.

A Javanese melody called Ricik-Ricik[5] (pro-

[5] Adapted from William M. Anderson, *Teaching Asian Musics in Elementary and Secondary Schools* (Adrian, MI: The Leland Press, Box 301, 1975), © permission.

142   Asian Arts

nounced ree-chik-ree-chik, "Softly Raining") is approximated on our scale by the notations in Figure 5–57.

Indonesian notes are designated with numbers rather than letters. In this music 3, 5, 6, 5 stands for F, A, B flat, A, and so on. The first melody *(a)* is played by two instruments one octave apart. For the second melody *(b)* an instrument plays the same note twice to each beat. Both melodies can be played on xylophones, glockenspiels, melody bars, or metallophones. In Javanese music the most important instruments are the rhythm instruments, or gongs. In this piece the large gong *(G)* is played only on the 8th and 16th beats. The medium gong (g) on beats 2, 4, 6, 8, 10, 12, 14, 16 and the smallest gong *(g)* on 3, 5, 7, 11, 13, 15. Besides gongs, use cymbals, triangles, or improvised gongs such as pot lids.

The first eight notes are repeated before going on to the second eight notes, which are also repeated before beginning the melody over again. The sequence is repeated many times. The music presented here is a vast simplification of Javanese music, which even in a "simple" piece has many layers of melodies being played.

There are several gamelans in the United States. Arrangements can often be made for having students see and sometimes play the instruments. They are located at the University of Michigan, the University of California at Berkeley, Wesleyan University, the University of Hawaii, Oberlin College, the Indonesian Embassy in Washington, D.C., the Uni-

FIGURE 5–55. A student gamelan accompanies the play. A metallophone, xylophone, finger cymbals, and gongs keep the beat.

FIGURE 5–56. A kindergarten audience sees Rama victorious over Rawana.

Ricik-Ricik (Softly Raining)

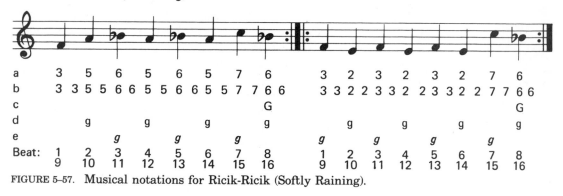

a	3	5	6	5	6	5	7	6	3	2	3	2	3	2	7	6
b	3 3	5 5	6 6	5 5	6 6	5 5	7 7	6 6	3 3	2 2	3 3	2 2	3 3	2 2	7 7	6 6
c								G								G
d		g		g		g		g		g		g		g		g
e			g		g		g		g		g		g		g	
Beat:	1 9	2 10	3 11	4 12	5 13	6 14	7 15	8 16	1 9	2 10	3 11	4 12	5 13	6 14	7 15	8 16

FIGURE 5–57. Musical notations for Ricik-Ricik (Softly Raining).

versity of Wisconsin, Brown University, Cornell University, Chicago Field Museum, California Institute of Art in Valencia, San Diego State College, the University of Santa Cruz, U.C.L.A., and the State University of New York at Binghamton.

Batiks

FIGURE 5-58. Contemporary Javanese tulis batik with a peacock design. Drawn entirely by hand with a tjanting. Collection of Susan Walton.

No one knows exactly when and where batiks were first made. But it is significant that the word that denotes this particular way of decorating cloth is Javanese. *Batik* is derived from *titik*, meaning "drop." Many centuries ago the basic method of using wax to resist applications of dye was introduced to Java from India, where wood blocks dipped in wax had been used in the decoration of cloth. In Java the craft of making batiks was raised to a fine art that has not been surpassed anywhere in the world. The Javanese invented a tool, the tjanting (pronounced chänting), which is a small copper bowl with a fine spout and a bamboo handle. This tool provides a reservoir for melted wax and is used as a drawing tool that permits the wax to be applied in extremely fine lines and dots.

Originally the art was developed and used by the women in royal families to make hand-decorated clothing, and certain patterns were only allowed for court use. Eventually, however, the making of batiks became widespread, daughters learning the techniques and patterns from their mothers. In this way, designs were passed down unchanged over many centuries. Batiks were worn by men and by women as head coverings, shawls, and sarongs (a wraparound skirt worn by both men and women). The original dyes, applied to a creamy, off-white cloth (a color created by soaking the cloth in coconut oil), were a deep blue made from indigo and a beautiful brown made from soga bark, a color rarely found outside of Java. (See color plate 17). Now dyes of many colors are used.

Making batiks by hand with a tjanting is a slow, meticulous process. Fine hemp or cotton cloth is used. The cloth is prepared by careful washing, light starching, and beating with a wooden mallet to make the cloth very smooth and supple. A special formula of resin and wax is applied to the cloth in intricate patterns with a tjanting. The wax is first applied

144   Asian Arts

to one side, and then the cloth is turned over and the design is applied in wax on the other side to be sure that the protection is complete. Then (if the piece is to be made in the earliest traditional colors) the cloth is dyed in indigo. All unwaxed areas will turn blue. When the cloth is dry, some of the wax is removed, revealing cream-colored undyed areas. (Where the wax is not removed, the designs will remain cream.) Those areas to remain blue are waxed with the tjanting, and the cloth is then dyed soga brown. After this final dye the cloth is rinsed in hot water to remove all the wax, revealing a completed design in cream, blue, brown, and dark navy blue where the brown combined with unwaxed blue areas.

The designs consist of both geometric shapes and shapes derived from such natural forms as flowers, foliage, birds, butterflies, animals, and fish. There are Indian and Chinese influences in some of these designs, reflecting two of the many different ethnic contributions to Javanese culture. The garuda, a mythical bird that carried the god Vishnu, is a common motif, and so are the phoenix and Nagu, the dragon. However, all these forms are very highly stylized. When Java came under Muslim influence, the Muslim religious law forbade representation of natural forms; these highly stylized and decorative forms were a way of complying with this law. Many designs have names and meanings stemming from their early use in court life. Some designs were used only by particular families, and some were made for special occasions such as marriages.

It sometimes took as long as six months of work to finish an especially fine sarong, which measures about 3½ by 7½ feet. In the middle of the nineteenth century, a new process was invented to speed up the making of batiks. Ribbons of copper formed into the desired designs are soldered into blocks called *tjaps*. The tjap is dipped in the hot wax and pressed onto the cloth. In this way, six sarongs can be made in one day. This method, done by men, still requires a great degree of skill. The blocks have to be very carefully placed for the design to appear continuous and like the hand-drawn batiks. Tjap batiks are less expensive and not valued as highly as the tjanting batiks. A piece of work stamped "Batik tulis" has been done by hand. If it is stamped "Batik tangan," a tjap has been used.

The intricate beauty of the Javanese batiks has very nearly caused their extinction. As the cloth has become popular throughout the world, imitations made by machine methods have been mass-produced in great quantities. The copied designs do not have the beauty or wearing quality of the hand-made fabrics, but since they are cheaper, they have almost eliminated the market for the real batiks. Tjanting batiks are becoming more and more scarce, and fewer and fewer women in Java learn this meticulous and demanding craft. There are artists in Java, however, who are making a great effort to keep this craft, which has contributed so much to the art of the world, from dying out.

Making Batiks

There has been a great interest in the art of batik in recent years, and many excellent books are available on the subject. It is not too complicated for upper elementary students to make simple designs, and it can be an exciting experience for them. Safety precautions must be carefully followed, however, in any project that involves hot plates and melted wax. It is essential to have adult supervision at every table using the hot wax. If students are absorbed in their work, they may not notice water running low in the double boiler arrangement or other dangerous situations. Parents will often help out in their children's classrooms for special projects such as this.

The batiking process described here is a much simplified version of that used in Java. Students should first work out a design on newsprint. They may want to make a decorative piece for a wall hanging or batik a T-shirt or an African dashiki. (Directions for making a dashiki are given in Chapter 2.) It would be expensive to buy enough tjantings for a large group of students. The best way for students to begin to learn the art is to apply the wax with brushes. In their designs they must consider this and work with wider lines and broader areas of color then if they were using a fine drawing tool such as the tjanting.

Before beginning, students must work out the se-

FIGURE 5-59. Sara, eleven, applies melted wax to the areas that will remain white. Wax is always melted in a pot that is placed in another pan of hot water over the burner.

quence of colors they are going to use. This is the most difficult part of the project. They must realize two principles. First, in dyeing they must go from light colors to progressively darker ones. Secondly, a second dye will combine with the first one to produce a new color. Suppose the first dye is yellow. The parts to remain yellow are waxed. Now, if the student expects to be able to have blue in his design he will be disappointed, because when he puts the yellow cloth in blue dye he will get green. Some possible sequences are: from yellow to orange to red to brown or purple; from light blue to medium blue to purple to black, or from blue to green to brown or black.

Cotton cloth, such as old sheeting, is excellent for batiks. New cloth should be washed and ironed before using. Avoid permanent press materials; they do not take dyes very well. Sketch the design lightly on the cloth, using a stick of charcoal (pencil lines will not wash out).

Really fine batiks use special formulas of beeswax, paraffin, and resin. Beginning students do very well with paraffin alone, which is also the least expensive. Before the final dye it can be cracked easily, making the distinctive veined effect found only in batiks. (Javanese artists did not originally try for this effect, however; they tried instead to eliminate any accidental qualities in their best batiks.) The wax is best melted on an electric stove burner or hot plate. An open gas flame is less safe. Place a hot plate on a sheet of metal or asbestos. Wax is always safer heated in a pot or coffee can, which is set in another pan of water over the heat source. *Never heat wax directly over the fire. It is highly combustible if it gets too hot.* Be sure, if the pot has a handle, it is turned so that no one will hit it and upset the pot. The wax is hot enough when it penetrates cloth easily. Test it on a scrap.

Protect the work table with newspaper. Place the cloth on a piece of wax paper. The wax paper prevents the cloth from sticking to the newspaper. If a shirt or dashiki is to be batiked, open up the garment and put newspaper and wax paper inside so that the design can be done on one side at a time without spotting through to the other side.

Brushes once used for batik cannot be used again

FIGURE 5–60. Sara has dyed the cloth blue. Now she applies wax to the parts to remain blue before she dyes it purple.

FIGURE 5–61. A flower design by Deborah, eleven, using a sequence of white, yellow, red, and brown.

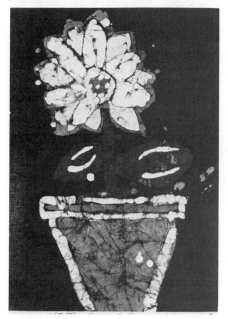

FIGURE 5-62. Geometric design by Kamala, age twelve.

FIGURE 5-63. A dashiki made by Jenny, age eleven. The color sequence is from white to orange to green.

for painting, so you may want to use old brushes. Put the brush into the hot wax, letting it get thoroughly hot. Take it directly to the cloth and make only two or three strokes. The wax cools very quickly and will not penetrate unless the brush is filled often with fresh hot wax.

First wax any areas that are to remain white. Be sure the wax has penetrated to the other side. If it has not, turn the cloth over and wax the other side, too.

Set up a separate table for dyeing. Protect it well with layers of newspaper. Using hot water and a tablespoon of salt, mix commercial dyes ahead of time. Cool the dye before using it; warm dye melts the wax. Plastic gallon milk containers with the tops cut off make good dye pots. Immerse the cloth until it is a shade darker than desired, since it will be lighter when it dries. Remove it from the dye and rinse it gently in lukewarm water. Do not wring it out; blot it between newspapers and then hang it up to dry in a shady place.

When the cloth is completely dry, wax those areas to remain the color of the first dye. Then the cloth is dyed a second color, rinsed, and dried. If a third color is to be used, the areas of the second color that are to be preserved are covered with wax first, and so forth.

If you want a veined pattern, gently crumple the fabric (which will crack the wax) before the final dye. The last dye seeps into these cracks, creating the veined effect unique to batiks. Dry the batik for the last time.

To remove the accumulated wax, place the batik between sheets of old newspaper (newspaper less than a week old may transfer ink to the cloth) and press with a hot iron, keeping the iron in motion. When the wax melts and is soaked up by the newspaper, remove the paper and place the cloth between new papers, iron again, and continue ironing and changing papers until all the wax is removed. (Although some books recommend boiling the cloth to remove wax, this can destroy the design if the dyes are not absolutely permanent.) In a wall hanging, some remaining wax may actually increase the brightness of the colors. However, an article of clothing may be somewhat stiff if the ironing does not remove all the wax. Dry cleaning will remove any wax residue. A dashiki or T-shirt should be ironed before it is washed the first time. Use a pressing cloth that has been dipped in a solution of vinegar and water. This helps make the color more permanent. Wash these items separately from other clothes.

A batik to be used as a wall hanging can be glued along the top to a ¼-inch dowel, or the dowel can be inserted in a fold sewn along the top. Hang it up with a short length of yarn tied to the dowel ends.

FIGURE 5-64. Sixth-graders Scott, Lori, and Amy wearing dashikis they decorated with batiked designs.

6

MEXICAN, CENTRAL AMERICAN, AND SOUTH AMERICAN ARTS

The Indians of the areas now known as Mexico, Central America, and South America had developed architecture and many arts and crafts to a high degree of skill during the centuries preceding the Spanish Conquest. Enormous stone temples of sophisticated design and construction, with richly carved and painted decorations, were created by Mayan, Toltec, Aztec, Incan, and Andean civilizations. Much of the artwork of these cultures was destroyed at the time of conquest, and much more disappeared as monuments and tombs were plundered over the ensuing centuries. However, from what remains we can appreciate the skill of the artisans of those times and the works they produced in clay, gold, and silver and with wool, feathers, and all available materials. In the contemporary popular arts of these areas, we see a mixture of these original arts with Spanish influences. Arts and crafts in great variety have continued to be handed down in the traditional manner.

150

Many arts are unique to particular villages according to the degree of isolation of the village and its resistance to outside influences.

Many pre-Conquest structures, as well as some of the surviving examples of arts and crafts, were inspired by religious requirements and beliefs. This is true of many of today's folk arts as well, and what to an outsider may be of purely aesthetic and decorative value may have been created for religious or magical purposes. However, many arts have lost their original purpose and, rather than being made by the people for their own use, are now created to be sold in the market.

Mexican popular arts abound in such variety that it is difficult to choose a few that are representative. Mexican arts are usually exuberant in their use of bright color and imaginative design. There is artwork in an endless variety of materials: bark, clay, wood, wool, metals, wax, and many other natural materials found in the environment. Examples of these arts are increasingly available in import shops.

Brilliantly colored yarn paintings are created by the Huichol Indians, who live high in the mountains of Nayarit and are direct descendants of the Aztecs. The yarn paintings are created for two purposes: some as religious tablets to be used as votive offerings to local deities, and some to sell. This distinction is traditional, and certain rules are followed in the design of the pictures depending on their intended use. The figures are *arranged* differently, although the animals, birds, plants, and people depicted are common to both types. The deer is a particularly important symbol and is seen frequently in the yarn paintings. Some of the pictures record legends or tell stories of village life. Although the designs are usually based on natural subjects, they are never realistic in color or form. The figures are highly stylized and sometimes quite abstract. The paintings, edged with a border of several colors, range in size from quite small to several square feet in area.

To make the paintings (traditionally men's work), beeswax is first warmed in the sun and then spread on thin boards. The picture is created by pressing

MEXICAN ARTS

Huichol Indian Yarn Paintings

FIGURE 6–1. Huichol Indian yarn paintings. State of Nayarit, Mexico. Collection of the author.

yarn into the wax with the thumbnail. The border is made first in three or more colors, each color several strands wide. Next, the figures are outlined with one or two colors, each only one or two strands wide. This outline is then filled in with contrasting colors. Rarely is a figure filled in with only one color. The background is done last and is usually a solid color. See color plate 18. The yarn is not applied back and forth; instead, it is made to follow the contours of the figures that define each space, reducing that space to a smaller and smaller area with one continuous strand of yarn until it is filled in. This creates a pleasing pattern in the yarn.

The Huichol also decorate gourds and maracas with yarn paintings in the same manner; and in a related art practiced by women, beads are pressed into wax to form designs on boards and inside gourd containers.

Making Yarn Pictures

FIGURE 6-2. Lee made a border of several colors first. Next he outlined his butterfly design. Now he is beginning to fill in the outline, following the inner contours of the butterfly wing. He uses scissors points to push the yarn into the wax.

Even a small yarn painting takes patience, and it is wise to start out on a small scale. The beauty of the art lies in part in completely covering the board. A board 6 x 8 inches is ample for a fifth or sixth-grade student. Use ¼-inch plywood, hardboard, or chipboard. Corrugated cardboard can be used if that is the only material available, but it is so flexible that sometimes the wax cracks off.

Although the Huichol work freehand or make a light sketch in the wax, it is better for students to work out a design first on paper that has been cut to the size of the board. Include a border in this design. In a piece this small, it is best to develop one central figure rather than many very small ones. When you are satisfied with the penciled design, transfer the design to the board with carbon paper. It will show through the subsequent application of wax.

Beeswax, available at art supply stores, is costly and can be somewhat extended with paraffin—but more than one part paraffin to two parts beeswax will result in a medium that is too hard. Melt the wax in a pan set in another pan of water over a hot plate or stove burner. (*Never* melt wax directly over the flame. It is highly combustible.) Using a wide, flat brush, spread the wax in an even layer on the board. If it becomes too thick in some areas, scrape it level again with a single-edged razor blade. Be careful to get wax all the way to the edges of the board.

Although the Huichol use their thumbnails to push the yarn into the wax, it is easier for students to use a popsicle stick, tongue depressor, or scissors points for this purpose. Follow the Huichol method of making the border first. Try not to round the corners but to get the yarn to turn sharply with the edges of the corner. After the border is done, outline the figures with one or two colors and then fill them in with bright contrasting colors. (See Figures 6–2 and 6–3.) The background is filled in last. The yarn is put on with the strands as close together as possible. It is applied to an area in one long continuous strand until that area is filled up, starting around the outer edges of that space and filling in towards the center, *never* from the center out. When an area is filled in, cut off the yarn close to the board, tuck the end into the wax, and fill in another area. The yarn is never crossed over adjacent strands to get to another area.

If wax is not available, white glue may be used as a substitute. Paint the glue on one small area at a time and press the yarn into it, keeping the top of the yarn soft and free of glue.

FIGURE 6–3. The wing tip has been filled in and the strand will be cut off flush with the rest of the yarn.

FIGURE 6–4. Yarn paintings by fifth-grade students. Clockwise from upper left: *Two Fish,* by Nick; *Bird,* by Alex; *Fish,* by Slavik; *Spider,* by John.

Amate Paper Cutouts

The amate paper cutouts made by the Otomí Indians of San Pablito in the Sierra de Puebla have a stark and unusual beauty that seems to convey some of the magic for which they were created.

The paper from which they are cut is made from the bark of the amate tree. Strips of bark are boiled in a water and ash solution until they are soft. Then they are laid, criss-crossed and overlapping, on a smooth board and pounded with stones until the fibers mesh together. The paper, which is strong and crisp, has a beautiful surface; the texture of the bark shows clearly. Both brown and white papers are made. This is an ancient art stemming from pre-Conquest times, when the paper was used for clothing and later for keeping records. The amate paper is now used to make symmetrical cutouts for magical purposes—to protect crops, to rid a place of evil, to guard the home, or to bring health or illness (as a punishment or to harm an adversary).

The designs frequently use human forms (which sometimes represent spirits) and also reflect elements of nature that are important in the lives of the Otomí people: agricultural plants, domestic and wild animals, and birds. The figures, however, are

FIGURE 6–5. Amate paper cutout made by Otomí Indians of San Pablito, Sierra de Puebla, Mexico. Collection of the author.

FIGURE 6–6. Pajaro del Monte, "bird-of-the-mountain" cutouts. Otomí Indian, San Pablito, Sierra de Puebla, Mexico. These cutouts are kept in the home as protection against all evil. They are made both in the two-headed and in the more powerful four-headed forms. Collection of the author.

not realistic but have added fanciful or symbolic ornamentation. A common design often shows a standing man combined with animal or plant forms (see Figure 6–5). Other traditional motifs include the two-headed or four-headed bird-of-the-mountain (Figure 6–6), which protects the home; and the Lion Spirit, which is buried with the dead and is believed to lead the spirit of the deceased to fresh water and fruit. Bark cutouts are also used as tokens of gratitude to the earth for a good crop.

In planning their designs, students may want to refer to *Design Motifs of Ancient Mexico* by Jorge Encisco (see the bibliography). This book contains many design ideas, some geometric and others derived from natural forms. None of them are realistic. Students should be encouraged to use their imaginations. The emphasis should be on fanciful decorative designs rather than realism.

To simulate the heavy, textured amate paper, begin with a piece of brown wrapping paper or brown craft paper. Pieces of brown paper bags can also be used very successfully. Fold the paper in half. Using the fold as a center line, chalk in *half* the form of a bird, animal, person, or pleasing shape. After the design is drawn on the folded paper, cut it out while it is still folded, as shown in Figure 6–8. Open up the design (it will now be symmetrical) and crumple it thoroughly to form irregular patterns in the paper. Carefully spread it open again, place it between two sheets of wax paper, and iron it.

Protect the table with a pad of newspaper. A second application of wax paper may be needed to deepen the color and bring out the pattern. As the wax melts, it creates a stiff paper product with some of the amate paper's color, texture, and feel.

The cutout is greatly enhanced by careful mounting. Apply white glue very sparingly to the chalky side of the cutout and mount it on white paper. The white paper should then be centered on a larger mat of brown construction paper.

The textured paper lends beauty to even the simplest designs. This is one project that allows all students to achieve satisfying results.

Making Symmetrical Cutouts

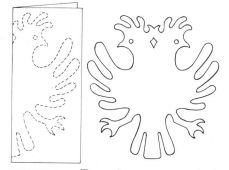

FIGURE 6–7. To make a symmetrical cutout, draw half a figure on a folded piece of brown wrapping paper. Cut it out while it is still folded, and then open it up to reveal a completed symmetrical figure.

FIGURE 6–8. Alice, age ten, cuts out a lion design from the folded brown paper.

FIGURE 6–9. Alfred crumples up his design.

FIGURE 6–10. After crumpling up her design, Eileen spread it open again and is ironing it between sheets of wax paper.

FIGURE 6–11. A sun design by a fifth-grade student. A hole puncher was used to add a lacy quality.

FIGURE 6–12. An abstract design by a fifth-grade student.

FIGURE 6–13. A four-headed bird-of-the-mountain by Helen, age nine.

The amate paper made by the Otomí Indians is purchased by the people of Ameyaltepec, Xalitla, and other villages and used for making highly decorative paintings. These paintings are often available in import shops in the United States. They usually show flowers, birds, animals, or scenes of village life and are painted with brilliant, sometimes fluorescent, paints. The paintings are very fanciful—flowers of many colors bloom from the same stalk, leaves may be blue or orange as well as green, fancy birds have plumage never seen in the real world, horses may be turquoise blue, and spots of color leave the figures

FIGURE 6–14. Amate paper paintings, Mexico. Collection of the author.

and trail in lines over the bark. Sometimes the painting is surrounded with a border of geometric designs. The background is never painted—the colorful figures stand out against the rich brown, beautifully textured, hand-made paper. See color plate 19.

To make these paintings, prepare the paper first. Cut a rectangle with rounded corners from brown wrapping paper or a paper bag. Crumple it thoroughly in your hands and then iron it out between wax paper.

Before they plan their designs, students should see some bark paintings if possible or study examples in books. They should note the highly fanciful, decorative quality of the designs. The design may be drawn lightly on the prepared brown paper with

Making Paintings on Prepared Brown Paper

FIGURE 6–15. Third-grade students working on their "bark" paintings. Angela is working on the first step, drawing the lines with black ink. Thea is working on the second step, filling in the designs with bright tempera paint and fluorescent colors. The background is not painted.

FIGURE 6–16. This "bark" painting by David captures the spirit of imaginative design.

a pencil. Then begin the painting by outlining the design with a fine brush and black paint or India ink. Next, when the ink is dry, fill in the figures with color *leaving some of the black outline showing*. Use tempera paint in the brightest colors available: magenta, turquoise, yellow-green, pink, orange, purple, and white. The tempera paint may be supplemented with small amounts of the more expensive water-base fluorescent paints found in art supply stores. The background is *not painted*—the textured brown paper provides a beautiful contrast to the brilliant paint. If you have trouble getting the paint or ink to stick to the waxy surface, stir in a drop or two of liquid soap or detergent.

FIGURE 6–17. Four "bark" paintings by third- and fourth-grade students: *Flower*, by Jeannie; *Bird*, by Sarah; *Flower with Border Design*, by Laura; and *Butterfly*, by Lisa.

Clay Figures from Tonala and Metapec

The art of making clay vessels and figures has played an important part in Mexican life from earliest times. Of the many arts and crafts in Mexico, it is the most widely engaged in. The style of work is as varied as the many villages and towns that specialize in works of clay, and pieces are so distinctive that the villages where they originated can easily be identified. Many different techniques are used, but usually the items are made entirely by hand. The clay pieces are fired in kilns constructed in the artisan's yard. These kilns are made of brick or adobe and fueled with wood or oil.

Tonala, in the state of Jalisco, is an important pottery center. The people there produce many different forms of pottery: plates, jugs, tiles, and figures. Most of them are decorated in a style unique to Tonala. Particularly appealing are small animal figures: horses, cats, fish, turtles, and birds of many kinds—owls, ducks, toucans, and pigeons. They are painted in subtle grays and earth colors with overall free-flowing designs of leaves and flowers, butterflies, dots, swirls, and lines, that seem to combine all that is joyous in nature. See Figure 6–18 and color plate 20 for examples of Tonala clay animals.

Metapec, in the state of Mexico, has long been famous for its pottery. Many artisans make items of clay, which range from functional pottery for domestic use to very ornate "trees of life," which are fanciful interpretations of the Garden of Eden. There

FIGURE 6–18. Clay figures from Tonala, state of Jalisco, Mexico. The animals and birds, decorated with fine brushwork, seem to combine all that is joyous in nature. (The little owl's back is decorated with flowers and a butterfly.) Collection of the author.

are statues of saints and of skeletons, animals, toys of all kinds, candlesticks, and masks. Most of the pottery is unglazed. After being fired, it is either left in its natural state or painted in brilliant colors.

The clay suns of Metapec are especially delightful. In many variations they seem to express benevolent and life-giving energy. Timoteo Gonzales of Metapec claims to have been the first potter to make the now famous Metapec suns. These suns range in size from seven inches to two feet across. The

FIGURE 6–19. Lise, age eleven, paints flowers and vines on a cat.

rounded form is made by pressing a slab of clay over a mold. Facial features are created from pieces pinched from a roll of clay and then added to the rounded form. Then rays are shaped from balls of clay and are attached around the edge of the sun. Slits are cut for the mouth and over the eyebrows. In some suns decorative perforations are also made around the rim, just inside the rays. Sometimes the sun is left undecorated after firing, and sometimes a base coat of white is painted with floral designs in bright colors, with touches of gold paint. (See color plate 21.)

Making Clay Animals and Birds

Students can form simple animal shapes of clay (the Tonala figures are streamlined with only a suggestion of features, legs, or feet). After drying for two weeks the pieces should be fired in a kiln, and then decorated with tempera paints. Use a very fine pointed brush when painting the designs. After the paint has dried thoroughly, it can be protected with a coat of shellac or polymer medium. Apply the polymer medium with a very light, flowing touch. Scrubbing with the brush will make the tempera colors mix and run. Be sure to wash the brush immediately after use.

FIGURE 6–20. Ellen and Lucy apply polymer medium as a protective finish to their decorated whale and mouse figures.

FIGURE 6–21. Three sculptures, inspired by Tonala clay pieces, by sixth-grade students. From left: *Bird*, by Lise; *Cat*, by Lanette; and *Mouse*, by Lucy.

Children of all ages enjoy making sun designs. Young children may form their suns freely from a fist-sized piece of clay. They can start by making a ball of the clay and flattening it with their fists. The rays can be pinched out around the circumference of the disk (pinching works better than trying to attach pieces) or indicated by pressing fingers or thumb all around the edge. A face may be incised

FIGURE 6–22. Clay sun design from Metapec, State of Mexico, Mexico. Nineteen inches. Collection of the author.

FIGURE 6–23. A group of first-grade sun designs. Each sun is unique and radiates an energy all its own.

FIGURE 6–24. Christine painted her sun with a base coat of white tempera and is now adding decorations with gold paint.

FIGURE 6–25. Heidi applies a protective coat of polymer medium to her sun design.

with a pencil point, poked in with fingertips, painted in later, or not indicated at all. After drying for two weeks, the pieces can be fired in a kiln and then painted with tempera paints. Figure 6–23 shows a group of first-grade sun designs. Each sun is unique and radiates an energy all its own.

Older children may want to study the Metapec designs, but they should also be encouraged to use their imagination in making a design of their own. The largest of the Metapec suns requires a great deal of clay. For a class of fifth or sixth-grade students, suns approximately nine inches across are probably about the right size.

The clay is first rolled out to an even slab by using a rolling pin and two sticks of about ½-inch thickness. Place the sticks one foot apart and put a baseball-sized lump of clay between them. Roll the clay out to form the basic slab. Next, to create a raised form, cut the lip off a paper bowl and invert it on a piece of newspaper. Then lift the clay slab and press it gently down on the bowl. If the clay has been rolled out large enough to extend an inch or so beyond the bowl, you can cut rays in the edge with a table knife. If not, form and add on rays, taking great care that the clay is well joined. Place the ray somewhat up on the rounded form, not just butting the edge. The joining should be as thick as the main body, or cracks may form and the rays may break off during drying.

Now that the basic shape is formed let imagination guide the students in creating their own sun designs. If the sun is to have features, these may be put on with additional clay. Make a long roll of clay and cut sections from it to form eyebrows, eyelids, nose, and mouth. Eyes and mouth may be cut out instead, or a combination of these methods may be used. Two holes may be pierced in the top of the sun (not in a ray) and later, after the sun is fired, a string pulled through and tied. In this way the sun can be hung up.

The suns should be dried for two weeks and then fired in a kiln. They can then be left in their natural clay color or painted with tempera paint. It is best to paint a base coat first of one solid color (in Metapec it's usually white) and to add further designs when

FIGURE 6–26. Three sixth-grade sun designs after having been fired in the kiln. They can be left this natural clay color or decorated with tempera paints.

this has dried. A protective layer of shellac or polymer medium should be applied when the paint is thoroughly dry. Follow the directions for application of polymer medium given in the project for making clay animals.

Artisans in many parts of Mexico make a great variety of brightly colored ornamental items of tin: flower arrangements to be used as votive offerings, countless toy animals and figures, boxes, decorative sun designs, masks, candelabra, lanterns, and elaborately framed mirrors. The sculpture is cut from flat sheets of tin. If it is to be a three-dimensional sculpture, it is then folded to form the figure. Before being folded it is often embossed (lines are pressed into the tin either as decorations or to create features, fur, feathers, or other details on the figures). After being folded, some parts of the sculpture are joined with solder. The pieces are usually painted with bright transparent paints made of powdered pigments and lacquer: turquoise, magenta, yellow, red, and green. (See color plate 22.)

Tin Sculpture and Boxes

FIGURE 6–27. Ornaments, a rocking horse, and a box—a small sampling of the great variety of items made from tin and sold in the markets of Mexico. Collection of the author.

Although Mexican artists make very fine sculpture, utensils, and jewelry in gold, silver, and copper (arts developed to a great height in pre-Columbian times), tin, which is inexpensive and easily shaped, is the metal of the people. With skill, imagination, and a sense of humor, folk artists have realized its potential to the fullest.

Making Aluminum Ornaments, Sculpture, and Boxes

Although tin is difficult for young students to handle, they can make small sculptures resembling tin work from aluminum TV dinner trays and pie plates. Or, much better, if there is an offset printing company in the community the discarded sheets of aluminum may be used. Use the lightest weight sheet (0.005 of an inch) and polish it first with steel wool and scouring powder to remove the ink.

The simplest sculptures to make are the ornaments cut of a flat piece of metal and embossed. (See the butterfly, birds, and sheep in Figure 6–27.) Plan a design first on paper. When you have one that pleases you, cut it out, place it on a piece of aluminum, and trace around it with a pencil. Cut it out of the aluminum with scissors.

The next step is to emboss it. Turn the design over on a thick pad of paper and press designs into the back of the aluminum. Use a pointed instrument that will not leave ink or graphite marks in the lines (such as an old ball point pen that has no ink or the pointed handle of a small paint brush). This will create raised designs on the other side. The flat Mexican tin designs, which are usually made to be hung as ornaments, have a wire soldered to the back for this purpose. A small hole can be pierced at the top of the aluminum and string slipped through for hanging up the piece. The ornaments can be left as they are or colored with bright permanent marking pens.

In designing a three-dimensional figure, such as a standing animal, it is a good idea to experiment first with heavy paper. Cut a flat one-piece shape that will make a standing figure when it is folded. For an animal, a good beginning is a thick capital *H* shape, with the center line wider than the sides. When folded down, this forms an animal body and legs. The pattern can then be refined in shape. The

FIGURE 6–28. Diagram of a tin rocking horse. Cut on the heavy lines. Emboss designs on the inside of the body and on the head and tail. Use designs such as those indicated here in thin lines, or use your own ideas. Bend the body in a gentle curve so that it will stand on the rockers. The slots in the head and tail are inserted in the slots in the body with a touch of glue.

164   Mexico, Central and South America

head is cut out separately and inserted in a slot in the body. A touch of model cement makes the joining more secure.

Figure 6–28 is a diagram of how to make a Mexican tin rocking horse similar to the one in Figure 6–27. It shows you how a sculpture looks before being folded. It can be changed in shape and proportions to form a rocking animal of any kind. When you have devised a pattern, trace around it on aluminum and cut it out. The piece should be embossed before folding. The more decorative lines the better—this both strengthens the aluminum and, if the piece is from a cake or pie tin, obliterates any pre-existing raised patterns or trade marks on the aluminum. It is especially important to emboss the rockers, curving them inward to strengthen them. If the horse is out of balance because the head is heavier than the tail, stick a wad of chewing gum or oil-base clay under the tail end.

Additional pieces of aluminum can be added to a basic form with fast-drying model cement or an epoxy or super-strength glue. These can form feathers, horns, tails, and so on.

Small decorated boxes are often made of tin and can be made of aluminum as well. Use the patterns given in Figures 6–30 and 6–31. For the box, cut out on the solid lines. Emboss the side panels by pressing with a tool on what will be the inside of the box. Fold on dotted lines in this order: Fold flaps A in flat against the side. Fold flaps B in half-way

FIGURE 6–29. Embossed aluminum ornaments by sixth-grade students. Clockwise from upper left: *Fish,* by David; *Butterfly,* by Kate; *Box,* by Lisa; and *Lion,* by Paul.

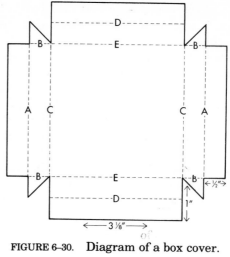

FIGURE 6–30.   Diagram of a box cover.

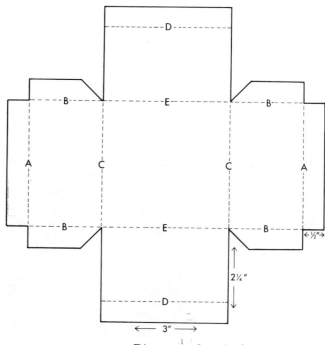

FIGURE 6–31.   Diagram of a tin box.

(at right angles to the side). Fold sides up at *C.* Fold flaps *D* in flat against side. Fold sides up at *E.* Put glue on outside of flaps *B* and insert them under flaps *D.* For the box cover, cut, emboss, and fold in same sequence and manner as for box. The aluminum will not take repeated folding without cracking, so it is important to get the fold right the first time. This is most easily done by placing a ruler on the line to be folded and pulling the aluminum up against the ruler. Color can be added to the embossed designs with permanent marking pens.

ARTS OF CENTRAL AMERICA AND SOUTH AMERICA
Cuna Indian Molas

The Cuna Indian women of the San Blas Islands off the coast of Panama decorate their blouses with beautifully designed and sewn cotton panels called molas. (Although *mola* means "blouse" in their language, it has come to mean the panel itself.) This tradition has been carried on for over 100 years. Girls begin to learn this skill from their mothers or grandmothers when they are seven or eight years old.

When making a mola, a Cuna woman first bastes together several layers of brightly colored cotton cloth. She creates the design by cutting away pieces of cloth and exposing the layers beneath. The edges of the cuts are skillfully turned under and sewn with almost invisible stitches. In some areas of the design, material may be appliquéd to sections that have previously been exposed, and small areas may be underlaid with a piece of cloth that does not extend under the entire work. The cloth surface is therefore cut into and built up in a sculptural way. A really fine mola may take many weeks to complete.

There is a great variety of subject matter in the designs. The molas most frequently have stylized designs based on the natural world: birds, animals, fish, leaves, and flowers. Some designs are based on Cuna mythology or religious beliefs. Others may be inspired by dreams or fantasies. A few are purely geometric in design. Whatever the subject matter, the design forms an elaborate labyrinth of color. Characteristic rounded slot shapes surround and are internal to the main figures. Although red, orange, or black frequently dominates a color scheme, the

FIGURE 6–32. Cuna Indian Mola, sikwi (bird) design, from the San Blas Islands, Panama. Collection of the author.

whole range of colors is used in making molas. A predominately red mola may also have flashes of bright green, blue, or yellow. Turn to color plate 23. This fine mola shows a bird and a tree or plant design with leaf and flower forms. It is made of three main layers of cloth: red, green, and then red again. The pink has been appliquéd on the bottom red layer, and then red has been appliquéd on top of the pink. Small pieces of yellow, blue, and purple, underlay the top red layer in many areas. This example is typical of the very complex Cuna molas which are executed with great skill and are unique in conception and design to this tiny part of the world.

Making Paper Molas

Students at the junior high level may wish to create a mola in the same manner as the Cuna Indians. The sewing required is too intricate for most elementary school children. However, molas made by using successive layers of colored paper are very satisfying and challenge enough. Whether they are made of paper or cloth, the design is created in the same way, with layers of color.

It is not possible to work with all the colored papers together at once. Cut into the piece that is to be on top first, working either with pointed scissors or a flat lino cutting tool or X-acto knife. In the latter case, place the paper to be cut on a thick pad of newspaper. The first shape cut out should be larger and less defined than the shapes cut in succeeding layers. Place the second piece of colored paper under the first cutout, lining up the outside edges, and paper clip them together. Then, with a pencil ¼ inch or so out from the edges of the first cutout, define the shapes more accurately and cut them out. The third piece of paper may be another color or repeat the first color.

Figure 6–33 shows the steps in making a four-layer mola. In *a*, the turtle shape and slot designs

FIGURE 6–33 *a, b, c, d.* Diagram of four steps in making a paper mola design. This is a yauk (sea turtle) design, adapted from a mola in the collection of Captain Kit S. Kapp.

a

b

c

d

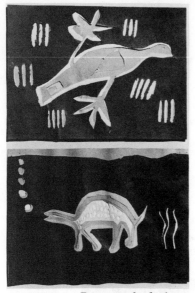

FIGURE 6-34. Paper mola designs: *Bird*, by Rachel, age ten, and *Turtle*, by Debbie, nine.

have been cut out of the first piece of paper. In *b,* a second piece of paper of a contrasting color has been slipped underneath and a dotted line drawn where it will be cut out. In *c,* the second layer of paper has been cut out and a third layer put underneath. Lines have been drawn on the third layer where it will be cut out. In *d,* the lines in the third layer are cut out and the fourth piece of paper, which is the same color as the first, has been slipped underneath.

This is one art that is easier to understand as one begins to work, and it may be a good idea to experiment with scraps of paper first, cutting simple shapes to see how successive layers are exposed.

In a completed mola design, the sandwich of layers should usually total at least three colors. Additional colors might be added by slipping small pieces of paper under particular areas for emphasis. Some very effective molas, however, use only two colors with a small bit of embroidery to create an eye on the figure. In the paper molas the eye would be glued on. When all the cutting is complete the layers are glued together with white glue.

FIGURE 6-35. Geometric paper mola design by Sarah, age nine.

Carved Gourd Designs

Gourds are used as containers and utensils in many South American countries. They are often highly decorated with carved designs. The people of the Andes Mountains have made gourd containers for at least 4,000 years. Especially fine work is done in the Peruvian Andes. Here the gourds are not only

FIGURE 6–36. A gourd decorated with traditional designs. Ink has been rubbed into the carving to emphasize the design. Cochas Chico, Huancayo State, Peru. Courtesy of Baobab, Ann Arbor, Michigan.

FIGURE 6–37. Two carved gourds by Cesar Aquino Veli, of Cochas Chico, Huancayo State, Peru. *Bird with Fish,* collection of the author. *Woman with Child,* courtesy of Baobab Ann Arbor, Michigan.

decorated and used as useful containers; they are also carved to be sold as sculpture.

The traditional designs on the containers are of village scenes and are very complex. People, animals, houses, and geometric designs form a rich overall pattern. The gourd is frequently dyed before being carved. This emphasizes the design by increasing the contrast between the gourd surface and the carved areas. Sometimes a black ink made of burnt leaves or grass mixed with animal fat is rubbed into the carving. In another method of decoration the dry gourd is first burned in some places with a glowing eucalyptus ember. Deep black areas are thus added to the natural golden orange color of the gourd. The artist brings out the design by incising with a sharp tool, creating lighter, almost white lines. (See color plate 24.)

The village of Cochas Chico, Huancayo State, Peru, is becoming well known for its decorated gourds. Using the method of burning some areas of the gourd, one man, Cesar Aquino Veli, turns the whole form of the gourd into an animal or hu-

FIGURE 6–38. *Flute Player,* made in the family of Juan Garcia Veli, Cochas Chico, Huancayo State, Peru. Courtesy of Baobab, Ann Arbor, Michigan.

man form. No longer made into a container, the carved gourd becomes a bird sitting on its nest, a mother with her child, or an animal figure. This was an innovation in an ancient art. Others now also decorate gourds in this way, but Cesar Aquino's work continues to be among the finest of the carvings. The burning ember is used like a delicate tool, and the carving is sure and incredibly fine, whether it is a feather pattern on a bird or the decorative edge of a woman's cloak.

Making Gourd Designs

If gourds are available in your community, buy the ones with a smooth surface; those with a textured or bumpy surface are difficult to work with. The gourds must be obtained six to eight months before the project is to be done and dried thoroughly. (Any dry place where air circulates freely will do.) An excellent arrangement is to place the gourds on a window screen that is supported off the floor in a raised horizontal position. If a screen is not available, turn the gourds frequently so that air reaches all sides equally.

It would be too dangerous for students to incise the hard gourds with a sharp tool. There is another method, however, that gives pleasing results. Clean the gourds of any dirt or mold accumulated during drying by scrubbing them with a scouring pad and water. Dry each gourd again thoroughly. Cover the entire surface (except perhaps any large area that will remain a natural color in the final design) with black crayon. If the gourd is at all damp it will resist the crayon, so it must be perfectly dry. The crayon should be applied with heavy pressure so as to completely cover the gourd. With the thumb or palm of the hand, polish and smooth the crayon coating to form a glossy black surface. (An alternate way of doing this is to melt black crayon in a tin over water and paint the gourd with the melted wax. This is quicker but does not produce quite such a smooth, glossy surface.)

Now study the shape of the gourd and decide what the design will be. Different gourds will suggest different solutions to this problem. Then, using a nail or the flat linoleum cutting tool, scrape through the crayon layer to expose the gourd underneath. First

FIGURE 6–39. The gourd was first covered with a smooth coating of black crayon. Then, using a linoleum cutting tool in a scraping (not cutting) motion, a student makes fur lines on the back of his animal figure.

outline the general design and then add as many details as possible—fur lines, delicate feathers, fish scales, geometric patterns, and clothing and features if it is a human figure. If the design is not as you wish, simply cover the gourd with black crayon again and start over.

Remember that it is not necessary to cut *into* the extremely hard gourd surface; the linoleum tool should be used *only* in a scraping, not a cutting, motion. Young students using a cutting motion could hurt themselves because the rounded surface causes the tool to slip easily.

If gourds are not available in your community, you can make an acceptable substitute with old electric light bulbs. This shape is quite similar to the most common gourd shape.

FIGURE 6-40. Three decorated gourds by sixth-grade students. From left to right, birds by Lana, Ellen, and Kay.

Cover the light bulb with five layers of paper dipped in wheat paste. (See directions for making papier mâché in the appendix.) Be very careful to tear (not cut) the pieces of paper to be applied so that seams will not show, and use rather small pieces (approximately one inch square). Carefully smooth down each piece of paper to make an even surface with no bumps or lines. When the papier mâché is dry, sand it with medium and then fine grade sandpapers to reduce surface irregularities. When it is smooth, cover the entire gourd with a coat of orange, yellow, or gold crayon. Proceed as you would with the gourd by applying a thick coat of black crayon over the first color. The design is created by scraping through the black crayon to the light colored layer beneath. The light bulb "gourd" is not balanced to stand on end. If it is to be displayed in a vertical position it will have to be placed in a stand made from a piece of modeling clay.

Gold Sculpture of Pre-Conquest Peru, Colombia, Ecuador, Panama, and Costa Rica

The art of making jewelry and sculpture in gold and silver reached extremely high levels in Central and South America before the Spanish Conquest. Countless treasures were melted down and sent back to Spain as bullion. Few of these pieces survive, but enough have remained for us to catch a glimpse of this beautiful work. We can only guess at what was made that we can never see.

In the area now known as Colombia, artisans cast very heavy sculptures that required great skill and knowledge of metallurgy. Equally awe-inspiring are the delicate, tiny sculptures that have been uncovered in Ecuador. The priceless gold and silver work of Peru is perhaps the most well known, because it was the first discovered in the New World. Large

FIGURE 6-41. Panamanian frog, excavated in Costa Rica. Circa 500–1500 A.D. Gold surfaced copper. Bequest of Robert H. Tannahill. Courtesy of The Detroit Institute of Arts.

quantities of gold sculpture were also cast in Panama and Costa Rica, and pieces are still being found in excavations there.

Several methods were used in making gold and silver sculpture. Much work was cast using the lost-wax method. The double-headed eagle pictured in color plate 25 was made by this method. The little Panamanian frog in Figure 6–41 was made of cast copper and surfaced with gold. It was excavated in Costa Rica. Little balls in the eyes make them ring like bells. Sculpture was also created of gold or silver hammered into sheets of paper thinness and decorated with repoussé designs. In repoussé work, the thin metal is pushed up from the back, which makes raised designs on the front. (See the lines that create the woolly coat on the silver alpaca, Figure 6–42.) Sometimes fine wires of gold or silver were braided, twisted, or coiled and added to the sculpture to form hair, ornaments, or designs.

Using these methods, artists made a great variety of gold objects. Many sculptures were created in honor of the Sun God or for other religious purposes. Gold pieces were also made for self-adornment and for use in the households of the wealthy: pendants; ear and nose ornaments; figures of people, birds, fish, and animals; cups, and other utensils. Masks of sheet metal were attached to mummy bundles. They were usually almost flat, with only a gentle curve. The stylized repoussé eyes sometimes had turquoise or shell centers attached with wire. Some masks were circled with radiating snake designs symbolizing the sun's rays.

Although working in gold is obviously impossible, students enjoy making designs in light cardboard or tagboard. Brushed with gold or silver paint, this resembles the work made of thin sheets of metal.

In making cardboard sculpture, students should cut out a basic shape first. They can make raised designs by cutting more pieces of cardboard and gluing them to the base. Cotton string can also be used: braided, twisted, or coiled, it can be glued to the cardboard to form designs like those made of gold wire in the pre-Conquest sculptures.

Students can design pendants, masks, or sculp-

FIGURE 6–42. Alpaca. Sheet silver. Peru. Courtesy of the American Museum of Natural History.

Making Gilded Cardboard Sculpture

FIGURE 6–43. Sculpture and pendant designs of gilded cardboard by fifth-grade students.

FIGURE 6–44. Butterfly pendant by
Ruth, age ten. The butterfly body and
wing designs were made by braiding
and coiling string.

tures of people or animals. The animal shapes may
be cut out and folded into standing figures. Experiment first with heavy-weight scrap paper until you
have a pattern you like, and then trace around it
on the cardboard and cut it out. (See the lion and
turtle in Figure 6–43.) Feathers, scales, fur, eyes,
whiskers, and so forth are cut out of cardboard or
formed from a piece of string and glued on. Remind
students that any feature or design on the cardboard
sculpture must be *raised* for it to show after it's
been painted.

When the sculpture is finished, it should be
painted with gold or silver tempera paint or gold
polymer. The added layers of cardboard and string
give an effect very much like that of repoussé work.

PLATE 1 (right)   Adinkra cloth from Ghana. Photograph taken at the "In Praise of Hands" exhibition of crafts from around the world at the Ontario Science Centre, Toronto, Canada, 1974.

PLATE 2 (below)   Adire eleko cloth from Oshogbo, Nigeria. A hand-drawn pattern made with cassava starch and indigo dye. Collection of Museum of African Art, Highland Park Community College.

PLATE 3 (above)   Indigo blue tie-dyed fabric
from Togo. Collection of Museum of African Art,
Highland Park Community College.

PLATE 4 (right)   An antelope dance mask, worn
by the Zamle Society, Guro, Ivory Coast; and a
highly abstract Kplekple mask, commonly called
"moon mask," Baule, Ivory Coast. Courtesy of the
Plymouth House Galleries, Plymouth, Michigan.

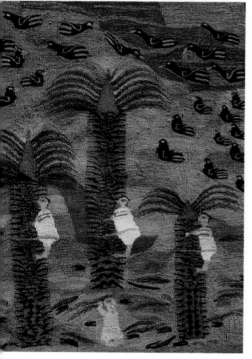

PLATE 5 (above)   Winged scarab amulet of blue faience, c. 18th Dynasty (1580-1321 B.C.). Modern stringing. Courtesy of Kelsey Museum of Archaeology, The University of Michigan.

PLATE 6 (left)   *Palm Pruners* by Soad Radouan, 13 years old. A tapestry woven at the Ramses Wissa Wassef Centre, Harrania, Egypt. Courtesy of Middle Earth, Ann Arbor, Michigan.

PLATE 7 (left) *Hen with Chickens*. A detail from the border of the mosaic pavement of Beth-Alpha Synagogue, Hefzibah, Israel. Early VIth century. Photograph by Palphot-Holyviews Ltd., Jerusalem, Israel.

PLATE 8 (below) *The Young Shoemaker and the Lion Before Bahram*. From a manuscript of the Shah-Nameh by Firdausi. Iranian, Timurid School, mid-15th century. Opaque watercolor and gold leaf on vellum. When the Shah's lion became loose, the shoemaker ran and climbed on his back, holding him by the ears until the keeper came. (Fortunately, the lion had just been fed!) Courtesy of the University of Michigan Museum of Art.

PLATE 9 (above) Kurpie leluja wycinanki design from Poland, early 20th century. Signed by Czeslawa Konpka. Originally a bright color, it has faded with age. Collection of the author.

PLATE 10 (right) Ukranian pysanky, from the collection of Mrs. Cyril Miles.

PLATE 11 (above) *Housewarming*. Straw inlay panel, Zhlobin, Byelorussia. Collection of the author.

PLATE 12 (left) A framed pressed flower arrangement from East Germany with gentians, primulas, wild geraniums, clover, sedge, and grasses; and a bookmark from West Germany with buttercups, clover, wild geraniums, and sedge. Collection of the author.

PLATE 13 (opposite, above) *Chrysanthemums and Rock*, color woodcut from the *Mustard Seed Garden Manual of Painting* by Wang Kai, 19th c. edition. Courtesy of the University of Michigan Museum of Art.

PLATE 14 (opposite) Gold-leafed lacquerware containers from Burma. Collection of the author.

PLATE 15 (above)   Marble box, inlaid with
lapis lazuli, carnelian, jade, tiger eye, agate, and
other semiprecious stones. Made in Agra, India.
Collection of the author.

PLATE 16 (right)   A kayon and Arjuna, wayangs (shadow puppets). Courtesy of A.L. Becker
and Judith O. Becker.

PLATE 17 (above)   Indonesian tjap batik. Detail of a sarong in cream, soga brown, and indigo blue. c. 1925. Collection of the author.

PLATE 18 (left)   Huichol Indian yarn paintings. State of Nayarit, Mexico. Collection of the author.

PLATE 19 (left)   Amate paper paintings, Mexico. Collection of the author.

PLATE 20 (below)   Clay figures from Tonala, State of Jalisco, Mexico. Collection of the author.

PLATE 21 (right)   Clay sun design from Metapec, State of Mexico, Mexico. 19″. Collection of the author.

PLATE 22 (below)   A small sampling of the great variety of colorful items made from tin and sold in the markets of Mexico. Collection of the author.

PLATE 23 Cuna Indian mola, sikwi (bird) design, from the San Blas Islands, Panama. Collection of the author.

PLATE 24 Two carved gourds by Cesar Aquino Veli, of Cochas Chico, Huancayo State, Peru. *Bird with Fish,* collection of the author. *Woman with Child,* courtesy of BAOBAB, Ann Arbor, Michigan.

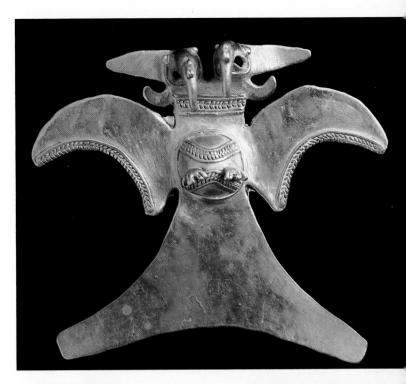

PLATE 25   Double-headed eagle
pendant. Panama, c. 900-1400
A.D. Cast gold. Courtesy of the
Detroit Institute of Arts.

PLATE 26   Seed necklaces from
Puerto Rico. Collection of the author.

PLATE 27 (above)   Navajo rug, woven with a
mixture of natural fleece colors, a yellow dye from
plants found on the reservation, and a commercial
red dye. Collection of Mr. and Mrs. Richard I. Ford.

PLATE 28 (right)   *Holyman,* Navajo sandpaint-
ing by E. Hunt. Collection of the author.

PLATE 29 (above)   Mato-tope's buffalo robe, Mandan, c. 1836. Horses, warriors, and a sunburst painted by a Mandan chief. Courtesy Bernisches Historisches Museum, Abteiling für Völkerkunde, Bern, Switzerland.

PLATE 30 (left)   Buckskin bag, decorated with porcupine quillwork in geometric and thunderbird designs. The lower part of the bag is decorated with a mallard duck pelt. Sauk and Fox, c. 1820. Courtesy of the Chandler-Pohrt Collection.

PLATE 31 (right)   Woodland Indian beadwork.
From left, beadwork sash, Chippewa, Wisconsin,
c. 1890; heddle woven bead sash, Potawatomi
Reservation, Kansas, c. 1885; beadwork garter,
Chippewa, Wisconsin-Minnesota, c. 1890. Cour-
tesy of the Chandler-Pohrt Collection.

PLATE 32 (below)   *Polar Bear and Cub in Ice,*
by Niviaksiak. Sealskin stencil print. Cape Dorset, Baffin Island, June 1959. From the collection
of Eugene B. Power. Copyright 1959. Reproduced
by permission of the West Baffin Eskimo Co-
operative Limited, Cape Dorset, Canada.

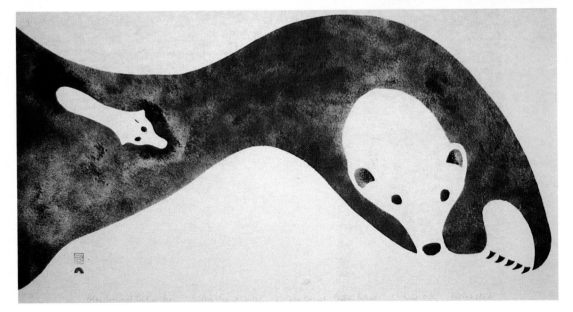

7
ARTS OF
THE CARIBBEAN
ISLANDS

The projects chosen for this chapter illustrate several different characteristics of the arts and crafts of the Caribbean islands. The necklaces created from seeds of island trees and shrubs are made in many of the other islands besides Puerto Rico, and they symbolize the natural beauty common to them all.

Maracas, rhythm instruments first made by the Indians who were the original inhabitants of the islands, represent the all-pervading musical traditions that have been enriched over the centuries with contributions from many different cultures.

The steel designs of Haiti illustrate a modern rather than traditional art. These designs originated on one island and make ingenious use of scrap metal rather than a naturally found material. The designs often explore concepts concerning humanity's relation to nature and to the spiritual world.

177

SEED NECKLACES OF PUERTO RICO

Puerto Rico is the smallest, eastern-most island of the Greater Antilles, situated in the Caribbean Sea. Before Columbus came in 1493, the Indians living on the island called it Boriquen (boh-ree-KEN). It was a green and fertile island with mountains in the center and coastal lowlands. The Tainos, a peaceful, agricultural people, lived in villages and raised corn and sweet potatoes and gathered the island fruits. It is believed that few Tainos survived the Spanish rule, although more may have hidden in mountain caves than was once believed. Much of their culture remained to influence the lives of all who live on the island: their cultivated vegetables, their arts of hammock and basket weaving, such musical instruments as maracas (round gourds filled with seeds) and guiros (a bottle-shaped gourd played with a wire fork), foods and ways of cooking them, and a feeling of love for the land that is shared by Puerto Ricans today.

FIGURE 7–1. Seed necklaces from Puerto Rico, containing (from the left) seeds from the earpod tree, alternating with red granate (red sandlewood); camándula (Job's tears); flamboyan (datelike), red granate, earpod, and matos gris (gray niker seeds); and tamarind (zarcilla seeds).

When the Taino population diminished, slaves were brought from Africa to do the work for the Spaniards, and so the culture of Puerto Rico became a mixture of African, Indian, and Spanish influences.

In 1898, after the Spanish-American War, Spain ceded Puerto Rico to the United States. Once again, a new, dominant culture was brought to bear on the island. Since 1952 Puerto Rico has been a commonwealth; it elects its own governor but has ties to the United States. Puerto Ricans are United States citizens at birth.

Puerto Ricans are proud of their island and their roots in Taino culture. Ancient ruins on the island have monuments of incised stones from pre-Columbian times. They depict the Taino gods, called cemies. Smaller figures of clay and wood have been found in excavations. By Spanish accounts, the Indians also made figures of gold. Craftsmen today make replicas of the stone and clay sculptures, and the Taino designs are used in modern fabrics.

Perhaps the most well-known Puerto Rican folk art is that of the carved wooden santos (SAN-tohs, meaning saints). The Spaniards brought Catholicism to the islands, and each town had a patron saint. Santos have been made for over 300 years, and until recently, most families had santos that were handed down for generations. A santo might be the village or family patron saint or one that brought special healing powers. Originally they were decorated with natural pigments. By the nineteenth century, santos were painted in many colors and sometimes included metal parts as well as wood. The sculptures are recognized for their unique beauty, and many are now in museum collections.

The African heritage in Puerto Rico is perhaps most clear in its many contributions to the music of the island and in the annual Fiesta de Santiago Apostol (Festival of St. James the Apostle) held in the village of Loíza Aldea. Historically, the village population was predominantly of African descent. The festival is famous for its feathered and horned masks, carved from coconuts and made only in this area. Singing satirical ballads and dancing the African bomba, the villagers depict history: the story of the conqueror and the conquered, in a mixture of love and hostility, fun and solemnity that represents many aspects of the Indian, African, and Spanish heritage of Puerto Rico.

San Juan, the capital of Puerto Rico, is built on an island. A modern metropolitan area with high-rise buildings has grown up across the bridges from the ancient sixteenth-century city of Old San Juan, and industrialization is changing the lives of Puerto Ricans. But still the beautiful tropical landscape is not far away, and there is a growing awareness of its value and a concern that industrialization make no further inroads. A recent attempt to begin copper mining was prevented by pressure from many people who value the natural qualities of their land.

Several of the trees and plants found on the island are known only in Puerto Rico. There are also many beautiful flowering trees, such as the flamboyan trees with large red blossoms, and the jacaranda with its violet-blue flowers. One variety or another is blooming throughout the year. Children in the country are familiar with many trees and plants and use them in their games. The seed of the mango fruit is made into dolls. It is large and flat and oval, and some varieties have a covering of long fibers. The children polish the fibers off the front and draw faces on them, combing the rest of the fibers into hair around the face. There are canna lilies, which are called maraca plants because the fine, hard seeds are gathered and put into gourds to make maracas (see next project). And there are games played with the algarrobo seeds. These one-inch seeds are oblong, dark red, and very hard. They grow in long pods on tall trees. A hole is made in the seed, and a heavy string is put through it and tied. Then children take turns swinging their algarrobo seed against their opponent's until one of the seeds breaks. This is much like the game of conkers that used to be played in England and in rural United States with horse chestnuts.

Along the rivers in marshy ground grow the camándula plants. They have shiny, pearly gray seeds (also called Job's tears) with a natural hole just right for stringing, and children make necklaces of them. *Camándula* means rosary beads, and they have also been used for rosaries for many years.

Necklaces made from native seeds and beans are sold in the tourist shops in San Juan. The two most commonly used seeds are the camándulas (both in natural colors and dyed) and the small, brown tamarind or zarcilla seeds. There are the smooth, brown, striped oval seeds from the ear pod tree and the shiny, bright red granate (or red sandlewood) seeds. The flamboyan has a datelike seed frequently used in necklaces. Beads are also sometimes made of coffee beans. From vines growing near the beaches come the softly striped and satiny gray niker seeds, or matos gris (see color plate 26).

The beads made from all these seeds speak of the land most tourists never see.

We can learn from Puerto Rico to see and use what is in our environment. Look both indoors and out for seeds that can be used for necklaces. Perhaps you have never noticed before how many seeds are thrown away or passed by and how beautiful some

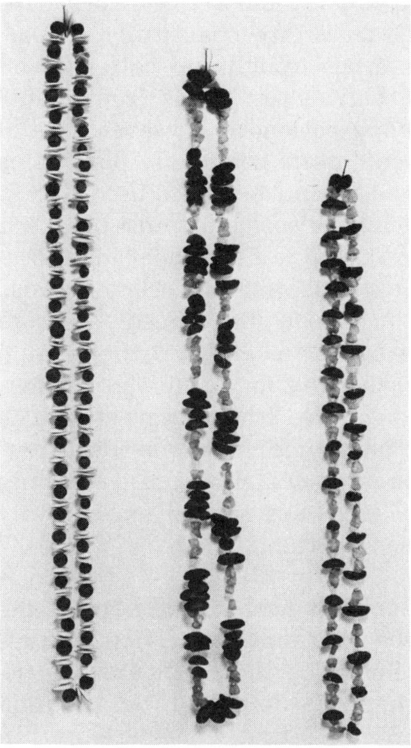

Making Seed Necklaces

FIGURE 7–2. Necklaces made by fourth-grade students. From left: Jenny's is made of allspice and acorn squash seeds, Bill's alternates yellow corn with coffee beans, and Amy's uses corn and coffee beans in a different arrangement.

FIGURE 7–3. A sampling of some seeds suitable for necklaces. Clockwise from top left: striped sunflower seeds, allspice, cantaloupe, coffee beans, acorn squash, apple, pumpkin, and watermelon. Acorn cups fill the center.

of them are on close inspection. Save apple seeds, shiny, brown, and much like the Puerto Rican zarcilla seeds. Squash, watermelon, and pumpkin seeds make fine necklaces. Separate the seeds from the pulp, wash them, and spread them out to dry on wax paper (they will stick to other papers). In the stores you can buy sunflower seeds with subtle gray stripes, round brown allspice seeds, and coffee beans (perhaps from Puerto Rico). Sometimes a grocer has spoiled produce that you can use: frozen corn and peas can be used for beads. They will dry to half their original size, so in stringing them you must make the necklace twice as long as the final length you wish.

Outdoors, look for seeds on ornamental shrubs or seeds that have fallen from trees. Acorn cups or husks, from oak trees, are beautifully shaped, smooth and brown inside, rough and patterned on the outside. (Some berries and seeds from plants and shrubbery may be poisonous, however. One of these, the castor bean, quite commonly planted, is highly poisonous and should never be used. If you do not know a plant, check with a botonist or poison control center before using it. For proper identification you will need leaves as well as berries or seeds.)

If the seeds are too hard to push a needle through (this is true of coffee beans and allspice), they should be soaked for several hours in warm water before you make the necklace. Use a heavy carpet thread. Think of a pattern for stringing your beads—alternate size and shape or colors. However, sometimes especially beautiful seeds are noticed more if only that one kind is used for the necklace.

ISLAND MARACAS

Music plays an important part in the lives of the people of the Caribbean Islands. It is a rich mixture of many cultures, including Indian, Spanish, African, French, British, and American. From the Indians came two instruments that were developed in pre-Columbian times and are still in use today: the guiro and the maraca. The guiro (gwee-roh) is made from a hollow bottle gourd that has lines incised on it. When the tines of a metal fork are scraped over the ridges, it makes a rasping sound. Maracas were used by Indians throughout the islands and in Mexico and South America as well. They are made of hollow gourds or the large, hard-shelled fruit of the calabash tree. Small seeds are put in the gourds and a handle is attached. Sometimes island scenes are painted on contemporary maracas, and sometimes designs are cut into the surface of the gourd while it is still green. Maracas are usually used in pairs and are shaken to the rhythm of a dance or to accompany a song.

Several kinds of guitar-like stringed instruments are made on the islands, often by hand in the villages. One of the most popular is the cuatro, which is a four or five double-stringed instrument. Perhaps the most widely known instrument from the area originated in recent years in Trinidad. During World War II percussion instruments were made of steel oil drums cut down into pans, which could receive a fine tuning. Notes are played by hitting different areas of the pan. Steelbands, which play with great skill, are now popular on many of the Caribbean islands.

Each island has its own particular musical heritage resulting in different styles, but much of the music played and sung is strongly African in origin with Spanish overtones. Under Spanish rule, slaves were not allowed to talk while they were working,

FIGURE 7-4. Island maracas. From left: two carved maracas from St. Thomas, collection of Irene Tejada; a carved and painted maraca from Cuba, collection of Mrs. Juanita Lopez; one painted and two carved maracas from Puerto Rico, collections of Yolanda Marino and Irene Tejada.

¡Temporal!
(Hurricane!)

Spanish and English
Text by Ruth Gomez

Puerto Rican Folk Song
Arranged by Elsa Adamson

Tem - po - ral, _____ tem - po - ral, _____
Hur - ri - cane, _____ hur - ri - cane, _____

a - llá vie - ne el tem - po - ral. _____
it is com - ing-the hur - ri - cane. _____

¿Qué se - rá _____ de Puer - to Ri - co
What will be - come of Puer - to Ri - co

cuan - do lle - que el tem - po - ral?
when the hur - ri - cane ar - rives?

FIGURE 7–5.

but they could sing. They developed songs to record history and keep it alive, to pass information, and to comment on current events. This is a tradition that has carried on. There are religious songs, love songs, and work songs, but perhaps one earmark of Caribbean songs is that they frequently recall memorable events of the past or comment on present political or social conditions.

After making maracas, students may want to learn the song we have included here and emphasize the beat with their maracas. This folk song is very

184 Caribbean Arts

popular in Puerto Rico and probably came into being to memorialize one of the terribly devastating hurricanes that periodically do great damage to the islands.

This type of song is called a "plena" and is of African origin (see Figure 7–5).

Maracas can be made quite successfully from papier mâché. Blow up a round balloon to about five inches in diameter. Tie the end to keep the air in. Apply at least four layers of torn newspaper dipped in wheat paste. (See appendix for directions for using wheat paste.) The pieces should be no larger than two-inch squares if there is to be a smooth surface. Do not cover the knot.

After several days, when the papier mâché is thoroughly dry, pop the balloon with a pair of scissors or a pin at the place where it is tied. (This is fun— the balloon will pull away from the inside of the globe, making mysterious crackling noises that go on for some time.) Remove the broken balloon.

Put a teaspoonful of dried split peas, rice, other smaller seeds, or very tiny pebbles into the hole. Insert an eleven-inch piece of ½-inch dowel into the hole and all the way up to the top of the globe.

Making Maracas

FIGURE 7–6. Applying newspaper dipped in paste to a balloon. Smaller pieces than are shown here would result in a smoother surface.

FIGURE 7–7. Michael listens to his balloon "talk" inside the papier mâché shell. (When the balloon is popped, it pulls away from the dry shell, making crackling sounds.)

FIGURE 7-8. Maracas made by third-grade students Roy and Chris.

FIGURE 7-9. Second and third graders sing a Spanish language song, accenting the rhythm with their maracas.

Place the maraca upright on its handle, and hammer a large-headed tack through the papier mâché into the dowel at the top. Now apply three more layers of newspaper dipped in wheat paste to the area where the globe joins the handle, using narrow strips in a vertical fashion and lapping the paper well down over the dowel. One more layer to the whole maraca will cover the tack and give added strength.

When the maraca is dry it can be painted with tempera paints. A good method is to give one base coat of a solid color, and let it dry before painting on a design with a fine detail brush. Students may want to try a typical island scene with palm trees and ocean or some design of their own. After the paint is thoroughly dry it should be protected with a coat of shellac.

HAITIAN DESIGNS IN STEEL

Haiti, "land of mountains" in the Arawak Indian Language, has had a long and often tragic history resulting in a mixture of Indian, Spanish, African, and French cultures. An uprising against colonial rule in 1791 began a long struggle towards self-rule by the largely black population that was brought to Haiti from West Africa as slaves during both Spanish and French rule. In 1804 Haiti won complete independence from colonial rule, but the next century brought internal struggles and occupation by the United States from 1915 to 1934.

The unrest and extreme poverty had not allowed for much artistic development. But when an art center (Centre d'Art) was opened in 1944, art blossomed. The center was opened at the suggestion of DeWitt Peters, who had come to Haiti from America as a teacher, and it was supported by the combined efforts of American and Haitian authorities. Many people came forward or were discovered who had been working privately at art for many years. They were unschooled primitive painters who had to earn their living by working at another job such as taxi driver, house painter, or barber, but who were devoted to painting whenever they could find time and afford materials. The art center brought fame to these painters, and other young people found in art a means of expressing the unique beauty and spirit of Haiti. Many Haitian artists became known worldwide.

One man who was touched by this new respect for art was Georges Liautaud. When he was discovered in the early 1950s, he was a blacksmith. He made tools and iron crosses for the tombs in the cemeteries. The iron crosses were of original designs, and when it was suggested by people from the Centre d'Art that he make iron sculptures he began to create mostly flat metal figures that are now prized in museums around the world. He has become one of Haiti's most famous artists. The figures portray a mixture of Catholicism and voodoo (a folk religion of African origin) that is unique to Haiti and often expressed in Haitian art. They represent spirits that embody fears and joys and sometimes a fine sense of humor.

The sculptures are usually made from steel oil drums. These are opened and flattened to a three-by six-foot piece of metal. Precise drawings are transferred to the metal and the shape is cut out with chisels, a large hammer, and shears. The sculptures emphasize the contours, or silhouettes, of forms. Sometimes designs are pierced through the

FIGURE 7–10. The Haitiian steel designs often merge human and animal forms. This design by Louis Bruno appears to be part human, part rooster, and part fish. Collection of the author.

FIGURE 7–11. Steel sculpture by Seresier Louisjuste. From the collection of Frances Crowe. Photograph by Nathaniel D. Smith.

FIGURE 7–12. Steel sun design by J. P. Bernard. Collection of the author.

Silhouette Designs

FIGURE 7–13. Peter cuts his design out of cardboard with an X-acto knife.

metal. It is an art of many meanings. Animal and human forms are often combined in one sculpture. One of Liautaud's favorite spirits is Maîtresse La Sirène. He portrays her as part woman, part fish, sometimes part bird or goat. She is a goddess of love and symbolizes universal woman.

Many other artists in metal followed. Murat Brierre became the first to make designs from the round ends of the steel oil drums. Three brothers, Janvier, Joseph, and Seresier Louisjuste, have become well known in the 1970s. Their work is almost lacy, an intricate combination of men, birds, animals, and gods that is usually contained within the boundaries of the original square, rectangular, or round piece of metal chosen to work with (see Figure 7–11). In some sculptures, surface designs are worked into the metal with a chisel, but in general the great dramatic effect is from the silhouette cut in the strong, hard steel.

The students should first work out their designs with pencil and paper. The elements most frequently seen in the Haitian designs are people and all forms of nature. These are sometimes a religious expression, a merging of human and animal forms characteristic of voodoo spirits. In some designs it is more an integration of plant, animal, and human forms that seems to express a joyful closeness to nature. Students choosing similar themes for their designs might think of them as symbolic of a new ecological consciousness of the interdependence of all forms of life.

Students may want to consider a design that is enhanced because it conforms to a particular shape: round, square, or rectangular. Although the edge may be cut into, enough edge should be retained to suggest the original form.

It is helpful to cross-hatch areas that are to be cut out later. This helps students see that the design must all be connected and that connecting parts must be thick enough so that they do not break in cutting. The cutting is difficult, and it is better not to try a design that is too delicate or lacy—cardboard does not have the strength of steel!

When the penciled design is ready, place carbon

paper under it and clip both the design and the carbon paper to a piece of black railroad board or other lightweight cardboard. Draw over the design with a pencil to transfer it to the cardboard. Include the cross-hatching as a guide for what is to be cut away.

With an X-acto knife (or single-edged razor blade) start cutting out the design in the center and work toward the edges. Work on an old magazine or thick pad of newspaper.

Sometimes the Haitian steel designs also have surface lines cut in with a hammer and chisel. Names are usually signed on the steel in this way, and some interior lines are added to the design as well. You can do this on the cardboard by placing a screwdriver (or the head of a large nail) on the cardboard and tapping it with a hammer.

The cardboard will have white edges where it is cut. It will look more like steel if it is rubbed with dark brown shoe polish. This will stain the edges and also add the warmer tones seen in the metal sculptures.

FIGURE 7–14. Sandra rubs brown shoe polish on her cardboard design to darken the cut edges and add warm tones.

FIGURE 7–15. Seventh- and eighth-grade silhouette designs inspired by Haitiian steel sculpture. Clockwise from top left: by Randall, Susan H., Susan G., Sandra, Kelly, and Laura.

8

ARTS OF
THE UNITED STATES
AND CANADA

Before the coming of settlers to North America, Native American arts had developed in the different cultural areas of the continent. These arts were products of those cultures and the different materials available in each environment. When traders came, some of these arts developed in new ways. For instance, when glass beads became available they were used instead of porcupine quills for decorative work. In some areas artwork also came to be produced for economic reasons instead of for personal use. This is the case with Eskimo prints and sculpture and with much of the Navajo weaving and Pueblo pottery.

Early American and Canadian arts were derived from several sources. Some, such as the making of applehead dolls, were adapted from Native American arts. In other cases, ideas were brought from Europe but were developed further on this continent. A few arts, like that of carving scrimshaw, came about because of new materials available through new occupations—in this case, ivory, a by-product of the whaling industry.

Archeologists believe that about 25,000 B.C., when the floor of the Bering Strait was dry land, people crossed from Asia to North America. The people who subsequently inhabited North America formed culture groups, which depended on different resources for food and shelter and therefore developed different ways of life. Art from four major areas will be discussed: the Southwest, the Central Plains, the Woodlands, and the Artic. These cultures were not completely isolated, however, and some arts were learned from other tribal groups. Materials not available in one area were sometimes acquired through trade. For example, the Plains Indians traveled to the Woodlands to get the valued porcupine quills to use for decorative arts.

All these groups lived in harmony with the natural world, using what their environment provided resourcefully and respectfully. Indian arts reflect Indian ways of living and traditions. Above all, they express a feeling of spiritual interdependence with all the forces of nature.

The Pueblo Indian culture is the oldest in the Southwest. The name *Pueblo* comes from the Spanish and means village. These Indians, who are settled farmers, live in close dwelling units of flat-roofed houses built of stone or adobe. Their ancestors lived in remarkable cliff houses, constructed in such a way that aesthetically they seem part of the mountains. These dwellings are still there after many hundreds of years. Current Pueblo tribes feel a continuity with their past that has never been broken in spite of foreign domination. The early Pueblo artisans did much fine work in pottery, basketry, weaving, and painting, and Pueblos still engage in these arts today.

Pottery making began as early as 300 B.C. The early clay pots were made for household and ceremonial vessels. Most were entirely utilitarian, but the people who lived in the Mimbres Valley of New Mexico painted black and white designs on their pottery.

NATIVE AMERICAN ARTS

Pueblo Indian Pottery and Outdoor Kilns

FIGURE 8–1. Polished black bowl with matte black design by Maria Martinez. San Ildefonso, New Mexico. Gift of Mrs. Ed. A. Ruggles. Courtesy of The Cleveland Museum of Art.

FIGURE 8–2. Black bowl with carved design. Santa Clara Pueblo, New Mexico. Gift of Mrs. Ed. A. Ruggles. Courtesy of The Cleveland Museum of Art.

Rabbits, turtles, lizards, and other lively drawings still bring to life the clay fragments that have been found in the area.

The tradition of making pottery has continued until the present day in many of the Pueblos. When the railroad brought both commerical pots for their own use and a market for their handmade wares in 1880, some of the Indians stopped making pottery for use in the Pueblo and began creating it as a piece of art for non-Indians. Although fewer Pueblos make pottery now, there has been a steady increase in artistic achievement among some of them.

Different tribes have developed distinctive styles of pottery because they use differing natural materials and because they are isolated by distance and language barriers. However, neighboring Pueblos often borrow ideas from each other.

Zuni pots of red clay are decorated with black designs painted on a white background. The intricate geometric designs have reduced bird shapes to lines and circles so abstract that a non-Zuni would never recognize them as such. Deer are also a frequent motif. At Taos cooking vessels are made of a clay that contains mica. When they are fired, the undecorated pots have a golden sheen. Hopi pottery is traditionally a creamy orange clay with black and red decorations.

In 1919 Maria and Julian Martinez of San Ildefonso invented a new style of pottery with designs of matte black painted over a polished black background. This Pueblo and that of nearby Santa Clara are now famous for this ware.

In the early 1930s, another style of pottery was created by Rose Gonzales of San Ildefonso. Her husband, while hunting, found a small piece of ancient carved pottery. Inspired by this, Rose developed carved pottery, which has become as famous as the black on black pottery. The pottery is usually decorated around the upper portion of the pot with traditional designs such as bird feathers, cloud symbols, and Awanyu, the plumed serpent (a Pueblo design since prehistoric times). The design is drawn on the pot and then clay is scraped away from around it, leaving the design raised. The carved out portion is usually matte, in contrast to the high polish of the pot and raised design. Both red pottery and re-duction-fired black pottery are made in this way at San Ildefonso and nearby Pueblos.

In all Pueblos the basic pots are made in much the same way they were in prehistoric times. Clay is dug from the ground, pulverized to a powder, and mixed with sand. It is then soaked in water and kneaded to the right consistency. A round cake is patted out to make the base of the pot. Thick coils of wet clay are rolled out and curled around, one on top of another, to form the pot. The pot is scraped and smoothed with pieces of gourd and set aside to dry. Earlier potters knew a glaze technique that is now lost. Potters now achieve a high gloss surface by applying several layers of slip (a liquid mixture of water and pure clay) and rubbing the surface with a smooth stone while it is still damp. These stones have sometimes been passed down within a family for generations. Some of them are believed to be dinosaur gizzard stones, found in the skeletons of prehistoric animals. For polishing, a stone is selected that fits the curvature of the pot.

Painted designs are applied with brushes made of yucca leaves. The leaves have been chewed until they are soft and the fibers have separated, and then they are trimmed to shape. The design is painted with slip or with natural pigments. There is no presketching; the designs are applied directly with the brush. They are usually based on symbols from nature, stylized or abstracted: rain, lightning, animal tracks, water, mountains.

A shallow pit is dug in the ground. A metal grate is laid in this, sometimes raised on tin cans to allow air circulation. The pots are stacked carefully, upside down, on the grate. A metal sheet, placed on top, protects them from direct contact with the fire. Then a fire of wood or cattle chips is built up in a mound over the pots and kept burning for several hours. At this point, if black ware is desired, finely powdered horse manure is thrown on the fire. This smothers the flame and creates a reduction firing; the lack of oxygen turns the pots black. When the firing is completed the pots are removed and rubbed clean with a dry cloth.

The finished pots are semiporous. In the Pueblos

this was desirable, because water seeping through kept stored water cool through evaporation. Most of the pots produced now are sold as decorative non-functional pieces only.

Making Clay Pots

Moist clay of any color may be used. First pat out a round cake about one-half inch thick to form the base of the pot. Using fingers and palms make a roll of clay about ½ to ¾ inch thick. Press the first roll down on the edge of the base coiling it around. Add more coils on top of the first, pressing them together as you go. This is easier if the bottom of the pot is placed on two small pieces of newspaper: the pot will then turn easily on the table. Smooth the coils together on the inside and outside of the pot as you work. To make the walls of the pot go out, place the coil so that it protrudes slightly beyond the outer edge of the coil beneath. To make it go in, place towards the inside edge. After building to the desired height and shape, smooth the pot carefully again on the outside with the fingers, while supporting the pot on the inside with the other hand.

FIGURE 8–3. Amy presses a coil of clay down on the base of her pot.

FIGURE 8–4. Jill has smoothed the coils in her pot together with her fingers. Sometimes using a tool, like a spoon, helps. She supports the inside of the pot with her other hand.

FIGURE 8–5. Danny carves a design in his pot with a linoleum cutting tool. This must be done before the pot is dry, at the "leather hard" stage.

FIGURE 8–6. Jenny polishes her pot by rubbing hard with a spoon before the clay is completely dry.

If the pot is to have an incised design, it should first dry to "leather hard" consistency. This is hard enough to hold its shape but not too hard to cut into easily. Use linoleum cutting tools to make the design. It is easier for young children to cut in a simple line design (Figure 8–5) than to try a more complicated raised design (with *background* cut away as in Figure 8–2).

While the clay is still leather hard, apply a coat of slip evenly with a brush. (Slip can be purchased at art supply stores.) If the clay has become too dry, this will flake off. Adding slip is not absolutely necessary, but if you polish the clay body directly, the sand that has been added to the clay may cause some scratches. While the slip is still damp it can be polished by rubbing the surface with a smooth stone or with the back of a spoon. You can keep unfinished pots at the leather hard stage by storing them in tightly closed plastic bags.

If there is a supply of wood and a proper place, the pottery can be fired outdoors in the Pueblo manner we have described. However, you can obtain good

Firing in an Outdoor Reduction Kiln

FIGURE 8–7. Third-grade students have built an outdoor kiln, using bricks. It is filled with layers of sawdust alternating with layers of pots. A final three-inch layer of sawdust will cover these pots.

FIGURE 8–8. The cracks between the bricks are filled with wet clay and then the fire is started in the kiln. The metal top is put on, and the long wait begins.

results with materials more easily found in modern city environments. Firing should take place on a windless, dry day.

For a class of about thirty, with pots measuring approximately four inches high, you will need seventy-two bricks and a heavy metal top measuring 19 x 19 inches. Place eight bricks in a hollow square (two bricks and the end of a third brick on each side) directly on the ground or asphalt. Place eight more on top of these, shifting them to cover the cracks of the first layer. Build up all nine rows. (See the finished kiln in Figure 8–8.)

Fill the bottom of the kiln with three inches of *dry* sawdust. Put in a layer of pots, spaced one inch apart. It is best to place them upside down. Cover with one inch of sawdust and proceed with the next layer of pots. Repeat until all the pots are covered and finish with a three-inch layer of sawdust on the top.

Now fill the cracks between the bricks with wet clay. Light the sawdust from the top so that it burns evenly. Crumpled newspapers will help it get started. Put the metal lid on top and weight it down if it doesn't lie flat. Leave the kiln burning until all smoking stops—this may take all day.

At the exciting moment when the kiln is opened the pots will be found all together in the bottom of the kiln if the firing has gone correctly and all the sawdust has burned. They are not high fired, and they will be porous and break if they are dropped, but they should all have become quite hard, turned black, and have retained a fine polish. Dust them off well with a cloth.

FIGURE 8-9. Four clay pots fired in an outdoor kiln by third-grade students Danny, Erik, Jenny, and Charlie.

Navajo Indians, now the largest tribal group in America, live in parts of Arizona, New Mexico, and Utah. Originally from the north, the Navajo were late arrivals in the Southwest. They learned sheep herding from the Spaniards and weaving from the Pueblos in the early eighteenth century. From this beginning, they became the greatest of all Indian weavers.

Early Navajo weaving was made into clothing in the form of blankets worn around the shoulders. Later, the Indians began to wear manufactured blankets, and weaving began to die out. However, the trading posts realized the commercial value of the fine work, and the Navajos began to weave saddle blankets and rugs to sell.

The early blankets were designed with stripes, edge to edge. The weaving made to sell became heavier so that it could be used for rugs. With this change came changes in design: new geometric shapes and borders. Over the past two hundred years, the Navajo have acquired skills through experimentation and handed them down through the generations; some designs have become very complex. There are now, in general, four categories of Navajo rugs:

1. those that use natural fleece colors—white, black, some brown, and gray (which is made by carding white and black fibers together);
2. those that use bright commercial dyes in many colors;
3. those that use natural dyes secured by gathering

Navajo Weaving

FIGURE 8-10. Navajo rug woven with natural fleece colors of white, black, and brown, with stripes of yellow made with dye from the chamiso plant. Collection of Mr. and Mrs. Richard I. Ford.

FIGURE 8–11. Navajo rug woven with a mixture of natural fleece colors (white, black, brown, and gray), a yellow dye from plants found on the reservation, and a commercial red dye. Collection of Mr. and Mrs. Richard I. Ford.

and boiling plants, berries, and roots found on the reservation, creating mostly soft pastel shades of brown, green, yellow, and pink; and

4. those that combine some of these elements in Yei designs, which are derived from designs used in sand painting ceremonies.

Different areas of the reservation have become famous for distinct styles and designs. But all weave basically in the ancient manner. Although some spun wool is now purchased commercially, generally sheep must be raised and the wool sheared, carded, spun, dyed, and rolled into balls. The loom is usually set up outdoors with the vertical warp strung between heavy logs suspended from trees or a wooden frame. The rug is woven by passing the weft over and under the warp threads and beating it down securely with a wooden comb. Heddles attached to every other thread open a shed to pass the weft through. A rug may take many weeks or months to weave, depending on its size. The design, no matter how intricate, is kept in the head of the weaver until it appears, wondrously, centered and perfect, row by row. (See color plate 27.)

FIGURE 8–12. Navajo Indian weaver in Monument Valley, Navajo Indian Reservation, Arizona. The loom is constructed of logs under a shelter that gives shade from the summer sun. The weaver is beating down the weft with a wooden comb. Photograph by Josef Muench.

In order to weave, a loom must keep the vertical threads, or warp, taut. A simple but effective loom can be made from a piece of strong cardboard. At third- or fourth-grade level a piece seven by ten inches is ample for a beginner. Cut notches, ½ inch apart and ¼ inch deep, at the top and bottom edges. Wind strong cotton twine around the cardboard: starting at the bottom notch on the left and leaving a "tail" ten inches long, carry the twine up to the top left notch, down the back, and up through the second bottom notch from the left. Continue in this manner until the loom is completely wound, leaving a ten-inch tail at the top right notch. These two tails are then pulled to the back and tied together to hold the warp tight.

The weaver can then proceed by passing yarn over the first warp, under the second, over the third warp, under the fourth, etc. At the end of the row the yarn circles the last warp and comes back, this time going over every thread it went under on the previous row (and under every thread it went over). Children will soon see that this creates a strong fabric that holds together.

Since the weft must go up over and curl under every warp thread (instead of going in a straight line), it takes more than seven inches of yarn to

Weaving on a Cardboard Loom

FIGURE 8–13. Tanya, age nine, weaving on her cardboard loom.

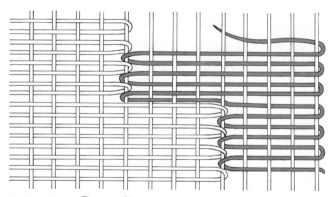

FIGURE 8–14. Dovetailing two colors in a weaving. Where the colors meet, each color circles the same warp thread before turning back.

weave a seven-inch width. Students have a tendency to pull the weft straight across, but unless *extra* yarn is added, the weaving will tend to pull in as it progresses and the sides will not remain straight.

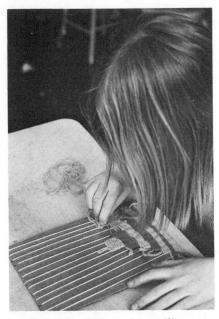

FIGURE 8–15. When dovetailing another color, using a needle helps in separating the weft in the parts already woven.

FIGURE 8–16. Three weavings by Amy, nine; Laura, ten; and Rebecca, nine.

To counteract this, students should add yarn by putting a "hill" into the weft, after it has been passed through the warp and before it is pushed down against the weaving. (See Figure 3–17 in Chapter 3, but use fingers instead of a fork to push the weft down.)

Before beginning to work, students should think about their design. If they want to make a striped pattern they should choose a few colors that go well together. These can alternate in sequence, or children can design a pattern that creates symmetry in some way—for instance, wide areas of color alternating with narrow areas, or a wide center color with several narrow stripes on either side.

When a piece of yarn has been woven in, start with a new piece at the place where the other ends. Yarn should never be tied; it creates unsightly lumps. If the yarn is packed down well with the fingers, the tightness will hold the weaving together. When it is completed, the weft ends are cut flush to the weaving and cannot be seen.

If a design is to be worked into the center, sketch a simple shape with a pencil on the cardboard behind the warp as a guide. When the weft reaches this outline it should turn and go back to the edge. Another color of yarn begins at the line and fills in the design, both yarns circling the same warp thread before turning. This is called dove-tailing. Figure 8–14 is a diagram of this process. Using a needle sometimes makes it easier to get between the weft threads (see Figure 8–15).

When the weaving is completed, the loom is turned over and the warp threads cut *in the middle* of the loom. Turn the loom face up again. Starting at the left bottom, release two warp threads and tie them in the overhand knot. See Figure 3–18 for how to make this knot. While the knot is still loose push it up against the weaving before tightening it. Proceed two at a time to tie warp threads until the bottom is completed. Then do the same for the top. The fringe may need to be trimmed, but leave a good length as part of the design so that it doesn't look "chopped off."

Navajo Sand Paintings

Until very recently, Navajo sand paintings were made only as an integral part of a religious cere-

FIGURE 8–17. Two Navajo men create a sand painting, Ganado, Arizona. Collections of the Museum of New Mexico, Santa Fe Railway photograph.

mony to heal the sick or mentally disturbed. Traditionally the Navajo believe that illness is caused by breaking taboos or in some other way being out of tune with the natural world. Tradition says the ceremony was taught to the Dineh (the Navajo word for themselves, which translated means "the People") by the Holy People, or gods, as a method to restore health of body and soul.

To bring a person back in tune with the universe, a medicine man will draw designs on the floor of a hogan (Navajo home), using materials he has gathered from the environment: pollen, crushed flowers, charcoal, pulverized sandstone, and other minerals. First, he spreads clean sand (or occasionally a buckskin) evenly on the floor. Then, with a skill born of many years of practice, the medicine man draws designs by letting these dry materials sift down from his fingers in designs that are traditional for each specific illness. He draws figures that represent the Holy People—elongated, straight-bodied figures. He represents the four directions: north, south, east, and west, and he draws some of the sacred plants: corn, beans, squash, and tobacco. Many other symbols of his natural and spiritual world are used: the bluebird (symbol of happiness), sun, moon, rain, lightning, reptiles. A rainbow, which protects the painting from evil, often surrounds it on all sides except the east.

FIGURE 8–18. Sand painting of a Holyman, by E. Hunt. This is a permanent design, not made for a healing ceremony. Collection of the author.

sun & eagle feathers

snake

lightning

eagle

corn

bluebird

FIGURE 8–19. Some symbols used in Navajo sand paintings.

The paintings range from small to as large as twenty feet in diameter. The biggest require the work of many men and most of a day to complete and are made in a hogan erected especially for that purpose.

Chants are sung for each element of the design as it is being made. They ask for the help of the Holy People and recount long myths about them to keep the stories in the minds of the people. The person to be cured, the family, and many friends gather to take part in the ceremony and gain strength from its performance. They believe that if the ceremony has been correctly performed, the patient will overcome the evil that is causing the illness and will again, in the Navajo words, "walk in beauty." The sacred painting must never be desecrated and therefore the medicine man scatters it to the four winds after the ceremony.

Although modern medical treatments are now available to Navajos, doctors sometimes invite medicine men to perform these ceremonies along with their treatment; doctors increasingly recognize that treating the mind as well as the body is important in helping people overcome illness. In this manner tradition and modern science work together to cure the whole person.

Non-Navajos, observing these ceremonies, used to marvel at the beauty of the sand paintings and wish that they could be preserved. At the urging of museums and for commercial reasons, the Navajos have recently begun making sand paintings on boards, using glue with the sand to make a permanent design. These are created as an art form quite separate from any religious ceremony.

Making Sand Paintings

If sand is available in your own environment, from the beach or at a sand pit, that is the best to use. Otherwise, it must be purchased at a building materials store. It can be colored by pouring a small amount of tempera paint into the sand and kneading it in well with your hands. Spread the sand out on newspapers, and stir occasionally with your hands as it dries to separate all the particles. If the sand

FIGURE 8-20. Eric, eight, drew his design with charcoal on a prepared board. Now he is applying glue to a cloud symbol.

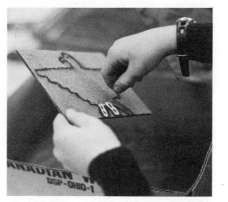

FIGURE 8-21. Sean, nine, has applied glue to the tailfeathers of his eagle design and is sprinkling colored sand on them. After the sand is applied, he will tap the board gently against the box so that loose sand falls back in.

FIGURE 8-22. Eagle design by Stephanie, age eight, includes broken arrow, symbol of peace.

FIGURE 8-23. Snake design by Ellen, age eleven.

paintings are to have the feeling of Navajo work, the colors should be subtle earth colors: the white of limestone, the yellow and brick red of sandstone, gray, black, and turquoise blue. (See color plate 28.) The sand should be separated by color into large, low containers.

Cut a piece of cardboard and paint the entire surface with white glue. Dip this into a container of natural (uncolored) sand, being sure to cover the entire piece. Tap it lightly, letting all unglued grains of sand fall back into the box.

While this sand is drying, work out a design. Students may want to use some of the symbols used by the Indians of the Southwest. The designs are highly stylized rather than realistic.

When the prepared board is dry, sketch the design lightly on the sand with charcoal. With a fine brush, paint a small part of one color area with white glue. Holding the board over one of the containers, drop the appropriate color of sand over the glued area. Tap the edge of the board lightly so that unglued grains fall back into the container. Then paint another small area and follow the same procedure, continuing until the painting is completed. The Navajo paintings are mostly line drawings. The design is beautiful against the natural sand background. This should be pointed out to the students so that they do not overwhelm the background with too much colored sand.

Plains Indian Buffalo Robes and Headdresses

It is hard to imagine the Great Plains of central North America as they were before Europeans came. Many millions of great bison, commonly called buffalo, roamed the prairie. Enormous herds, each numbering in the thousands, grazed peacefully or thundered on their northern and southern migrations. The earliest Indian tribes of the Great Plains area were seminomadic, living much of the year in mud and grass lodges on the edge of the prairie. They were farmers as well as hunters. Later, after horses had been introduced to the Indians by the Spaniards in the South, some groups of Indians became nomadic and followed the buffalo as they migrated. Tribes of at least thirty different language groups lived on the Great Plains.

The lives of all these tribes were dependent on this huge animal, and their cultures reflected its impact on everything they did. The bulk of their diet consisted of buffalo meat, both fresh and dried to last through the winter. The skins were made into coverings for their tipis, a shelter that was beautifully adapted to a nomadic life. Heavy winter skins with the fur left on became warm robes and blankets. Specially cured hides from younger animals became shirts and other clothing. Skins were also used as canvas, to record the history of the tribe and the exploits of war. These were painted with porous buffalo bone brushes and yellow paint from the buffalo gallstones (other pigments were made from minerals and plants). Buffalo ribs made sled

FIGURE 8–24. Engraving of a buffalo by George Catlin.

FIGURE 8–25. *Making the Buffalo Come.* Engraving of a Mandan dance by George Catlin.

runners, the horns became spoons, bones became hoes and hide scrapers, old tough hides became shields and moccasin soles, sinews became rope and thread. Scores of other products were made, too. They used every scrap of the buffalo, and every part of the Indians' lives, from birth through death, was affected by this huge animal. Even the buffalo dung was used for a hot, smokeless campfire in a mostly treeless prairie.

Religious ceremonies often centered around the buffalo. Animals, especially the sacred buffalo, were believed to have spirits that could be influenced through certain rites. There were ceremonies before the hunt to bring good hunting and ceremonies afterwards in thanksgiving. Plentiful as they were, at times the buffalo did not wander close enough to be hunted safely. Many of the Plains Indians tribes were constantly at war with each other, and hunters did not want to venture too far from their own villages. To bring the buffalo closer to the village, the Indians held dances. The nineteenth-century artist, George Catlin, traveled among the Indians and preserved their lives and ways with sketches and paintings. He described a buffalo dance in the Mandan village. Ten or fifteen men of the tribe would start the dance wearing their buffalo headdresses, which included the horns and completely covered their heads (see Figure 8–26). To the accompaniment of drums and rattles, the dancers stamped and pawed the ground, imitating buffalo sounds and movements. They continued without food until they were exhausted. When a dancer dropped because of fatigue, he was "shot" with a blunt arrow and pulled

FIGURE 8–26. Mandan buffalo headdress. Courtesy of the National Museum of Natural History, Smithsonian Institution.

warrior on horseback

tipi

thunderbird

sunburst

bear paw

buffalo

deer

turtle

FIGURE 8–27. A few Plains Indian designs used in decorating buffalo robes, drums, tipis, shields, and other items.

Designing a Buffalo Robe, or "Winter Count"

from the circle by onlookers, who pretended to cut him up for meat. While the exhausted dancer was resting he was replaced by a fresh dancer. The dance continued for days, if necessary, without interruption, until the buffalo were sighted. Figure 8–25, an engraving by Catlin, depicts this dance.

Painting was an important art to most of the Plains Indians, and buffalo skin was the usual canvas. Many tribes painted tipis with designs and historical events. Buffalo robes were decorated on the skin side. A man's robe was often designed with a sunburst or recorded his brave deeds in war. (See color plate 29.) A woman's robe was usually decorated with a geometric design. Some hides, called "winter counts," were kept as a history of the tribe. A symbol represented the most important event that had occurred each year: war, an eclipse of the sun, a smallpox epidemic, peace, or the coming of the white man. These symbols usually started in the center of the hide and spiraled out counterclockwise. Some of the hides record well over 100 years of history.

Because their lives were so entwined with the buffalo, the incredible slaughter of these great animals by the white man—for hides and sometimes just for sport—spelled doom for the Plains Indians. Even had they not been mercilessly pushed into reservations, the Indians' life as they had known it could not have existed without the buffalo. Now a unique life style is gone. What is left to us consists of a few examples of beautifully decorated hides and clothing and finely crafted tools and household items that are now preserved in museums.

However, the young descendants of these tribes are showing a renewed interest in the traditions, in the songs and dances and legends of their people, and a new commitment to the Indian concept of reverence for the land. Perhaps now that many people are truly concerned about saving natural resources, we can at last learn from the original inhabitants of North America how to live in harmony with nature.

Leather can be simulated with heavy brown wrapping paper, brown craft paper, or paper grocery bags.

Tear (do not cut) the shape of a buffalo hide from a large piece of this paper. Make designs with crayons. Indian robes frequently showed historic events, such as wars or buffalo hunts, or designs such as the sunburst of concentric feathered lines or geometric patterns. (See color plate 29.) Or the student can make a winter count of his own life by drawing symbols to represent events that were important each year: birthplace, illness, vacations, siblings born, pets acquired, and so on. The crayon should be put on with heavy pressure. When the drawing is finished, the paper is crumpled up in the hands and immersed in a bucket of water, to which a cup of brown tempera paint has been added. Knead the "hide" gently but thoroughly in the solution. Then remove it and spread it out to dry on newspapers. The crayon work resists the paint and will show well against the leatherlike surface. If it does not show, either the crayoning was too light, or there was too much paint in the solution. It can be rinsed and recrayoned when dry if necessary.

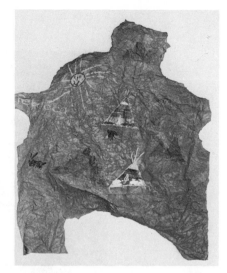

FIGURE 8–28. A brown paper "buffalo robe" by Rebecca, age six.

A headdress can be made with a large grocery shopping bag as a base. Cut the bag at the bottom at an angle, so that the side that will be at the back of the neck when worn will be longer than the front. Tape horns cut from corrugated cardboard to either side of the head. Apply at least three layers of newspaper dipped in wheat paste to the entire surface of the paper and the horns. (See appendix for mixing wheat paste.) To round out the horns, make a mash of sawdust and wheat paste and mold this to the cardboard horns. When the mask is dry, cut holes for eyes and nostrils. (The mask wearer will actually be looking through the nostril holes.) Paint the mask brown with tempera paint. A buffalo has long shaggy hair on top of his head and under his chin. A final touch is to glue excelsior, which has been dipped in brown paint and then dried, to the area between the horns and to the chin.

Buffalo dances are described in several books. Students should accompany the dancers with a drum beat. The Mandan dance described earlier can be used. The dance could end with great rejoicing when

Creating a Buffalo Headdress

FIGURE 8–29. A paper bag is used as a base for a buffalo headdress. On the right, Doug puts layers of newspaper dipped in Metylan (see appendix) on the bag to strengthen it. On the left, Jenny is giving her headdress a coat of brown paint.

several buffalo (nondancers imitating buffalo with their headdresses) appear in the distance.

FIGURE 8–30. A mixture of sawdust and Metylan is applied to a cardboard base to make rounded horns.

FIGURE 8–31. After painting, excelsior is added between the horns and under the chin. The headdresses, piled ready for a dance, look like a buffalo stampede!

FIGURE 8–32. Third-grade students Larkin, David, Amy, and Cynthia performing a buffalo dance.

Woodland Indian Quillwork

Just as the Pueblo Indians used the clay in their environment and the Plains Indians the buffalo, Woodland Indians knew and used their environment with wisdom, respect, and great skill.

There were about thirty major tribes in the area east of the Mississippi and north of what is now

Tennessee. They fell into two major language groups, the Iroquoian and the much larger Algonkian. Although there were variations in culture, they shared many things. Some tribes were primarily hunters and wild food gatherers. Deer and other game provided them much the same range of items as the buffalo provided the Plains Indians. Other tribes did a good deal of farming and raised corn, beans, squash, and pumpkins. Because the region was dominated by woods, the trees, especially the birch, were used for a great variety of products. From the birch came graceful canoes, covers for the wigwams, baskets, cooking pots, decorations for clothing, and cradles. Birch bark even provided material for an unusual pure art form done just for fun: pieces of paper-thin bark were folded several times and bitten along the edges in such a way that when they were opened up, geometric designs and snowflake patterns appeared! Other trees with special properties were used for toboggans, snow shoes, medicines, and even sugar (from maple sap). The Woodland Indians excelled in wood carving, and they produced many fine bowls, ladles, masks, clubs, and ritual objects.

A very fine art, known only in North America, was porcupine quill decoration. How inventive to take the quills of this spikey animal and use them so beautifully! This art, in use for about 200 years before Columbus, probably began in the East. Eventually it spread throughout the Plains, although there the quills had to be obtained from the East by trade. Although the quills are only five inches long and require great skill and patience to work with, large areas of clothing and other items were decorated in this manner.

A porcupine provided as many as 40,000 quills of varying thicknesses. These were plucked, sorted to size, washed, dyed, and the barb removed. By keen observation and experiment, the Indians developed many dyes by boiling plants, bark, and roots. The major colors used in designs were red, black, yellow, and blue, as well as the natural white.

The quills were softened in the mouth or soaked in water and then pulled through the teeth to flatten them. Sometimes the flattening was done with a

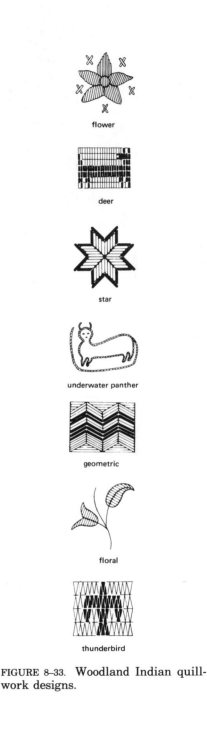

FIGURE 8-33. Woodland Indian quillwork designs.

FIGURE 8–34. Alison is holding a Woodland Indian sweet grass basket. The birch bark cover is decorated with a white porcupine quill floral design.

bone tool. There were many techniques for applying the quills to leather or birch bark: wrapping, in which they were twisted around strips of leather or birch bark; sewing with sinews; plaiting; and weaving on a loom. One method, which used unflattened quills, was to apply designs to birch bark by inserting the quill ends into holes punched in the bark with an awl and bending the ends over on the back (see Figure 8–34). Color plate 30 shows a buckskin bag in which many different quillwork techniques were used, including wrapping, zigzag bands, and sewing.

Two favorite motifs for quillwork designs were the thunderbird and the underwater panther—both spirit animals of great power. The latter was lynx-like; it had a long tail and great knowledge of medicines. Many designs were based on native flowers and leaves or geometric shapes.

The quillwork decorated both men's and women's clothing, moccasins, birch bark boxes, medicine bags, and pouches. Cradle boards for infants were often elaborately decorated. The leather on which the designs were sewn was frequently dyed dark brown or black to emphasize the bright colors of the quills.

The women did the quillwork. They took great pride in decorating clothing for their families. Quillwork was given as gifts during visits to other tribes. A woman gained recognition for her designs and was challenged to do even better. Thus the artists grew in skill, and the complexity of their work increased.

When beads were brought to this area by European explorers and traders, most quillwork was dropped. However, some tribes still make small birch bark and sweet grass boxes decorated with quills.

Making Quill Designs

Porcupine pelts are not readily available for doing quillwork, but flat toothpicks, dyed in various colors, give a similar linear effect.

Food colors make fine dyes. Place the colors in shallow containers and soak flat toothpicks in them until they have absorbed the dye. They should be a shade darker than desired because they will lighten as they dry. Remove the toothpicks and spread them to dry on newspaper.

However, it might give students a greater understanding of Indian art to make dyes from their own environment. Many dyes can be obtained from canned or fresh fruits and vegetables. If there is time to experiment, students should also gather leaves, berries, and flowers from their yards or vacant lots. If wild plants are used, be sure they are not on the endangered species list. Also caution students that many quite ordinary wild and ornamental plants are poisonous and must never be tasted or swallowed. Wash hands after gathering.

Crush the material and bring it to boil in a small amount of water. Boil for about half an hour and test with white paper to see if the dye is strong enough to give a good color. Many plants give no color at all or one other than expected.

Strain the liquid and simmer the toothpicks in this solution until they have taken a shade darker than the desired color. Here are some that work well:

Red: raspberries. Use only the juice drained from canned or frozen berries.

Pink: cranberries. Cook berries, keep them to eat, and use only the liquid.

Rose: beets. Cook and save. Use only liquid for dye.

Orange: onions. Use outside skins, which grocers throw away. Makes a very good dye.

Yellow: marigold flowers.

Green: grass. *Do not boil.* Rub *fresh grass* on toothpicks.

Blue: outer purple cabbage leaves boiled with a rusty nail or piece of iron.

Red-Purple: blueberry juice drained from canned berries.

Blue-Purple: outer purple cabbage leaves.

Brown: black walnut husks. Permanent; be careful of clothes.

These colors may not be very stable (they may fade in time). The Indians knew various natural mor-

FIGURE 8–35. Reinder, eleven, places a glued toothpick in position on his headband.

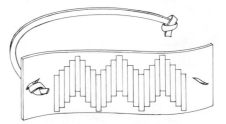

FIGURE 8–36. Diagram of a wristband with toothpick quill design. Toothpicks must be at right angles to the curve of the wristband, as here, or they may break. A leather thong, knotted at the ends, holds the wristband on.

FIGURE 8–37. Topher, eight, with his "quilled" leather wristband.

FIGURE 8–38. Reinder's headband is a striking design of red, blue, yellow, and green geometric shapes.

FIGURE 8–39. In Dawn's pendant, bright quills radiate from the center.

FIGURE 8–40. A pendant with a thunderbird design, by John, age ten.

dants that set the colors permanently. After simmering the toothpicks in the dye, spread them to dry on newspapers.

Many leather craft stores sell bags of scrap

leather at a very reasonable price. From these scraps, cut small pendant shapes, wristbands, head-bands, or chokers. Students should study examples of Indian designs—geometric, and animal, flower, and leaf shapes—and work out a design on paper. The dried toothpicks are then cut or broken in the desired lengths (try to match them by width; they taper at one end) and glued in place with white glue. A piece of leather that is to be curved while worn (such as a wristband, choker, or headband) must have the toothpicks glued in a position that is at right angles to the direction of the curve, or they will break when the leather bends. Bands may be tied by cutting thin strips of leather into thongs. Make a small cut at an angle in each end of the band, insert the leather thongs, and knot them at the ends (see Figure 8–36). Either leave two loose ends to tie, or make one thong the exact length needed with a knot at each end. Keep one end of the thong knotted in one end of the band, and "but-ton" the other end into the other slot each time it is to be worn.

For many centuries before the Europeans came to America, Woodland Indians made beads for personal adornment. They were made from natural materi-als: stone, fossils, bone, shell, copper, and pearls from fresh water clams. These materials were shaped and pierced as necessary. Beads were also made of bear teeth, and pendants were created from engraved shale.

The most well-known of the Indian beads is called wampum (a shortening of an Algonquin word). These beads were made by shaping and drilling quahog clam shells. They were cylindrical in shape and were both white and, less commonly, purple. They were considered very valuable, and used for many pur-poses beside adornment: in burial rituals, for ex-change at the making of treaties, as a document during the sale of property, and as history belts (with designs symbolic of important happenings worked into the beads).

When glass beads became available through trade with Europeans during the mid-seventeenth cen-tury, they replaced most of the hand-made beads.

Woodland Indian Beadwork

FIGURE 8–41. Woodland Indian bead-work. From left, beadwork sash, Chip-pewa, Wisconsin, circa 1890; heddle-woven bead sash, Potawatomi Reser-vation, Kansas, circa 1885; beadwork garter, Chippewa, Wisconsin-Minne-sota, circa 1890. Courtesy of the Chan-dler-Pohrt Collection.

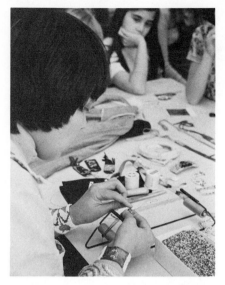

FIGURE 8–42. Joyce Tinkham, Native American, demonstrating beadwork to a sixth-grade class. She is wearing wide beaded wristbands of floral design.

FIGURE 8–43. Joyce explains the technique to Staci while Kathy watches.

They were made into necklaces and used instead of porcupine quill work in decorating clothing. Many of the same design motifs were used, but the beads allowed for both a wider range of colors and more intricate designs.

Beads were sewn onto clothing and they were also woven into colorful bands on looms. There were three types of looms: a simple wooden frame, a bow which held the warp taut, and a belt loom. The women used thread and needles that were also obtained from the trader. With the looms they made belts, garters, headbands, chokers, and bands to be applied to clothing. See color plate 31.

Beadwork came to be done by Indians throughout most of North America. Each tribe had characteristic designs, which used symbols meaningful to them, although there was also some borrowing of designs. The Woodland Indians were noted for fine naturalistic floral and leaf patterns.

Making Indian Beadwork

A loom can be made from any box. An ideal shape, however, is a cardboard container that is frequently used for holding fruit in the markets. It has two higher ends on which to wrap the warp, and lower longer sides, which makes access to weaving easier. They measure approximately 6 x 8 inches. If another box is used, cut the two longer sides lower.

You will need nylon thread for a good strong warp. When wrapping the warp around the box, make an even number of warp threads—this enables you to have an odd number of beads and consequently a center line in your design. The warping thread is wrapped firmly around the box and spaced slightly farther apart than the width of the beads. Wrap the warp close to the left side of the loom. This leaves a space at the right. Beads can then be kept in the bottom of the loom and picked up to the right of the band being woven. Secure the two ends of the warp by tying them together on the back of the loom.

Before beginning, work out a design with crayons and graph paper ruled in ¼-inch squares. It will be much larger than the beadwork and easy to follow. For the beginner a design nine beads wide (ten warp threads) and fifty to sixty beads long is sufficient to make a small wristband. Simple geometric designs that repeat are easiest for beginners. See Figure 8–45.

Beads are available in several sizes. Be sure they are of uniform size, because mixed sizes in the same

FIGURE 8–44. Cathy works on her cardboard bead loom. If the warp threads are wound on the left side of the loom, beads can be picked up to the right.

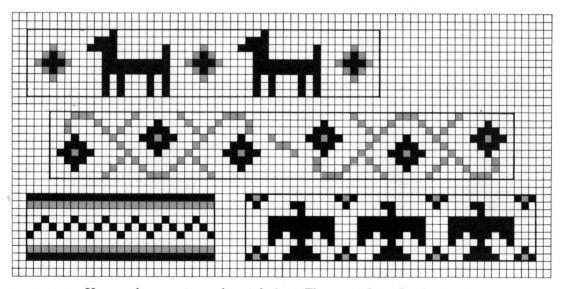

FIGURE 8–45. Use graph paper to work out designs. These are deer, floral, geometric, and thunderbird designs based on modified Woodland Indian beadwork designs.

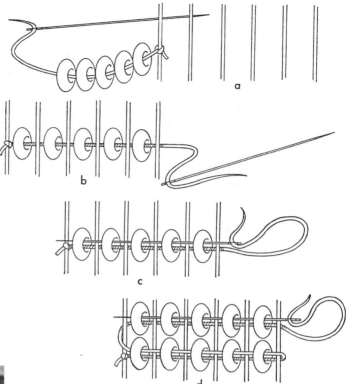

FIGURE 8–46. Diagram of the beading process.

FIGURE 8–47. Adam holds the beads in place with a finger of his left hand, while his right hand pushes the needle through on *top* of the threads.

piece cause bumpiness. Put the beads in a small shallow container or in the bottom of the loom itself.

After the loom is warped, thread a beading needle (available where beads are sold) and tie the end of the thread to the first warp thread on the left. (If you are left-handed, reverse this to the right side.) Follow your pattern and pick up the first row of beads by putting the point of the needle into one and tipping it up to let the bead fall to the base of the needle. Continue until all the beads of the first row are on the needle. Check to see that they are in the right order. Push the beads on the thread down to where it is attached to the warp, pass the thread and needle *under* the warp (Figure 8–46a), and push the beads up in the spaces between each warp thread (Figure 8–46b). Hold them there with the left forefinger. Bring the needle up to the top of the warp and pass it back through the beads (from right to left) *on top of the warp threads,* to the other side (Figure 8–46c). New beads are picked up and the same process followed (Figure 8–46d) until the pattern is completed. After finishing the last row, tie the thread to the outer warp thread and pass the end back through the beads in the row above.

When the beading is finished cut it from the loom, leaving at least two inches of warp threads. Take the threads of one end between the thumb and forefinger, twist them into a chord, and pull them to the back of the beadwork, securing them with a piece of masking tape. Do this on both ends, and tape the entire back of the beadwork to give it some firmness.

Leather scraps may be obtained from leatherworking shops. Be sure that they are soft enough to pass a sewing needle through easily. Place the beadwork on a strip of leather, leaving one half inch or more of leather at either end for attaching thongs. Sew the beadwork to the leather using an overcast stitch, bringing the needle up inside the outer warp thread and down around the leather edge. Sew all four sides of the beadwork. Felt can be used if leather cannot be obtained.

You can secure the wristbands in any number of ways, as Figure 8–48 illustrates: by using thongs and slits, commercial snaps, or buttons and buttonholes.

The last group of people to cross the Bering Strait and settle on the North American continent spread across the area that stretches from the Aleutian Islands in the west across the Artic to eastern Greenland. By outsiders they are called Eskimos, an Indian name meaning "eats raw flesh." However, the people of the Canadian Eastern Arctic prefer to be called Inuit, which in their language means "the people." In their small, isolated groups in that vast land of snow and ice and tundra, they frequently spent their lives without seeing any other inhabitants of the continent.

Two thousand years ago there were two main cultural groups, the Dorset and the Thule. These prehistoric tribes left evidence in the form of tools and artifacts that lead anthropologists to believe their culture was much like that of early historic times,

FIGURE 8–48. Sixth-grade beaded wristbands made by (top to bottom) Adam, Katya, Jenny, Nicola, Annette, and Kamala.

Inuit Stone Sculpture and Printmaking

FIGURE 8–49. *Bird,* by Isa Smilen, and *Seal,* by Joe Adamie Tuki, both from Inoucdjouac Co-op, on the East bank of Hudson Bay. Courtesy of Denali Arts, Inc., Ann Arbor, Michigan.

FIGURE 8–50. *Polar Bear,* by Niviaksiak, Cape Dorset, Baffin Island. From the collection of Eugene B. Power.

although more primitive. They were seasonal hunters; in the summer they lived on the land, fishing and hunting caribou and musk ox. In the winter they lived on the sea ice, hunting seal and walrus. The Thule were great whale hunters. Every man carved in ivory and stone in order to survive. Things were always made for a specific purpose: harpoons, knives, and tools. These were sometimes incised with lines that enhanced the shape. Saucers and lamp bowls were also carved from soft stone, and driftwood was carved into dramatic masks probably used in religious ceremonies.

The Dorset people made very small, smooth carvings from the tusks of narwhale and walrus and from seal teeth. The carvings were made with stone tools and were highly polished. These tiny, beautiful pieces were probably magical in purpose (for instance, to ensure good hunting). Worn as amulets, they depicted birds, walrus, bear, and other game.

The Inuit of those earliest days (and until recent times) lived in very small groups to increase their chances of successful hunting. Theirs was a barren and cold climate. Survival meant very hard work in the best of times, and they had to face starvation when storms or other disasters made hunting unsuccessful. And yet the Inuit seem to have had a warm and joyous spirit to share with those who have traveled among them. They endured long stretches of deprivation but took much pleasure in each other's company when bad times were over. They appreciated the stark beauty of their land. How much more joy the summer sun brings when it barely clears the horizon in the long dark winters! Animals were not merely adversaries or food—they were fellow inhabitants of the land. They were killed only when needed and then thanked for giving their lives. Atonement was sometimes made in some symbolic way.

In the nineteenth century, as contact with the outside world grew more frequent, changes began taking place. They did not face the defeat and removal to reservations experienced by the Indians to the south. The Inuit alone had the skills to survive successfully in the Arctic. White men who came as explorers frequently had to rely on the Inuit for survival. Rather, their lives were changed by the gradual encroachment of different cultures (Russian, Danish, Canadian, and American); new diseases (the common cold caused the death of thousands); and dwindling game. Some Inuit began living in larger settlements, often relying on government support to survive.

When different cultures begin to come together, new life styles begin to form. Inuit in some areas still hunt in the old ways, but they may use guns and gasoline-powered vehicles instead of harpoons and dog sleds. Some skills, such as carving, which were once developed only for their own use and pleasure, are now used for a new economic base to supplement hunting and trapping. At the same time, their carving gives great pleasure to countless numbers of people in other parts of the world.

This development of producing sculpture to sell began in 1948. James Houston, traveling on the coast of Hudson Bay, noticed some Inuit carvings in stone and felt there could be a market for them. The Canadian Handicrafts Guild sent Houston to Cape Dorset on Baffin Island in 1951 to encourage the Inuit in this endeavor. This was a new idea to them, since the Inuit had always carved in the past for a useful purpose. They had made objects to be used as tools or as ornaments for clothing, to be turned over in the hand and seen from every angle— not be be put in one stationary place and admired. Houston stayed at Cape Dorset for ten years, and over that period of time the sculptures became well known in the United States and Canada.

In the United States this was due in large part to Eugene Power, who in 1953 established a nonprofit organization, Eskimo Art Incorporated, which arranged with the Smithsonian to have a traveling exhibit of sculpture sent to museums throughout the country. This exhibit developed an interest in the carvings and a demand for them.

Although the concept of making artworks for sale was new to the Inuit, their sculpture is imbued with a completely Inuit feeling for animals, a remarkable capturing of the spirit of the bear or seal or bird portrayed. The sculptures of people show a deep affection for family life and relationships: for times of pleasure, times of backbreaking work, and times of incredible patience in hunting. The skillful carving is done with great sensitivity to form and respect for the solid quality of the stone. In the best of them, the forms as in the ancient ivory carvings, seem less to be imposed on the stone than discovered and revealed in it. The Inuit do not have a preconceived idea of what they are going to carve; they let the grain and structure of each individual stone suggest what is to be brought out.

In 1957 a new technique, printmaking, was introduced at Cape Dorset, and again the Inuit used this medium to express their own feelings in art. Two methods are used. In the first, large slabs of stone are cut and polished to a flat surface. A previously drawn design is transferred to the surface of the stone. Then the stone is chiseled away, leaving the design raised in relief. Ink is rolled onto this surface, paper is laid on and rubbed with the hands or a sealskin barren, and then lifted off. In this way as many as fifty prints are made from one design.

Another method, adapted from the Inuit craft of cutting designs out of seal skin for appliqué work, is to make stencils. Originally, designs were cut in flat, stretched pieces of sealskin. Ink was then daubed through the holes cut in this stencil to make

FIGURE 8–51. *Polar Bear and Cub in Ice,* by Niviaksiak, Cape Dorset, Baffin Island, June 1959. A print made from a sealskin stencil. It is unusual in that the bears are created in negative space—the ink is applied only to the water and small details on the bears. From the collection of Eugene B. Power. Copyright 1959. Reproduced by permission of the West Baffin Eskimo Co-operative Limited, Cape Dorset, Canada.

the designs on the paper placed underneath. (See color plate 32.) Now the Inuit use paper prepared with wax for the stencils so that seals will not have to be killed for this purpose.

Frequently the prints are visual representations of spirit forms. In Inuit mythology, animal and human forms and activities fuse, and the prints often show these spirits that inhabit the sea and the land.

The prints are designed by both men and women, but men usually cut the stones and apply the inks for printing. The prints and sculpture made at Cape Dorset are now sold by the Inuit through their own cooperative organization. Several other Inuit communities, such as those at Holman Island, Baker Lake, Port Harrison, Povungnituk, Lake Harbour, and Pangnirtung, are also producing art.

The Inuit use soapstone, whalebone, and other materials in their environment for carving their sculpture. In the urban environment it is sometimes possible to find an artificial sandstone, which makes a fine medium for young students to carve. If there

Carving Artificial Sandstone

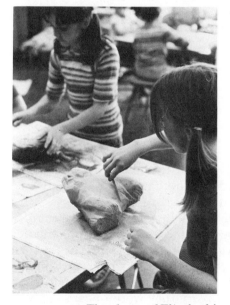

FIGURE 8–52. The shape of Elizabeth's sandstone suggested a bear, and she is bringing out the shape by scraping with a pair of scissors.

FIGURE 8–53. Jeannie uses sandpaper to smooth her sculpture of a bird.

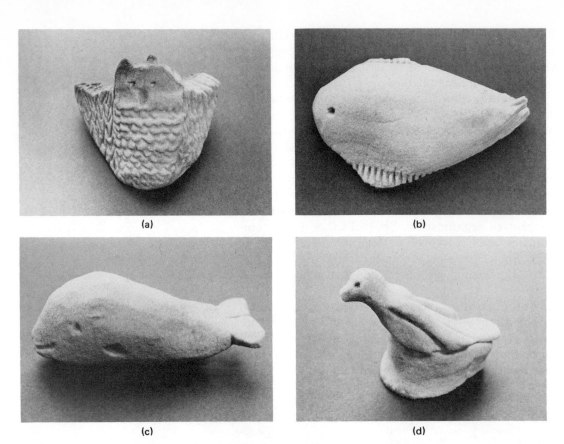

FIGURE 8–54 *a, b, c, d.* Some fourth-grade sandstone sculptures. *(a) Owl,* by Laura; *(b) Fish,* by Lisa; *(c) Whale,* by Masashi; *(d) Bird,* by Jeannie.

is a metal casting foundry in the area, it may use a process that makes molds out of a manmade sandstone. After the molten metal has been poured into these molds and cooled, the mold sand is broken away and discarded. Most foundaries are only too glad to have it put to creative use.

The mold sand will be in many irregular chunks. If the chunks are too large, saw them into smaller pieces. Before proceeding, the student should turn his piece and view it carefully from every angle. The ancient Inuit believed there was a form already inside the piece of ivory they were to carve. It was only to be discovered and released. The success of the final piece may be in this initial process of looking at the form and being in tune with what it suggests. The mold sand can be carved easily with table knives, forks, or other tools. In fact, it can be carved too easily. It should be *gently* scraped to bring out the form. It is easy to take too much off at once—and there's no putting it back.

Place the mold sand on a pad of newspaper. As the sand accumulates from scraping, dump it into a wastebasket at regular intervals or it will soon be tracked around the workroom. Lines can be etched in the sculpture with a nail. The piece should be lightly smoothed with fine sandpaper. To prevent sand from coming off the surface of the finished sculpture, seal it with a coat of shellac or fixative spray.

Older children (from sixth to ninth grades) may find it more challenging to work in a harder medium. Plaster alone or mixed with vermiculite may be a better choice for them.

To mix the plaster follow the directions given in the appendix. For texture, and to make the material a little easier to carve, you may want to add vermiculite to the plaster—stir in up to one-third of the total volume. The plaster can then be poured into waxed cardboard milk containers or better yet, since it will produce more natural shapes, into plastic bags. If you pour the plaster into plastic bags, you can shape the form slightly as the plaster sets. Let it harden overnight and remove the plaster from the containers.

Then turn the piece of plaster and look at it from all sides to see what forms are suggested by the shape. Carve on newspaper, and dump the scrapings frequently in some container. Plaster dust can create an unbelievable mess! Many different tools can be used. A hammer and chisel can be used for cutting a rough form. The flat, oval shaped linoleum cutting tool works very well in carving the plaster. Files and rasps can also be used if the plaster is thoroughly dry (if it is damp, it will clog the files). However, carving with a linoleum tool is made easier by very quickly running the sculpture under water. This softens the plaster somewhat and makes it less dusty to work with. After roughing out the form, work closer and closer to the final shape. Try to

Plaster Carving

FIGURE 8–55. Plaster carvings by sixth-grade students: *Whale,* by Mike; *Seal,* by Jason; and *Kayak,* by John.

make the sculpture interesting from every angle, not just one side. Also, if the students study some examples of Inuit work, they will realize that the sculptures keep the solidity of the stone; the Inuit make no attempt to carve delicate, spindly shapes. Minor holes and mistakes may be corrected by mixing a small amount of plaster and applying it to the area, which should be dampened first.

Tools used in carving plaster should be thoroughly cleaned after use, because plaster is highly corrosive to metal.

When the carving is completed it should be sanded with fine sandpaper until as smooth as possible. Then it can be given a coat of liquid black shoe polish. It may need a second coat. This will give a smooth, slightly shiny black surface. Inuit soapstone sculpture is rubbed with oil, which gives the stone a smooth black surface. In the final step, carefully add a few details, such as eyes or flipper lines, by cutting through the black surface to the white plaster beneath with a nail or pin.

Printmaking

Carving a stone block for printing is a long and tedious process. But students can create their design in relief by a different method. First, study Inuit prints and get a feeling for the subject matter. It ranges from superbly delineated birds and animals that are easily identified to supernatural animal spirits that often combine human and animal characteristics. Some are very humorous, some quite frightening, and others radiate wild beauty.

After a student has drawn a design on paper, he or she should transfer it to a smooth piece of rubber innertubing (another item to be found in our urban environment). This can be done by thoroughly chalking the underside of the design, which turns it into a kind of white carbon paper. Place the design, chalky side down, on the piece of rubber and trace over the design with a pencil, pressing firmly. Then cut out the shape with scissors. Some interior design lines may be made by cutting off a portion, such as a wing, and then placing it slightly away from the body so that a line or space will be formed when printing. (See the wings on the birds in Figure 8–63.) Eyes may be made with a hole puncher.

FIGURE 8–56. Dawn, age ten, applies ink with a brayer.

FIGURE 8–57. Inking bare spots (caused by depressions in the rubber) with a finger.

FIGURE 8–58. She places the paper on the inked block and rubs it vigorously.

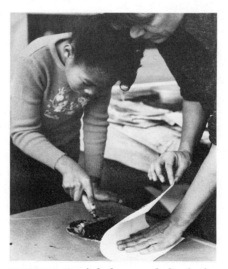

FIGURE 8–59. Dawn checks to see if the block was well inked and the print is good.

FIGURE 8–60. A helper peels back the paper so that more ink may be applied to the block.

FIGURE 8–61. Dawn examines her finished print.

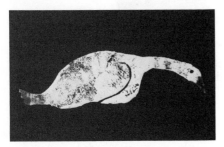

FIGURE 8–62. *Goose,* by Dana, nine. A second color was blended into the beak and tail before printing.

FIGURE 8–63. *Birds,* a print by Sarah, ten.

After the piece has been cut out, glue it to cardboard with white glue to make a printing block. One side of the rubber may have ridges or texture; be sure this is glued down and the smoothest surface is up.

After the block is thoroughly dry, cut away any extra cardboard, leaving only a small edge around the rubber. This will make it easier to keep all the ink on the rubber when you are inking the block.

Squeeze out some waterbase printing ink onto a flat surface. A floor tile or piece of window glass is fine. With a brayer, roll the ink until it forms an even, slightly sticky surface that "crackles" as the brayer passes over it.

With the inked brayer, apply ink to the raised rubber design, being careful not to get any on the cardboard base (Figure 8–56). If the rubber is not completely flat, there may be depressions that don't receive the ink. In that case apply the ink with your index finger. First pat the finger up and down in the ink and then use the same *up and down* motion on the rubber (smearing back and forth will give a different surface texture than the rest of the block) (Figure 8–57).

Place the paper to be printed on the inked block. Rub the paper carefully with the side of the hand (or the smooth bowl of a spoon), feeling for every part of the block (Figure 8–58). Check to see if you have rubbed enough by holding the paper firmly at the bottom and peeling down only the top half (Figure 8–59). Then replace the top and peel back the bottom. If you need more ink, add some while a helper peels back half the print at a time (Figure 8–60). It is better to work this way than to discard poorly made prints. Once the paper has been lifted completely, it is not possible to replace it accurately.

Many prints may be taken from one block. You can create interesting colors by rolling a new color over the first one on the block. If an entirely new color is desired, the block should be cleaned with a damp cloth only (washing in water will disintegrate the cardboard). A more permanent block can be made using a waterproof glue and a wood base.

Some of the Inuit prints are a solid color. Others grade one color into another. This adds a texture and emphasis of form. Students can add an area of color by blending a second color into the edge of the first with the brayer or with their index fingers.

Sometimes the block is effective if it is printed several times on one piece of paper to form a group, such as a school of fish or a flock of birds (see Figure 8–64).

FIGURE 8–64. *Narwhals,* by Mike, ten. One block was printed three times to make this group.

Wherever there are children, there will be dolls. When the early settlers came to North America, they made dolls for their children from materials they found in their new environment: there were dolls made of twigs, corn cobs and corn husks; dolls made of straw, of wood, and of nuts. These materials were supplemented with precious scraps of cloth and rags from old clothing.

The Indians already living on this continent also made dolls for their children, sometimes to instruct them in the names and attributes of their gods and sometimes for play. Young Indian girls learned to make and decorate clothing by dressing their dolls. The Iroquois Indians, living in what is now the northeastern part of the United States and Canada, made doll-like figures (thought to have been created for sacred rituals) that used dried apples for heads. The early settlers learned this art from the Indians.

Although the bodies were made in many different ways, the significant part of this kind of doll was the head, which was made from a carved apple. As the apple dried, it softened and wrinkled into amazingly lifelike expressions, especially of old age. The applehead doll became a tradition with early settlers and was made in many parts of Canada and America, especially in New England and Appalachia. Ap-

EARLY AMERICAN FOLK ARTS

Applehead Dolls

FIGURE 8–65. Applehead doll made by Mrs. Leah Rae Greenberg, Toronto, Ontario. Exhibited at the *In Praise of Hands Exhibition,* Ontario Science Centre, Toronto, 1974. From the collection of Leah Rae Greenberg.

plehead dolls have become popular again in recent years and are made by many craftspeople, less as dolls for children to play with than as finely crafted dolls made only for display. They are a reminder of the past when dolls were not mass-produced in factories and advertized on television but lovingly made by hand by a father or mother, an aunt or a grandmother, to fit the needs of a particular child.

Making Applehead Dolls

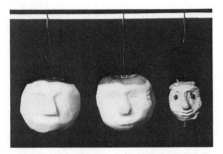

FIGURE 8–66. Stages in making an applehead. From left to right: the first step is to carve the nose by cutting a triangular shape and making flat planes on either side of it. In the center apple, the nose has been refined, eye area deepened, and slits cut in for eyes. "Crows-feet" add a twinkle to the eye. A slit has been cut for the mouth, and ears have been carved on the side of the head. The third apple was dried for over three weeks.

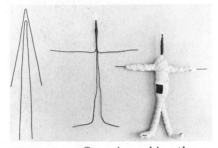

FIGURE 8–67. Steps in making the applehead doll body. Two pieces of wire, one 20 and one 13 inches, are bent in half. They are taped together at the neck and the arms and legs bent out. Then the wire is wrapped with crepe paper or rags secured with tape.

Choose a large apple and peel it, leaving some skin around the stem and blossom ends. Make as smooth a surface as possible. Carve a face into the apple, beginning with the nose: with the point of the knife make a triangular cut in the middle of the apple about ¼ inch deep. Cut a flat plane on either side of this to bring the nose out. Cut out a piece underneath the nose also (see the apple on the left in Figure 8–66). Gently soften the lines of the nose by scraping it with the knife. Deepen the eye cavities to create a brow, and make a slit for each eye. Scraping three lines that radiate out from the eyes will make laughter lines or "crows-feet." As with the eyes, cut just a slit for the mouth, about ⅛ inch deep, either straight or curved in a smile. As it dries, it will open up. You can make a lower lip by scraping a shallow line parallel to and beneath the mouth. Ears may be carved in the side of the head, although this is unnecessary if hair is to cover that part of the apple. The middle apple in Figure 8–66 shows one in which the carving has just been completed. The third apple has dried for over three weeks.

If you wish the apple to remain a light color, immerse the head in lemon juice for a few minutes to prevent it from turning dark. Hang the apple up to dry by poking a wire through it, from the bottom to the top. Bend over an inch of wire on the bottom so that the apple will not slip off, bend a hook in the top, and hang it over a line. After it is hung up, sprinkle it heavily with salt to hasten the drying and prevent the growth of mold. You will need to lay newspaper underneath to catch the drips.

The apple takes three to four weeks to dry, depending on the humidity in the air. Do not hang it in direct sun, but do hang the apple where you can see it, because it is fascinating to watch the slow changes taking place in the figure you have carved. After the first week or two, the apple will become somewhat pliable. Using your fingers, pinch the nose, cheeks, and chin a little more to your liking.

The hands should be cut from another apple, which has been cut in ½-inch slices. Cut mitten shapes at least twice as large as you want for the final size. Dip them in lemon juice and sprinkle them well with salt. Set them to dry by inserting toothpicks or short lengths of wire into the apple pieces and sticking the other ends into corrugated cardboard or styrofoam. After they have dried for three or four days, they will become like soft leather, and the fingers can be cut into the mitten shape with scissors.

While the applehead is drying, the rest of the doll can be made. The body is made over an armature of wire. Take two lengths of 18 gauge wire, one twenty inches long and one thirteen inches long, and bend them in half. (See Figure 8–67.) Next, place these bent wires together. Pinch the ends at the bend with pliers to make the bend as sharp as possible, and then wrap them together with plastic electrical tape for 1½ inches to form a neck. Spread up the shorter wire to make arms, separate the legs, and bend up the feet. Finally, wrap the arms and body with strips of crepe paper or rags to fill out the shape. Secure the ends of the wrapping with tape. Leave the neck and ends of the arms unwrapped. Wrap down one leg and out the foot almost to the end. Bend the last ¼ inch of wire and clamp it with pliers against the wrapping to keep it from slipping off the foot, and then wrap back up the leg to the body. Secure the end of the wrapping with tape, and do the other leg in the same way.

To make clothing, use scraps of material appropriate to the character you have in mind. Follow the diagram for marionette clothes in Figure 4–42. Shoes may be made from scraps of leather glued to the padded feet.

When the head has dried, put it on the doll by pushing it down over the wire neck. First, remove

FIGURE 8–68. Applehead dolls by Kreig, twelve, and Lisa, ten. Kreig cut the hat from scraps of leather. Lisa's lady wears a tiny yellow flower in her hair.

FIGURE 8–69. Gandalf the wizard, by Hudson, age eleven.

the wire it was hung on and enlarge the hole in the apple, if necessary, with the point of a scissors or a nail. Put glue on the neck before inserting it. Glue the ends of the arm wires also and insert them into the hands. Whole cloves are pushed in for eyes. Hair may be made from cotton, untwisted yarn, or fleece. Eyeglasses can be shaped of thin wire and secured by poking the wire ends into the head under the hair. Such details as jewelry, hats, ties, and pipes add to the realism of the doll.

An applehead doll is even more interesting if it appears to be engaged in some activity, such as playing a musical instrument, knitting, or walking with a dog. Students can use all kinds of scrap materials to make chairs, books, knitting needles, guitars, or other miniature items.

Scrimshaw

The art of scrimshaw, carving in whalebone and ivory, was practiced by most of the sailors that went on the long sea voyages searching for whales. Carving in ivory certainly was not new. It had been done for centuries by people all over the world with the ivory of elephants, hippopotami, walrus, and whales. But scrimshaw is a nautical term, and it applies to the art as practiced by the whalemen in the eighteenth and nineteenth centuries.

FIGURE 8-70. Scrimshawed whale's tooth made by E. C. Starbuck for his uncle, Captain E. Smith, circa 1840. Courtesy of the Whaling Museum, New Bedford, Massachusetts.

The colonists first engaged in whaling in the middle 1600s. Whales were valued for their oil (for lamps) and for their meat. When a whale was sighted from the land, men put out in small boats to harpoon the animal and bring it ashore. These were baleen whales. *Baleen* is the name for the long strips of flexible material (not bone but more like the composition of fingernails) that hung down in their mouths, acting as food strainers and collecting small marine life from the ocean. Baleen, discarded at first, was later used for scrimshaw and also for many other articles, especially corset stays.

It wasn't until the 1700s (when the search for the sperm whale, which ranged much farther out to sea, brought about deep sea whaling) that scrimshaw began to flourish. It is an excellent example of an art arising from the materials at hand. This whale was much sought after, because it had more and better oil. It also had teeth, which the baleen whales did not. Because it was not of commercial value, this ivory was used by the whalemen to make scrimshaw. By the late eighteenth century, great whaling ships from New England went out all over the world. They stayed out until all their barrels were full of oil—often several years. There were long boring stretches of time when the sailors' work was done and there were no whales in sight. This time was often filled with making items from the whale teeth and bones. Made captive on their ship by the sea, the artist-prisoners whittled and carved and sawed beautiful items of great variety either to give to their loved ones when they returned or to use themselves.

The fine example of scrimshaw illustrated in Figure 8–70 includes a poem that gives ample evidence of the homesickness and boredom that afflicted many sailors, young and old:

While on the seas my days are spent,
In anxious care oft discontent,
No social circles here are found,
Few friends to virtue here abound,
I think of home, sweet home, denied
With her I love near by my side.

When will kind fortune set me free,
That I can quit the boisterous sea,
I love my friends, I love the shore,
I long to leave the oceans roar,
Then home sweet home shall be my pride
With her I love near by my side.

Perhaps these feelings were alleviated somewhat when the sailors became absorbed in their intricate, time-consuming art. The teeth were smoothed to a satin polish and then incised with fine drawings. These designs were perhaps most frequently whaling scenes, but they also portrayed birds, fish, flowers, romantic recollections of home, and political events.

Scrimshaw also refers to more sculptural pieces made of the ivory or whalebone: tools (pie crimpers, knitting needles, thimbles, handles for silverware), toys and games (such as chess pieces), letter openers, boxes, baskets, canes, and candlesticks. Some of the loveliest engraving was done on corset stays.

Whale teeth are deeply ridged. These ridges first had to be whittled, scraped, and sanded smooth by the scrimshander (one who makes scrimshaw). Sharkskin, glued to a piece of wood, made a good sandpaper. When the tooth was smooth and polished to a fine finish, it was engraved. A design was worked out first on paper, the paper was placed on the tooth, and the design was transferred by lightly pricking along the lines with a pin. Sometimes the design was drawn on freehand. Sailmakers' awls and needles, sharpened to a fine point, were used to engrave the lines. When done, the lines were emphasized by filling them with pigments—lampblack could be made aboard ship, and sometimes other pigments were purchased and brought on board to use. The sculptured objects, such as pie crimpers and chess pieces, needed more equipment. The most used tool was the jackknife, with which the sailors could do very delicate carving. Fine saws, small hammers and chisels, and even in some cases hand-powered lathes were also used. The sailing ships touched at ports all over the world, and fine woods were also used in combination with the whalebone and ivory. Beautiful writing desks and inlaid boxes were made of these materials.

So thorough were the whaling ships in their pursuit of oil that whales became very scarce. The discovery of petroleum probably came just in time to save them from extinction. However, they are still hunted and several species are endangered. International efforts are now being made to protect them.

The art of making scrimshaw, so much a part of the life on board the sailing ships, declined rapidly. But some artists today have revived the art. They use ivory from other sources, and since most other ivory-bearing animals should also be protected, they are always looking for substitute materials. One such material is ivory nuts from the South American ivory palm tree. When the nuts are baked, they become hard and closely resemble ivory.

The engraving on scrimshaw is incredibly fine and takes a good deal of patience. Making a pendant-sized piece is a good introduction to the art. Plaster can substitute for ivory. Mix the plaster as described in the appendix. Using a teaspoon, drop spoonfuls of plaster on waxed paper. The plaster pieces should dry for a day or two, being turned over occasionally after they are hard.

Sand the plaster to a pleasing smoothness, taking off any bumps or irregularities. With a ¼-inch drill bit, drill a hole at the top. (A rotary hand drill can be used, but too much pressure on it may crack the plaster. A power drill is better but should be operated by a parent or teacher.) Sand again, using the finest available sandpaper.

Next, draw around the plaster on a piece of paper, so that you can work out several designs to fill that particular shape. After drawing around the plaster, give the plaster two coats of white shellac. Let the first dry well before applying the second. While waiting for the shellac to dry work on your designs. You may want to use a nautical theme, but subject matter of all kinds was used by the scrimshanders. Remember that the lines are very fine and you will want lots of details—perhaps rows and rows of little waves or flower designs with delicate leafy vines.

After choosing one of your designs, copy it onto the shellacked and dried plaster with a pencil. Mistakes can be erased and redrawn. Then, using a pin or a small nail with a sharpened point (sharpen by rubbing at an angle on a whet stone), engrave the design into the plaster. When the design has been engraved, blow off any accumulated plaster dust.

The whalemen used lampblack to darken the engraved lines, and that is easy to do. Light a candle

Making Plaster Scrimshaw

FIGURE 8–71. Ricky engraves his plaster pendant with a sharpened nail, while John R. collects soot from a candle flame by holding a ceramic tile over it. He will rub the soot into his engraving.

FIGURE 8–72. Plaster scrimshaw pendants. From left to right: by Jack, John P., Lisa, and Alison, fifth-grade students.

and hold a ceramic tile or white ceramic saucer just above the tip of the flame. Soot will accumulate on it. (Observe safety precautions with the candle. It should be in a secure holder, preferably on a large sheet of metal. Keep papers away and don't leave it lighted while unattended.) It is difficult to rub the dry soot down into the engraved lines, so it should be mixed with a little cooking oil. Simply rub your finger in the soot and then into a little dab of oil, mix them together, and then rub this mixture into the engraved design. Make more lampblack as it is needed. Because the plaster has been shellacked, the lampblack will come off the surface with a clean cloth, staying only in the lines. Use a leather thong, ribbon, or piece of yarn to complete the pendant.

APPENDIX

SOME COMMON PROCESSES

Papier Mâché

The basic method for making objects of papier mâché is simply to apply paste to torn pieces of paper and press them onto a base.

The base may be constructed of boxes, tubes, cardboard, or rolled or bunched newspaper. These items can be used separately or combined and taped together into a new shape. Or the base may be a blown-up balloon (to create a spherical shape) or a plastic bowl or container. In the latter case the bowl should be given a light coat of petroleum jelly so that it can be removed easily after the papier mâché has dried.

Wheat paste, which is most commonly used for making papier mâché, is available at wallpaper stores and craft supply stores. Sift the dry paste into a bowl of water while constantly stirring the mixture, until it reaches a smooth, thickened, creamy consistency. Mix only what is needed for the project at hand; it does not keep well.

There is a new product, called Metylan, which can be used instead of the traditional wheat paste. It has the advantage of keeping indefinitely. It is mixed in the same manner as wheat paste, but it has to set fifteen minutes before being used. For strong papier mâché, mix Metylan using somewhat less water than is suggested on the package. It is used in the same manner as the wheat paste.

Apply the wheat paste or Metylan to both sides of *torn* pieces of newspaper. The edges of torn pieces tend to blend and make a smooth surface, whereas cut pieces of paper leave noticeable ridges. Overlap these pieces of newspaper on the object. Try to smooth out all the wrinkles. Large pieces of paper can be applied to large flat surfaces, but rounded or small sculptures should be made with small pieces of paper to avoid wrinkles. A strong piece will need four layers. After the first two layers are applied, let it dry a day or two before applying the third and fourth layers. It is easier to be sure each layer has completely covered the object if different papers are used. For instance, alternate layers of white and colored newspaper, or alternate newspaper with industrial strength paper toweling.

If a very smooth finish is desired, the papier mâché can be lightly sanded after it has completely dried. It is then ready to be painted or decorated. A final coat of shellac, varnish, or polymer medium will strengthen the papier mâché.

Plaster of Paris

Have containers into which the plaster is to be poured set out on newspaper before mixing the plaster.

Put water into a plastic pail or bowl in an amount slightly less than the quantity of plaster needed. Sprinkle the dry plaster into the water *(without stirring it)* until it stops disappearing into the water and begins to form a large island of dry plaster. Then stir the plaster with your fingers, being sure it is smooth and there are no lumps. It should be a slightly thickened, creamy consistency. Immediately pour the mixture into the containers that have been set out. Tap the filled containers several times to level the plaster and make bubbles come to the surface. If the plaster hardens too quickly to pour, you have added too much plaster. Do not try to dilute it with more water. You will have to discard it and start over with a new mixture.

Do not rinse hands, tools, or containers in the sink, because the plaster will clog the pipes. Rinse your hands and tools in a bucket of water. When the plaster has settled, pour off the clear water. Then wipe out the container with newspaper or paper towels. If a flexible plastic pail is used, the plaster may be cracked out easily after it is dry.

When students are working with plaster, cover tables with newspaper and frequently dispose of plaster dust or chips. Plaster is easily tracked around a building once it gets on the floor.

Plaster that has been dipped in water is easier to carve, but getting it too wet will weaken it.

Repairs may be made by mixing and adding small amounts of new plaster to a dampened piece.

Glass Cutting

A glass cutter is an inexpensive tool. Buy one with a knob at the end of the handle. Place the glass to be cut on a pad of newspapers. Hold the tool in an almost vertical fashion, between thumb and fingers. Press down firmly but not too hard and make one continuous pull across the glass. You can feel the tool bite into the glass slightly if you are applying enough pressure. (Some people grip the cutter in a fist hold, with the thumb on the tip of the knob end. This hold gives a little more pressure.) The tool will have scored a white line on the glass. Turn the glass over and press with your thumbs along this line, or tap gently along the line with the knob on the cutter handle. The glass should come apart. Roll the cutter blade through a drop of oil each time it is used to keep it running smoothly.

To cut the glass to a particular size, measure the piece to be cut and make small guide marks with the glass cutter at the top and bottom edges. Place a ruler on these guide marks and run the glass cutter down along the ruler.

BIBLIOGRAPHY

Chapter 2   *General African Arts*

DUERDEN, DENNIS, *African Art*. Feltham, England: Hamlyn Publishing Group Ltd., 1968.
An excellent introduction to African art, ancient and modern. Beautiful color plates of sculpture, architecture, adinkra cloth, and contemporary painting.

GLUBOK, SHIRLEY, *The Art of Africa*. N.Y.: Harper and Row Publishers, 1965.
A fine introduction for young people, showing a great variety of arts. Excellent black and white photos.

JEFFERSON, LOUISE E., *The Decorative Arts of Africa*. N.Y.: Viking Press, 1973.
Excellent, comprehensive, and copiously illustrated book on a great variety of African arts, from metal work, carving, and fabric design (including adinkra cloth and symbols) to dress, hair styles, and many other decorative arts.

MONTI, FRANCO, *African Masks*. Feltham, England: Hamlyn Publishing Group Ltd., 1969.
Full-color photographs of many types of masks with explanatory text.

NEWMAN, THELMA R., *Contemporary African Arts and Crafts*. N.Y.: Crown Publishers, Inc., 1974.
Excellent book for use in the classroom. Covers all areas of contemporary crafts. Photo of aluminum panel by Olatunde, photos of contemporary fabrics: adire eleko, adire eleso (tie-dye), adinkra, and others. Description of processes involved in all these arts. Chapters end with brief suggestions to help the reader engage in similar art processes.

PARRINDER, GEOFFRY, *African Mythology*. Feltham, England: Hamlyn Publishing Group Ltd., 1967.
Fine photographs of bronze panels and a bronze leopard from Benin, Nigeria; brass from the Ashanti people of Ghana; carved wood Yoruba panels from Nigeria; beadwork; and carvings and masks from many other tribal groups. The book describes the myths and ways of life behind the art work and also relates many delightful animal fables.

SIEBER, ROY, *African Textiles and Decorative Arts*. N.Y.: Museum of Modern Art, 1972.
Beadwork, jewelry, clothing, body decoration, and textiles. Includes many examples of weaving, applique, painted cloth, tied-and-dyed fabrics, and adire eleko.

WAHLMAN, MAUDE, *Contemporary African Arts*. Chicago, Ill.: Field Museum of Natural History, 1974.
Wide range of contemporary arts, including a chapter on aluminum panels by Asire Olantunde.

WILLIAMS, GEOFFRY, *African Designs from Traditional*

Sources. N.Y.: Dover Publishers, Inc., 1971.
Black and white prints and drawings of traditional African designs used in many different media from all over the continent.

African Textiles

ASH, BERYL AND ANTHONY DYSON, *Introducing Dyeing and Printing.* N.Y.: Watson Guptill, 1979.
Methods of dyeing and printing with examples from Africa as well as other areas of the world.

BROOKS, LOIS, "Workshop: Adire Eleko." Craft Horizons, August 1971.
An illustrated article on adere eleko techniques. See also general bibliography for books that include information about adire eleko.

GLOVER, E. ABLADE, *"Adinkra Symbolism,"* A chart. N.D.D. A.T.D. ERSA Faculty of Art, University of Science and Technology, Kamasi, Ghana. Published by The Center for Open Learning and Teaching, 1976. P.O. Box 9434, Berkeley, California 94709.
The chart shows many adinkra symbols and their meanings. See also books in the general bibliography for this chapter for photographs and descriptions of adinkra cloth.

MAILE, ANNE, *Tie and Dye Made Easy.* N.Y.: Taplinger Publishing Co., 1971.
See also the books in the general bibliography that have examples of African tie-dyed fabrics.

Egyptian Arts

"An Egyptian Hieroglyphic Alphabet of 2500 B.C." (chart). N.Y.: Metropolitan Museum of Art, 1967.

DAVIS, PETER, *"Experiment in Harrania."* School Arts Magazine, October 1963.

FORMAN, W. AND B., AND WASSEF, RAMSES WISSA, *Tapestries from Egypt, Woven by the Children of Harrania.* London: Paul Hamlyn, 1961.
This is a beautiful book with sixty-six full-color plates of Harrania weavings and of the young weavers themselves. In a short commentary, Professor Wassef describes his experiment at Harrania, which was not only to revive a craft, but to do so in a way that protected and nurtured the innate creativity of the children.

GLUBOK, SHIRLEY, *The Art of Ancient Egypt.* N.Y.: Athenium, 1962.
Well illustrated introduction for young children.

HARRIS, J. R., *Egyptian Art.* London: Spring Books, 1966.
Surveys Egyptian art, describes how craftsmen worked. Color illustrations of sculpture, reliefs, and painting.

SCOTT, JOSEPH AND LENORE, *Egyptian Hieroglyphs for Everyone.* New York: Funk and Wagnalls, 1968.

Chapter 3

An excellent introduction to hieroglyphs, beautifully illustrated.

VILIMKOVA, MILADA, *Egyptian Jewelry*. London: Paul Hamlyn Publishing Group, Ltd., 1969.
Describes development of jewelry from prehistoric times through to the last dynasty and subsequent Greek and Roman influence. Ninety beautiful color illustrations.

Israeli Arts

FORTINER, VIRGINIA J., *Archaeology as a Hobby*. N.J.: Hammond and Co., 1962.
For students who have become interested in archaeology and want to know more about it and perhaps get involved in field work in their area.

GLUBOK, SHIRLEY, *Art and Archaeology*. N.Y.: Harper and Row, Pub., 1966.
A beautifully illustrated book describing the work of archaeologists in many countries, including Israel. Explains methods of working in many different environments and tells of the hard work involved, of inspired and accidental discoveries, and of the art that has been found in the search for more knowledge about the past.

KATZ, KARL; KAHANE, P. P.; AND BROSHI, MAGEN, *From the Beginning, Archaeology and Art in the Israel Museum*. Jerusalem: Reynal and Co., 1968.
Archaeological discoveries from prehistoric times up to the more recent past. Photographs of work in clay, bronze, stone, glass, gold, and silver from the museum's collection. Contemporary art work also shown.

ROTH, CECIL, *Jewish Art*. Jerusalem: Massada Press, 1971.
A beautifully illustrated book with an anthology of articles by experts in their fields. The book covers over 3,000 years of Jewish art on five continents and includes many arts, from architecture and sculpture to painting, pottery, illuminated manuscripts, and ritual objects.

RUTLAND, JONATHAN, *Looking at Israel*. N.Y.: Lippincott, Co., 1970.
A general book on Israel for the young student.

UNESCO, *Israel, Ancient Mosaics*. New York Graphic Society, 1960.
Thirty-two large color plates of mosaics in Israel with helpful preface and introduction by Meyer Schapiro and Michael Avi-Yonah.

Persian Miniature Painting

BUSH, SYLVIA T., *"An Artist's Search for Colors."* Design Magazine, Midwinter 1973.
An article telling what is known about the materials used by Persian painters and their sources and preparation.

UNESCO, *Iran, Persian Miniatures, Imperial Library*. New York Graphic Society, 1956.

Beautiful color reproductions of Persian paintings in their original dimensions. The preface by Basil Gray and introduction by André Godard describe the art in general and the miniatures reproduced in the book.

WELCH, STUART CARY, *Persian Painting.* N.Y.: George Braziller, 1976. Paperback.
Brilliant color reproductions of paintings from five Royal Safavid manuscripts of the sixteenth century. The introduction gives a history of Persian miniature painting, and each color plate is accompanied by very helpful comments that explain the story illustrated and point out delightful details that might otherwise be missed.

Swedish Arts

PLATH, IONA, *The Decorative Arts of Sweden.* New York: Charles Scribner's Sons, 1948.
A well-illustrated survey of Swedish arts, past and present: textiles, ceramics, wall paintings, and artwork in glass, metal, and wood.

RYCRAFT, ELEANOR AND CARROLL, *Rycraft Scandinavian Cookie Stamp Recipes.* 4205 S.W. 53rd St., Corvallis, Oregon: Rycraft, 1971.
A small booklet of recipes that accompanies Rycraft's clay cookie stamps.

Polish Wycinanki

GACEK, ANNA ZAJAC, *Wycinanki, Polish Folk Paper-Cuts.* 4 Green Street, New Bedford, Mass.: Sarmatia Publications. 1972.
Paperback, with history of wycinanki and instructions for making Kurpie leluja and gwiazdy designs, Lowicz designs and other regional types of papercuts.

JABLONSKI, RAMONA, *The Paper Cut-Out Design Book.* Owings Mills, Md.: Stemmer House Pub. Inc., 1976.
A sourcebook for creating and adapting the heritage of American folk art, Polish wycinanki, Chinese Hua Yang, Japanese kirigami, German Scherenschnitte and others. An excellent introduction to paper cutting from many cultures.

Wycinanki, Polish Cut-Outs. 813 Trombley Rd., Grosse Pointe Park, Mich.: Friends of Polish Art, 1972.
A booklet with a short history of the art and many photographs describing Kurpie and Lowicz cutouts and how to make them.

WYTRWAL, JOSEPH A., *The Poles in America.* Minneapolis, Minn: Lerner Pub. Co., 1969.
This book begins with a short history of Poland but is concerned for the most part with the many contributions of Polish-Americans to art, music, literature, industry, education, science, and sports in America, from earliest colonial times to the present day.

Chapter 4

Ukrainian Pysanky

COSKEY, EVELYN, *Easter Eggs for Everyone*. Nashville, Tenn. Abingdon Press, 1973.
Egg lore and legends from many cultures. One chapter deals with eggs decorated with the wax batik process, among them the pysanky, with very complete directions for making them.

FERENCE, CECELIA, *Making Ukranian Pysanky*. P.O. Box 295, Saline, Michigan 48176. Published by Cecelia Ference, 1975.
Excellent booklet describing Ukrainian customs at Easter and giving instructions for making traditional pysanky. Illustrated with many designs. All necessary supplies are available at this address.

JORDAN, ROBERT PAUL, *Easter Greetings from the Ukrainians*. National Geographic, April 1972.
Beautifully illustrated article on pysanky making among the Ukrainian-Americans of Minneapolis and St. Paul, Minnesota.

LUCIOW, JOHANNA; KMIT, ANN; AND LUCIOW, LORETTA, *Eggs Beautiful, How to Make Ukrainian Easter Eggs*. 2422 Central Avenue, N.E. Minneapolis, Minnesota 55418. Published by Ukrainian Gift Shop, 1975.
A very comprehensive, beautifully illustrated book on making Ukrainian Easter eggs. All necessary supplies are available from this source.

Supplies are also available at Hanusey Music Co., 244 W. Girard Ave., Philadelphia, Pa. 19123; Ukrainian Book Store, P.O. Box 1640, 10207–97 St., Edmonton, Alberta T5J 2N9, Canada; Globe Merchandise & Supplies, 6720 Michigan Ave., Detroit, Michigan 48210. When inquiring for supplies at any of the above sources, send a stamped self-addressed envelope for a price list.

German Flower-Related Arts

BAUZEN, PETER AND SUSANNE, *Flower Pressing*. N.Y.: Sterling Pub. Co. 1972. Originally published by Verlag Frech, Stuttgart-Botnang, Germany.
Excellent small book with directions for pressing flowers and framing them under glass or plastic. Many other projects using pressed plants with cloth, wood, fiber, glass, and resin. The book also describes methods of preserving plants with lacquer, printing with plants, and using them as stencils.

FOSTER, LAURA LOUISE, *Keeping the Plants You Pick*. N.Y.: Thomas Y. Crowell Co., 1970.
Illustrated with drawings by the author. Describes methods of pressing and preserving plants and many projects to make with them.

KULL, A. STODDARD, *Secrets of Flowers, The Message and Meaning of Every Flower*. Brattleboro, Vt.: The Stephen Greene Press, 1976.

The folklore and symbolism of many flowers.

RUSSELL, FRANCIS, *The World of Dürer.* N.Y.: Time-Life Books, 1967.
A biography of Dürer, beautifully illustrated with many of his paintings, woodcuts, and engravings.

Italian Marionettes

BAIRD, BIL, *The Art of the Puppet.* N.Y.: Macmillan Co., 1965.
A beautiful, comprehensive book, describing puppets from ancient to modern times in many different countries. Long, beautifully illustrated chapters on the evolution of Punch and Judy and on the Orlando puppets.

CURRELL, DAVID, *The Complete Book of Puppetry.* Boston: Plays Inc., 1974.
History of puppetry in many lands, its uses in schools, and directions for making various kinds of puppets, marionettes, and stages.

D'AMATO, JANET AND ALEX, *Italian Crafts, Inspirations from Folk Art.* N.Y.: M. Evans and Company, Inc., 1977.
Describes traditional Italian folk arts in many media and gives detailed instructions for many projects based on these crafts, including marionettes.

WALL, L. V.; WHITE, G. A.; AND PHILPOTT, A. R., *The Puppet Book.* Boston: Plays, Inc., 1965.
Oriented toward puppet plays as a valuable part of school curriculum. Excellent directions for making all kinds of puppets and stages and ideas for plays and improvisations.

Chinese Arts

Chapter 5

ECKE, TSENG YU-HO, *Chinese Calligraphy.* Boston: David R. Godine, Publisher, 1971.
A history of calligraphy, description of methods, and photographs of calligraphy and their translation from an exhibit at the Philadelphia Museum of Art.

SCHACHNER, ERWIN, *Step-By-Step Printmaking.* N.Y.: Golden Press, 1970. Paperback.
Directions for making woodcuts, linoleum cuts, and other kinds of prints. Very fine illustrations from many sources, ancient and modern.

SMITH, BRADLEY AND WENG, WAN-GO, *China. A History in Art.* N.Y.: Harper and Row, 1976.
Beautifully illustrated with a great range of Chinese arts: early pottery and pictographs; sculptures in stone, bronze, jade, clay; calligraphy; woodcuts; and paintings.

SZE, MAI-MAI, *The Way of Chinese Painting, Its Ideas and Techniques with Selections from the Seventeenth Century Mustard Seed Garden Manual of Painting.* N.Y.: Random House, 1959. Paperback.
The illustrations include many woodcuts from The Mus-

tard Seed Garden Manual.

WOLFF, DIANE, *Chinese Writing: An Introduction*. N.Y.: Holt, Rinehart and Winston, 1975.
An excellent introduction to Chinese writing and calligraphy. Illustrated with photographs and with calligraphy by Jeanette Chien. For young students.

Japanese Arts

AIDA, KOHEI, *Sumi-e Self Taught*. Tokyo: Japan Publications, Inc., 1968.
Well-illustrated instructions for doing Japanese ink painting: animals, birds, flowers, and landscape.

BASHO, MATSUO, *The Narrow Road to the Deep North and other Travel Sketches*. Translated from the Japanese with an introduction by Nobuyuki Yuasa. Baltimore, Md.: Penguin Books, 1966.
Five travel sketches by Basho, greatest of haiku poets. As he traveled through Japan by foot and horseback, he wrote of his adventures and the places that inspired his haiku.

HENDERSON, HAROLD G., *An Introduction to Haiku*. Translations and Commentary. Garden City, N.Y.: Doubleday and Co., Inc., 1958. Paperback.
The best anthology for classroom use.

LEWIS, RICHARD, *In a Spring Garden*. N.Y.: The Dial Press, 1965.
Beautifully illustrated by Ezra Jack Keats (Western style). A collection of twenty-three haiku selected for appeal to young children.

MIKAMI, TAKAHIKO, *Sumi Painting*. Tokyo, Japan: Shufunotomo Co. Ltd, 1965.
Covers the same ground as the book by Aida.

TERAKAZU, AKUYAMA, *Treasures of Asia, Japanese Painting*. Cleveland, Ohio: Skira, distributed by The World Publishing Co., 1961.

The Poet-Painters: Buson and His Followers. An Exhibition organized by Calvin L. French. The University of Michigan Museum of Art, Ann Arbor, 1974.
Although called a "catalogue" of the exhibit, this is really a very informative, beautifully written book with many fine illustrations.

YAMADA, SADAMI, *Sumi-e in Three Weeks*. Tokyo: Japan Publications Trading Company, 1964.
Well-illustrated instructions for doing Japanese brush painting.

Burmese Arts

BIXLER, NORMA, *Burma, A Profile*. N.Y.: Praeger Publishers, 1971.
A general book on Burma.

NEWMAN, THELMA R., *Southeast Asian Arts and Crafts*. N.Y.: Crown Publishers Inc., 1977.

The first chapter discusses Southeast Asian arts in general and some similarities in these arts arising from shared influences. The book describes many arts and how they are done, including the lacquerware process, with many photos.

Arts of India

SCHULBERG, LUCILLE, *Historic India.* N.Y.: Time-Life Books, 1968.
Well-written and beautifully illustrated with color photographs of the Taj Mahal, Moghul miniature paintings, and ancient sculpture.

Indonesian Arts

ANDERSON, BENEDICT R. O'G., *Mythology and the Tolerance of the Javanese.* Cornell, N.Y.: Modern Indonesia Project Monograph Series, 1965.
A rather technical essay but illustrated with pen drawings of sixty-five wayangs. These are very helpful in drawing the puppets.

ANDERSON, WILLIAM M., *Teaching Asian Musics in Elementary and Secondary Schools.* Adrian, Mich.: The Leland Press (Box 301), 1975.
Excellent introduction to playing Javanese gamelan music. Well illustrated.

BELFER, NANCY, *Designing in Batik and Tie Dye.* Worcester, Mass.: Davis Publications, Inc., 1972; Englewood Cliffs, N.J.: Prentice-Hall, Inc., 1977.
Gives a well-illustrated history of the art of batik in Java and a description of contemporary designs and methods.

BRANDON, JAMES R., *On Thrones of Gold.* Cambridge: Harvard University Press, 1970.
A complete description of wayang kulit, its history and performance. Includes three plays, written as they are performed, with stage directions concerning the movement of the puppets, musical accompaniment, and the dhalang's songs and narrations. Illustrated.

KELLER, ILA. *Batik: The Art and Craft.* Rutland, Vt.: Charles B. Tuttle Co., Pub., 1969.
Gives a well-illustrated history of the art of batik in Java and a description of contemporary designs and methods.

NEWMAN, THELMA R., *Contemporary Southeast Asian Arts and Crafts.* N.Y.: Crown Pub., 1977.
Photographs and description of making shadow puppets and of a performance. Also contains a well-illustrated chapter on history and techniques of batik in Java.

REINIGER, LOTTE, *Shadow Puppets, Shadow Theatres and Shadow Films.* Boston: Plays Inc., 1970.
A brief description of wayang kulit and the history of shadow puppets from other countries. Directions for con-

struction of many kinds of shadow puppets and theatres.

SCOTT-KEMBALL, JEUNE, *Javanese Shadow Puppets.* Trustees of the British Museum, Shenval Press, 1970. Paperback.
Especially fine color illustrations of puppets. Describes the performance of a play, the puppets, and the human qualities they symbolize. Tells how the craftsmen make the puppets.

ULBRICHT, H., *Wayang Purwa—Shadows of the Past.* London: Oxford University Press, 1970.
Excellent small paperback on all aspects of Javanese shadow puppets.

Wayang Kulit: The Shadow Puppet Theater of Java. Baylis Glascock Films, 1017 North La Cienega Boulevard, Los Angeles, California 90069, 22 minutes, color.
A beautiful film, showing both puppets and gamelan in action.

Chapter 6 *Mexican Arts*

ENCISO, JORGE, *Design Motifs of Ancient Mexico.* N.Y.: Dover Publications, Inc., 1953.
Helpful black and white illustrations of ancient designs arranged by subject matter.

HARVEY, MARIAN, *Crafts of Mexico.* N.Y.: Macmillan Publishing Co., Inc., 1973.
Chapters on weaving, reed work, metals, clay, wood, and paper, describing these arts and giving directions for making some of the items described.

LENZ, HANS, *"Paper and Superstitions."* Artes de Mexico, Myths, Rites and Witchery. No. 124, Ano XVI, 1969, page 93. Amores 262, Mexico 12, D.F.
This article is primarily on amate paper cutouts, their historical beginnings, and contemporary use.

SAYER, CHLOË, *Crafts of Mexico.* N.Y.: Doubleday and Co., 1977.
Full-color illustrations of Mexican crafts with directions for making many of the items described—embroidery, lacquerwork, yarn painting, pottery, items of wood and paper, piñatas.

TONEYAMA, KOJIN, *The Popular Arts of Mexico.* N.Y.: Weatherhill, Inc., 1974.
Exceptionally beautiful color illustrations of many of the popular arts of Mexico: Huichol yarn paintings, amate paper cutouts and paintings, clay figures and pots of many kinds, tin sculpture, and many other arts.

Central and South American Arts

ANTON, FERDINAND, *The Art of Ancient Peru.* N.Y.: Putnam's Sons, 1972.
Comprehensive well-illustrated history.

ANTON, FERDINAND AND DOCKSTADER, FREDERICK J., *Pre-Columbian Art and Later Indian Tribal Arts*. N.Y.: Harry N. Abrams, Inc., 1968.
Beautifully illustrated in black and white and color photos. Architecture and art work in clay, metal, and textiles.

DOCKSTADER, FREDERICK J., *Indian Art in South America*. New York Graphic Society, 1967.
Well-illustrated history. Excellent photographs of art work in gold and silver, clay, basketry, and textiles. Notable in gold: mummy mask, Fig. 151; crown, Fig. 94; ornaments, Fig. 93; staff head, Fig. 14.

GLUBOK, SHIRLEY, *The Art of Ancient Peru*. N.Y.: Harper and Row, 1966.
Excellent book with illustrations of gold and silver sculpture, textiles, and ceramics.

KAPP, CAPTAIN KIT S., *Mola Art from the San Blas Islands*. Cincinnati, Ohio. K. S. Kapp Publications, 1972, Paperback.
Well-illustrated, comprehensive study of molas, their origin and development, how they are made, and an analysis of the many designs used.

KLOTZ, ROY, *"The Mola: Artistry in Cloth," Design* 73, no. 3, Mid-Winter 1972. Page 10.
A short, illustrated article on molas.

MATTIL, EDWARD L., *"The Cuna Mola," Everyday Art* 52, Spring 1974. Sandusky, Ohio. The American Crayon Company.
Small paperback booklet with many full-color illustrations of molas.

OSBORN, HAROLD, *South American Mythology*. Feltham, Middlesex, England: Hamlyn Publishing Group Ltd., 1968.
Black and white color photos of gold sculpture and jewelry, clay pots and figures, and textile work.

Caribbean Arts

Chapter 7

CHRISTENSEN, ELEANOR INGALLS, *The Art of Haiti*. Cranbury, N.J.: A. S. Barnes and Co., Inc., 1975.
Haitian history and culture from pre-Columbian times up through to the flowering of the arts in the middle of the twentieth century. Illustrated with many black and white and color photographs.

KURTIS, ARLENE HARRIS, *Puerto Ricans, from Island to Mainland*. N.Y.: Julian Messner, 1969.
A history of the island and its people, written for young children and illustrated with photographs.

Puerto Rico Reconstruction Administration, *Puerto Rico. A Guide to the Island of Boriquen*. The Puerto Rico Department of Education, 1940.
This book, written by Puerto Ricans, covers the history

of the island, its natural resources, government, arts, and cultural life, and takes readers on several descriptive tours of the island.

RODMAN, SELDEN, *The Miracle of Haitian Art.* N.Y.: Doubleday and Co., Inc., 1974.
The renaissance of art in Haiti that was fostered by the Centre d'Art. Biographical sketches of the most prominent painters and sculptors, illustrated with many black and white and color photographs.

Chapter 8   *General Native American Arts*

American Indian Art: Form and Tradition. N.H.: E. P. Dutton and Co., 1972.
An exhibition organized by Walker Art Center, Indian Art Association, The Minneapolis Institute of Arts. A catalogue of very fine examples of Indian art. Essays on art from each region, on the meaning of art in the daily life of the Indian.

APPLETON, LEROY H., *American Indian Design and Decoration.* N.Y.: Dover Pub., 1950.
Black and white drawings of the design elements of North and South American Indian regional groups.

BILLARD, JULES B., ed., *The World of the American Indian.* National Geographic Society, 1974.
Beautifully illustrated with color photographs. A comprehensive volume of Native American life from what we can guess of prehistoric times to the present. Gives a feeling for the many different Indian cultures, which were alike in their respect for and total use of environment.

BURLAND, COTTIE, *North American Indian Mythology.* London: Paul Hamlyn, 1965.
Color and black and white photographs of Indian arts and crafts and the rich mythology that helps in understanding the symbols used in much of the art.

DOCKSTADER, FREDERICK J., *Indian Art of the Americas.* N.Y.: Museum of the American Indian, Heye Foundation, 1973.
Black and white and color photographs showing the full range of Indian art, with text.

GLUBOK, SHIRLEY, *The Art of the North American Indian.* N.Y.: Harper and Row, 1964.
A good review of art for the younger child.

JONES, CHARLES, ed., *Look to the Mountain Top.* San Jose, CA.: H. M. Gousha Co., 1972.
Contemporary views on all aspects of Indian Heritage.

Pueblo Indian Pottery

BAHTI, TOM, *Southwestern Indian Arts and Crafts.* Las Vegas, NV.: K. C. Publications, 1966.
Along with other crafts, describes pottery-making pro-

cess and has photographs showing differing styles from sixteen pueblos.

BAYLOR, BYRD, *When Clay Sings.* N.Y.: Charles Scribner's Sons, 1972.
A beautiful book about the pottery of prehistoric Southwest Indians. Brings to life the spirit of these ancient peoples, their respect for and delight in all forms of life, and their relation to Pueblo people of today.

GILLETT, MARIAN, *The Enduring Art.* 16950 Tesoro Dr., San Diego, CA.: 1970. Super-8 color film of Rose Gonzales from San Ildefonso Pueblo making, polishing, painting, carving, and firing black on black pottery. With cassette.

Navajo Weaving and Sand Painting

RAINEY, SARITA R., *Weaving Without a Loom.* Worcester, MA: Davis Publications, Inc. 1966; Englewood Cliffs, N.J.: Prentice-Hall, Inc., 1977.
Many techniques for weaving without a regular loom, using a wide variety of materials.

TANNER, CLARA LEE, "Modern Navajo Weaving," in *Arizona Highways,* September 1964, Arizona Highway Department.
History of Navajo weaving and descriptions of all major regional styles with color photographs.

VILLASENOR, DAVID, *Tapestries in Sand.* Healdsburg, CA. Naturegraph Co., 1963.
Tells about the process of sand painting and, more importantly, the spirit behind it—the myths and stories handed down for generations that hold, distilled, the Navajo beliefs about man and his place in the universe.

Plains Indians Arts

CATLIN, GEORGE, *George Catlin Letters and Notes on the North American Indians,* Michael M. Mooney, ed. N.Y.: Clarkson N. Potter, Inc., 1975.
This book was originally published in 1841. It has been condensed and rearranged by the editor. Includes many engravings and paintings by Catlin.

GLUBOK, SHIRLEY, *The Art of the Plains Indian.* N.Y.: Harper and Row, 1975.
A well-written and illustrated book for children. Includes photographs of decorated buffalo skins, including a winter count; painted tipis, shields, and shirts; beaded moccasins; dolls; and paintings.

McHUGH, TOM, *The Time of the Buffalo.* N.Y.: Alfred A. Knopf, 1972.

MARTIN, CY, *The Saga of the Buffalo.* N.Y.: Hart Publishing Co., Inc. 1973.
This book and the one above by McHugh both deal with the natural history of the buffalo and especially its changing relationships to man, from its role in the life of the Plains Indians to its near extinction by the west-

ward movement of settlers to its present-day establishment in new herds through the efforts of the Canadian and U.S. governments.

MASON, BERNARD S., *Dances and Stories of the American Indian.* N.Y.: The Ronald Press Co., 1944.
This collection includes directions for performing three buffalo dances from the Sioux, the Cheyenne, and the Jemez tribes.

Woodland Indian Arts

The Art of the Great Lakes Indians. Flint Institute of Arts, 1973.
An exhibition organized by the Flint Institute of Arts. Chapters on the history, art, and culture of Great Lakes Indians and careful description of porcupine quillwork and methods. Excellent diagrams and photographs. I have drawn heavily from this book in writing this chapter.

HUNT, W. BEN and BURSHEARS, J. F. "Buck", *American Indian Beadwork,* N.Y.: Collier Books, 1951.
A comprehensive paperback of Indian beadwork methods. Includes many color illustrations of Indian designs.

RITZENTHALER, ROBERT E., and PAT, *The Woodland Indians of the Western Great Lakes.* Published for The American Museum of Natural History. Garden City, N.Y.: The Natural History Press, 1970.

Eskimo Arts

BURLAND, COTTIE, *Eskimo Art.* London: Hamlyn Publishing Group Ltd., 1973.
Eskimo art and culture from prehistoric times to the present day. Beautifully illustrated with many color and black and white photographs.

CARPENTER, EDMUND, *Eskimo Realities.* N.Y.: Holt, Rinehart and Winston, 1973.
Aboriginal Eskimo art, especially prehistoric ivory carvings. An analysis of what art is to the Eskimo. A different point of view. Mr. Carpenter believes true Eskimo art is interchangeable with the Eskimo's life. He does not feel the sculpture and prints made for sale are truly Eskimo art but are Western in concept and execution.

Eskimo Graphic Art 1960. West Baffin Eskimo Co-operative, Canada. Exhibition catalogue.

GLUBOK, SHIRLEY, *The Art of the Eskimo.* N.Y.: Harper and Row, Publishers, 1964.
Art in many different media, especially masks and ivory carvings. For younger children.

HOUSTON, JAMES, *Eskimo Prints.* Barre, Mass.: Barre Publishing Co., Inc., 1971.
How printmaking began in Cape Dorset in 1957. Mr.

Houston introduced the concept but believes the images and ideas created are "based on centuries of ancient Eskimo traditions, myths and skills."

Kenojuak. A two-reel color film produced by McGraw-Hill, Film Division, Distribution Center: Hightstown, N.J. 08520.
A very beautiful film about the Inuit artist, Kenojuak She tells of her sources of inspiration, and we are shown the process of making a print from its conception in the mind of the artist through to its being cut in stone and printed on paper.

SWINTON, GEORGE, *Sculpture of the Eskimo.* Greenwich, Conn.: New York Graphic Society, Ltd. 1972.
This book has 37 color photographs and 770 black and white photographs of sculpture. It covers the environment, history, and modern day culture of the Eskimo and traces the transition from making magical objects to making functional decorative objects for pleasure and market. Shows many styles and subject matters.

Early American Folk Arts

FLAYDERMAN, E. NORMAN, *Scrimshaw and Scrimshanders, Whale and Whalemen.* Conn.: N. Flayderman and Co. Inc., 1972.
A comprehensive and well-illustrated book on the history and art of scrimshaw.

Golden Book of Colonial Crafts. N.Y.: Golden Press, 1975.
Seventy craft projects from colonial times, with directions for making them with materials available today.

JONES, IRIS SANDERSON, *Early North American Dollmaking.* San Francisco: 101 Productions, 1976.
Beautifully illustrated book showing a great variety of dolls with instructions for making many of them, including applehead dolls.

JUNG, PAMELA F., *"Apple Dolls," Design* 74, No. 1. p. 14.
Illustrated article on the apple dolls of Mrs. E. E. Grannis of Lewiston, Idaho, and her methods of making them.

LINSLEY, LESLIE, *Scrimshaw, A Traditional Folk Art, A Contemporary Craft.* N.Y.: Hawthorn Books, Inc., 1976.
How scrimshaw is done today—tools, materials, and methods of contemporary scrimshanders.

INDEX